Mr. Smith Goes to China

Mr. Smith Goes to China

Three Scots in the Making of Britain's Global Empire

Jessica Hanser

Yale
UNIVERSITY PRESS
New Haven & London

William Daniell (1769–1837). *A View in China: Cultivating the Tea Plant,* 1810. Courtesy of the Yale Center for British Art.

in Britain and North America until the next decade, especially after the Glorious Revolution of 1688–89.[20] By 1703, the directors of the East India Company were claiming that tea drinking in Britain had caught on "among persons of all qualities."[21] To satisfy the growing demand for tea, the East India Company imported 1,765,694 pounds of tea in 1739.[22] This figure was "almost certainly . . . only a small fraction of the total consumption." Another two million pounds, "and probably more," was smuggled into the country and sold annually.[23] According to government estimates, traders working for various European East India companies brought three million pounds of smuggled tea into Britain between 1742 and 1745.[24] By 1743, tea drinking had become so widespread that when the government discussed "a new duty on tea, to be paid by every housekeeper for all the sons in their family," one contemporary observer, Horace Walpole, declared that "it will scarce be proposed; tea is so universal, that it would make a greater clamor

Published with assistance from the Annie Burr Lewis Fund and
from Yale-NUS College through grant number IG15-SR103.

Set in Bulmer type by Newgen North America, Austin, Texas.
Printed in the United States of America.

Library of Congress Control Number: 2018958483
ISBN 978-0-300-23608-8 (hardcover : alk. paper)

A catalogue record for this book is available from the British Library.

This paper meets the requirements of ANSI/NISO Z39.48-1992 (Permanence of Paper).

10 9 8 7 6 5 4 3 2 1

For Mom, Dad, Daniel, and Grandpa

Forgive me for mentioning the circumstance which I do, to show,
amongst numberless other instances, how a splendid act of government
may be linked with the conduct of very obscure individuals,
separated even from its seat, at a distance of half the globe.

—Captain Mackintosh to Mr. Rose, November 19, 1791

Contents

Preface

FROM THE SEVENTEENTH until the nineteenth century, the East India Company enjoyed a monopoly on trade east of the Cape of Good Hope, a monopoly bestowed and periodically renewed by the British government. The vast majority of the British people were not legally entitled to engage in trade with India, Southeast Asia, Japan, or China. While some entrepreneurial and well-connected individuals managed to obtain licenses from the East India Company to trade on their own accounts, many chose to ignore the Company's monopoly rights entirely. Most of the time, the Company could not enforce its monopoly, so private traders quickly became a normal feature of the commercial landscape of maritime Asia. The term "private trader" as used throughout this book refers to those individuals who conducted business in Asia but did not work for the East India Company. This book tells the history of British private traders operating between India and China during the second half of the eighteenth century.

We knew little about them until recently. Most studies on European commerce and imperialism in maritime Asia have taken the various East India companies formed by the British and Europeans as subjects. Although some of these studies—for example, those of Holden Furber, P. J. Marshall, Emily Erikson, and Søren Mentz—discuss "private trade," they tend to focus on the side businesses conducted by East India Company employees on their own account while giving short shrift to or completely overlooking independent private traders. These studies also typically focus on India, not China.

In the past few decades, however, historians have begun to pay much greater attention to private traders. American historians, like Jonathan Goldstein and James Fichter, led the way in large part because the United States had no equivalent to the East India Company; Americans who went to India and China were private traders by definition because commerce with Asia was open to every American citizen. Studies from the Chinese side of things, particularly the invaluable research of Paul Van Dyke, have breathed new life into the history of the Canton trade. Van Dyke's work has inspired a generation of scholars—Susan Schopp, Maria Mok, Lisa Hellman, and Benjamin Asmussen—to delve deeply into American, European, and Chinese archives to shed light on global commerce in China before the First Opium War (1839–42).

Mr. Smith Goes to China is part of this new wave of scholarship characterized by close, sustained examination of the lives of traders in maritime Asia and, more specifically, China. By placing private traders at the center of the story, this book turns the seemingly dry materials of ledger sheets into a compelling historical narrative that fundamentally alters our understanding of Britain's empire and global trade on the eve of the industrial revolution.

This book was not written alone. Over the past ten years, I have benefited from the kindness and generosity of many people and institutions. I have had the great fortune to work with two excellent editors at Yale University Press, Jaya Chatterjee and Mary Pasti, whose professionalism, attentiveness, and encouragement have made the publishing process a pleasure.

I received funding from Yale University, the Woodrow Wilson Foundation, the Taiwanese Ministry of Education, the U.S. National Security Education Program, the Fulbright Program, the Beinecke Rare Book and Manuscript Library at Yale, the Andrew Mellon Foundation, the Institute for Historical Research (London), the Yale Boswell Editions, the Yale Council on East Asian Studies, the History Project at Harvard University, the Yad Hanadiv Foundation (Israel), Tel Aviv University, the City University of Hong Kong, and Yale-NUS College (Singapore). This work was supported by Yale-NUS College through grant number IG15-SR103.

The staff of the British Library, Beinecke Library, and Surrey History Centre, especially Hedly Sutton, Margaret Makepeace, Richard Morel, and Diane Ducharme, showed me the ropes in the archives.

Timothy Barrett, Kate Teltscher, Huw Bowen, Mark Gamsa, Jordan Goodman, Sir Peter Crane, John E. Wills, R. Bin Wong, Kenneth Pomeranz, Benjamin Elman, Chen Kuo-tung, Hsu Ya-hwei, Susan Schopp, Maria Mok, Lisa Hellman, Eecheng Ong, Ho Gia Ang Le, Maria Taroutina,

Christine Walker, Emanuel Mayer, Taran Kang, Claudine Ang, Tan Tai Yong, Mate Rigo, Scott Cook, Bryan Van Norden, Naoko Shimazu, Trevor Burnard, James Fichter, Michael Puett, Pericles Lewis, Rebecca Tannenbaum, Charles Bailyn, Brian McAdoo, John Wong, Catherine Ladds, Annie Ruderman, Prasannan Parthasarathi, Peter Perdue, Robert Travers, Kathleen Wilson, Barbara Hahn, Robert Batchelor, Zhang Wanmin, and Zhang Longxi have given me valuable comments, criticisms, and encouragement at various stages of the project. My research assistants, Lai Yikpo and Mollie Saltskog, also provided valuable help.

That I was able to learn Chinese and translate the Chinese documents quoted throughout this book was the result of many hours of language instruction from extremely patient and encouraging teachers, including Philip Kuhn, Hu Jing, Paize Keulmans, William Zhou, Shen Jianhua, Su Wei, Lin Chiu-fang, and many other wonderful instructors at Yale University and the National University of Taiwan's International Chinese Language Program who made learning this challenging language a joy.

I am lucky to have been mentored by some outstanding scholars who helped me to become a researcher and teacher. Jonathan Spence taught me how to find a compelling story, Francesca Trivellato introduced me to the world of cross-cultural trade and microhistory, Nicholas Spence showed me how to do family history research, P. J. Marshall guided me through the East India Company's labyrinthine archives, and Paul Van Dyke taught me how to be a Canton trade historian. After finishing the PhD, I gained several wonderful new mentors—Naomi Lamoreaux, Adam Clulow, Tonio Andrade, and Paul Van Dyke—whose kindness and support for my work have meant so much.

When Keith Wrightson, my former PhD advisor, accused me many years ago of being "intellectually promiscuous," I was secretly delighted. He encouraged me to pave my own intellectual path and taught me how to write with humanity. I am grateful to have been his student.

Following the three George Smiths all around the world has required a great deal of travel. I am thankful to Rebecca and Greg Rice-Brensilver, Leora Hanser and Graeme Traynor, and Alison and Jeremy Cohen for providing me homes in Berkeley and London. The Xiao family—Maggie,

Shaw, Xiao Yu, and Kenny—treated me like a daughter and sister and gave me a refuge to finish writing my book in Taiwan.

Lastly, I am eternally grateful to my friends and family. I can only hope that this book is worthy of the time, energy, resources, and emotion that they have invested in me.

George Smith Timelines

George Smith of Madras

c. 1730	Born in Scottish Highlands
1754	Sails to Madras
1757	Is in China
1765	Makes Madras his permanent residence
1769	Marries Margaretta Aurora Munro in Madras
1779	Leaves Madras for Britain
1783	Returns to India (Bengal)
1791	Dies in Calcutta

George Smith of Canton

c. 1746	Born in Scotland
c. 1771	Arrives in China
1778	Marries Charlotte Smith née Peche and buys the country ship *Eliza* in Bombay
1782	Is kicked out of China by the East India Company and returns to Britain (Surrey)
1808	Dies in Stoke-next-Guildford, Surrey

George Smith of Bombay

1737	Born in Fordyce, Scotland
1757	Moves to Europe to work as a clerk
1768	Moves to Bombay
1784	Is supercargo of the *Lady Hughes*
1789	Leaves Bombay for Scotland
1790	Dies on the voyage

Mr. Smith Goes to China

Introduction

IN THE MIDDLE OF THE EIGHTEENTH CENTURY three Scots, all named George Smith, sailed from Britain to the East Indies to make their fortunes. Because they shared one of the most common British names of the time, contemporaries distinguished them by the port cities where they worked and lived. This book follows the lives of George Smith of Madras, George Smith of Canton, and George Smith of Bombay. While they might sound merely like a collective metaphor for the British empire in Asia, they were real; historians have long been aware of them. These three George Smiths have surfaced in the footnotes of many historical works, yet we know virtually nothing about them. They have (very understandably) been confused and mistaken for one another by so many historians that it can be extremely difficult to get their stories straight.[1]

What can be gained by learning about these obscure Scots and their shadowy lives? For one thing, their stories are compelling. For another, they offer us unique access to a world of global commerce and British imperial expansion during the second half of the eighteenth century. By following these George Smiths across the globe, we can see how imperial engagement in different parts of Britain's commercial empire simultaneously developed and intensified. The Smiths' stories also shed new light on Britain's first embassy to China in the early 1790s, in that the idea for an embassy as well as several of its key aims appear to have originated with the George Smiths. Lastly, and perhaps somewhat paradoxically, sustained focus on these three traders from Scotland reminds us that the empire was not merely the making of a handful of daring British men. The stories of the Smiths open our eyes to a wider array of actors, including Chinese and Indian mercantile and political elites, women, children, and local British communities, who also participated in the empire and partook of its fruits.

Officially, Britain and China had nothing to do with each other until the last decade of the eighteenth century, when the British government dispatched the Macartney Mission, its first state-sanctioned embassy to the imperial court in Peking (Beijing). The real action, as far as British traders were concerned, was not to be found in northern China, but in the south, in Guangzhou, the capital of Guangdong Province, known to European and American traders as Canton. By the time the British government decided to send an ambassador to China, British traders could already celebrate a century of lucrative commerce in Canton. The East India Company, granted monopoly rights by the English Crown in 1600 to trade east of the Cape of Good Hope, reached the southeastern coast of China in the early decades of the seventeenth century.[2]

The arrival of the British East India Company in China coincided with political upheaval in both the British Isles and China. In 1644, just two years after civil war had broken out in England (resulting in the beheading of King Charles I), the Ming dynasty (1368–1644) was overthrown by Manchu-speaking Jurchen tribes from the north. The new dynasty, known as the Qing, began ruling China right away, but the dynastic transition was violent, protracted, and disruptive. Ming loyalists, led by the Zheng family and based on the southeast coast of China, in Fujian Province, and Taiwan, succeeded in resisting the Qing until the 1680s. While the Qing government refused to open Chinese ports to foreign traders until political conditions had stabilized, the Zheng regime, looking to increase its military potential "through imports of English weapons and ammunition," allowed the East India Company to set up a trading factory in Taiwan in 1670 and in Amoy (Xiamen) several years later.[3]

When the Qing dynasty finally defeated the Zheng regime in 1683, the East India Company lost its trading privileges in Taiwan but obtained something it had been seeking all along: permission to trade at ports on the Chinese mainland. Canton quickly emerged as the preferred port of call for East India Company ships. In Canton, Company employees encountered a stable, well-managed bureaucracy devoted to supporting and regulating international trade. Complain as they might about corrupt Chinese officials, bribes, and high tariffs, the "Canton system," which lasted almost

Lamqua, attribution (Chinese, active dates 1825–60). *View of the Hongs at Canton,* 1825–35. Oil paint, canvas. Asia, China. Frame 22 1/2 × 32 × 2 inches (57.15 × 81.28 × 5.08 cm). Peabody Essex Museum, Museum purchase, Augustine Heard Collection, 1931. M3793. Courtesy of the Peabody Essex Museum, Salem, Mass. Photography by Mark Sexton and Jeffrey R. Dykes.

one hundred fifty years, until the First Opium War (1839–42), proved an orderly and efficient system for facilitating cross-cultural commerce.[4] That merchants from all over the world—Europeans, Armenians, Indians, Parsis (mostly also from India), and Americans—flocked to Canton and made great fortunes there testifies to the system's success.

The East India Company was not the only significant British presence in Canton. During the late seventeenth century, private traders arrived on the southern coast of China. These "free merchants," "country traders," and "interlopers" (as they were known by contemporaries) were not employees of the East India Company but lived and worked in the Company's shadow. By the early eighteenth century private traders—John Scattergood, for example—had formed close business relationships with

Chinese merchants in Canton, including Linqua, Anqua, Buqua Goldsmith, and the amusingly named Pinkee Winkee.[5] In 1715, Linqua and Anqua, Fujianese business partners who supplied the greatest part of the East India Company's cargoes and whose business networks extended to Dutch Batavia, modern-day Jakarta, sent Scattergood two pots of black tea and two pieces of taffeta silk to thank him for providing transportation to "our China men which went passengers on your ship both in their passage and at Madrasse."[6]

The flow of private traders to China increased dramatically around the middle of the eighteenth century, when, according to Holden Furber, they brought about a "commercial revolution" in the Indian Ocean.[7] During the 1760s, trade between India and China expanded—a process made possible by Britain's territorial conquests in India during the middle of the century. Private British shippers took advantage of "the newly found power and the expanded resource base" to create new Asian trade networks.[8]

The three George Smiths operated in this dynamic world of private trade and cross-cultural commerce in maritime Asia. This book did not start as a study of either the George Smiths or even private traders, however. It began as an exploration of Britain's economic and political relationship with China before the First Opium War. The East India Company's records in the British Library were the natural place to begin research, and it was in the Company's records that George Smith first appeared. He was in Bombay (today's Mumbai), Canton, the settlement that became Cape Town, Penang, Surrey, London, Scotland, Madras, Bengal, and Macao. George Smith seemed to be an irrepressible globetrotter. Who was this incredibly energetic and entrepreneurial business person? He was everywhere, yet his own records were nowhere to be found. His will, letterbooks, journals, and diaries have all vanished, but he was impossible to ignore. With time and further research in British, Chinese, and European archival materials held in the United States, England, Scotland, Australia, Taiwan, Sweden, Denmark, Hong Kong, and Macao, three different George Smiths emerged, all operating between India and China during the second half of the eighteenth century. Smith of Bombay even appeared in the Chinese records; he was called Taipan Shi Mie (大班士蔑).[9] The historical records revealed how these mostly unremarkable Smiths became embroiled in several remarkable events, including two financial crises in Asia, an armed conflict with the Chinese government, a military coup in Madras, a hostage crisis in Canton, the dispatch of two warships to China, official inquiries by the East India Company and Parliament into Indian affairs, and the planning of Britain's first embassy to China. The Smiths' experiences, thoughts, and actions structure this book.

Focusing on the George Smiths of Madras, Canton, and Bombay, in addition to those like them, gives a human face to otherwise complex and abstract macro-level processes, in this case, globalization and British imperial expansion in Asia. The microhistorical approach of this book not only populates "our models and theories with real people" while animating "abstract processes, histories and geographies," but also enables us to test "overarching (and too often idealized) premises with dynamic, embodied examples of past human behaviours."[9] A focus on the George Smiths makes it possible "to explore things otherwise inaccessible" and reminds us that "empires are built on the blood, sweat, tears and desires of people."[10]

Writing history from the perspective of the Smiths helps us to tell a new story about British imperial expansion in Asia. Through the Smiths we can imagine Britain's eighteenth-century empire not only as a commercial, cultural, or political entity defined by consumerism, trade, and the projection of military power across the globe but also as a financial entity, constituted and underpinned by countless financial transactions, credit relationships, and exchanges between Europeans and local elites on the geographical edges of empire. When things went awry, private individuals made new calculations and took action abroad as well as at home, pressuring and sometimes, but not always, convincing the metropolitan government to support their initiatives and intervene more aggressively in the wider world. While historians have long recognized the important connection between finance and imperialism, they have tended to focus on "gentlemanly capitalists," bankers, financiers, and investors based in England (specifically, in London) who, in their view, influenced imperial policies and facilitated imperial expansion by investing their capital throughout the empire.[11] By shifting our geographic focus to the port cities of maritime Asia, new economic actors and systems come into view. We discover that private traders and their clients were creating large financial markets in India and China by lending private British capital (i.e., silver) to Indian rulers and Chinese merchants. This financial system was built upon risky high-interest loans to Asian borrowers, eventually resulting in major financial crises in Canton and Madras. What looked like financial partnership and collaboration had an insidious underbelly and potentially damaging consequences for the participants. Mutually beneficial financial transactions and credit relationships could quickly morph into something different, something imperial; cross-cultural credit could quickly become colonial debt.

In the port cities of Madras and Canton the George Smiths show us how the machinations of private British capital and the levers of debt wielded by its masters helped to tip the balance of power at the micro-economic level in favor of the British. The process by which European empires became world powers has long attracted the attention of scholars. Some have explained the "Rise of the West" in "the East" by arguing for the superiority of European navies, militaries, technology, financial and corporate institutions, and even cultures. In so doing, they have searched far into the past to find the deep origins of European geopolitical success.[12] In the past few decades, however, many scholars have chosen to "re-Orient" themselves and instead emphasize striking similarities between European and Asian empires and societies until the nineteenth century. They contend that "the default setting for the bulk of recorded history . . . was one in which Asia was paramount."[13] According to the most current imperial scholarship, European power was "slight" and "based closely on interaction with Asians and Africans"; Europeans struggled "to find a place in Asian-dominated political orders."[14] But Europeans attempted and sometimes succeeded in altering the terms of economic and political engagement with Asian elites. Observing these subtle power shifts and seeing precisely how empires expand requires closely analyzing new kinds of cross-cultural encounters on the geographical edges of empire. By placing eighteenth-century British private traders at the center of the story, we are uniquely positioned to pinpoint the crucial moments and processes that enabled

Europeans to assert themselves more forcefully in Asia and ultimately to tip the balance of power in their favor.

The economic and political influence of British private traders reached well beyond the port cities of maritime Asia to the centers of British political power in London. Henry Dundas and Edmund Burke, two of the most important British statesmen of the time, received numerous letters and policy suggestions from private traders, including George Smith of Madras and George Smith of Canton. The Smiths' extensive correspondence sheds new light on Britain's first embassy to China. While it is widely believed that the British government decided to send an embassy to China to secure the lucrative tea trade and to open new markets to British exports, we still do not know why the British government suddenly turned its gaze eastward to China. Why did Henry Dundas, the right-hand man of Prime Minister William Pitt (the Younger) and de facto head of the governmental board overseeing the East India Company's affairs in India, decide to commence official diplomatic relations with China against the wishes of the East India Company? Private traders are central to the story of Britain's first embassy to China; they were its greatest advocates, and the idea for an embassy may have originated with them. In Henry Dundas, a fellow Scot, they found a sympathetic and energetic partner whose vision for an empire of free trade aligned with their quest for private profit and greater opportunity in Asia. Together, Dundas and the private traders planned Britain's first embassy to China.

The George Smiths also reveal the significant role Scots and Scottish economic thought played in Britain's China trade. Scots were undoubtedly ubiquitous across the British empire, including India.[15] According to one historian, Tom Devine, "When the statistical record for virtually any area of professional employment in the empire is examined, Scots are seen to be over-represented, and in some cases, like the senior military ranks in India, massively so."[16] In 1776, one English private trader working in India observed that "almost everybody in this part of the world is either Scotch or Irish."[17]

The three Scottish George Smiths demonstrate the importance of Scots, not just in Europe, America, India, and Australia, as numerous studies have already done, but in China as well.[18] Although a disproportionate number of private traders in China were Scottish, most studies on the Scots in Asia focus on India, "where issues of patronage, networking and Scottish Orientalism have been to the fore."[19] The little we know about Scots in China comes to us through the rich biographies and studies of the most famous opium smugglers and plant hunters of the nineteenth century, William Jardine, James Matheson, and Robert Fortune.[20] But keen interest in the decades leading up to the First Opium War, in the nineteenth century, Britain's first military conflict with China, has caused historians to overlook the eighteenth-century dimension of Scottish involvement in China. Even when Scots in China have caught the eye of historians, they have been mistaken for "private English" or "a jealous band of Englishmen resident in China."[21] "Private Scottish" or "a jealous band of Scotsmen" would be more accurate. Scottish private traders played a key role in developing new financial markets linking India and China. Through their relationship with Henry Dundas, they also influenced imperial policies made in London. Close examination of the three George Smiths and others like them confirms Scotland's "conspicuous and arguably disproportionate" impact on the development of Britain's eighteenth-century empire in Asia.[22]

Studying the George Smiths also brings the processes of globalization and its consequences for and connections among a variety of participants in Britain, India, and China into clearer view. The Smiths make visible the relationships and links among areas within as well as beyond Britain's imperial reach. Through the Smiths we see how growing consumer demand in Britain for an ancient Chinese product, tea, created commercial opportunities and financial challenges in Canton for both the East India Company and Chinese merchants. Liquidity problems in Canton were met in large part by private capital from Bengal, Bombay, and Madras, where the East India Company's military conquests in the middle of the eighteenth century made large fortunes for many British East India Company employees. The microhistorical focus on these three Scottish traders provides a global perspective that transcends narrow geographies of the British empire by bringing the entangled histories of Britain, India, and China together under one lens.[23]

The George Smiths serve as our guides through a global history of Britain's eighteenth-century empire, but this book is not simply about three Scottish men. It is also the story of their Asian trading partners, the nawab (prince) of Arcot in southeastern India and the Hong merchants in Canton, with whom the Smiths developed intimate long-term financial relationships. It is also the story of the Smiths' families and communities. The three George Smiths, like many Scots at the time, left home very young. They met their wives and lovers in India. Their children were born and raised in Madras, Bombay, Macao, and the Cape Colony (in modern-day South Africa); their sons and grandsons obtained employment in the East India Company's civil and military service; their daughters and granddaughters married Company and British Army men; and their sisters, widows, and unmarried daughters inherited substantial Eastern fortunes, which enabled them to live comfortably in Britain as independent fundholders and investors. It may, in fact, have been the Smith widows and daughters who ultimately benefited the most from family fortunes begotten in Asia. Financially independent single women and wives with trust funds enjoyed their wealth and lived off their investments "free from the interference, control, debts, or engagement of any husband."[24] The Smith families' extensive and enduring connection to empire demonstrates how "Britain's status as an imperial power became a part of the lived lives of Britons," including several generations of women and children.[25]

East Indian fortunes touched the lives of entire British communities. At the turn of the nineteenth century, boys in Fordyce, Scotland, with the surname Smith (there seem to have been many) received bursaries to study modern commercial languages, mathematics, and accounting under a "well skilled" schoolmaster. Fordyce residents with any surname obtained medical treatment at a new hospital. They also enjoyed the pastoral care of the parish minister. Funding for these important social services came directly from the coffers of George Smith of Bombay. He donated his private Indian fortune to serve the minds, bodies, and souls of his extended kin and neighbors and, in the process, brought the empire home.[26]

Were it not for the addictive Chinese drink tea (茶), Mr. Smith would not have gone to China. British subjects began consuming tea during the late seventeenth and early eighteenth centuries for various reasons, and this cultural practice, new to Britain, drew China, India, and Britain together.[27]

As it became increasingly difficult for both the East India Company and Chinese Hong merchants—that is, those with establishments handling foreign commerce—to finance the growing tea trade in Canton, British private traders stepped in to fill the financial gaps. The George Smiths show us exactly how this was done: through private British capital raised in India and used to make high-interest loans to Chinese merchants. This lending practice led to a major financial crisis in 1779, spurring private traders to use the power of the British state to intervene aggressively in Canton. Something similar was occurring in Madras at roughly the same time. This was no coincidence. The financial crises in Canton and Madras both reveal an imperial pattern in British trading outposts in India and China. Private financial entanglements were undermining local elites and extending British power in Asia.

Not long after the financial crisis erupted in Canton, the third George Smith of our tale, George Smith of Bombay, became entangled in another serious conflict with the Chinese government. When the gunner of Smith of Bombay's ship, the *Lady Hughes,* fired a cannon salute killing two Chinese men in a boat nearby, trade came to a halt and war nearly broke out.

These troubling developments in Canton were often on the mind of Henry Dundas as he contemplated the future of Britain's lucrative China trade and its place in Britain's burgeoning eighteenth-century empire. Under the advice of George Smith of Madras, George Smith of Canton, and private traders like them, he decided to send Britain's first embassy to China.

ONE

Tea and Finance

THE EIGHTEENTH CENTURY WAS, in many ways, Britain's Chinese century. China occupied a central place in British imperial imaginings about "the East" and drew British society in with its unique and sophisticated wares.[1] The wealthy decorated and designed their estates and gardens according to Chinese aesthetic principles, or at least a European interpretation of Chinese style, known as chinoiserie.[2] The rising middle class collected Chinese porcelain. The literati wrote of China's government, religion, and economy, and by the end of the eighteenth century, almost everyone drank tea.[3]

Were it not for tea, Mr. Smith would not have gone to China. British consumers, their cups of tea in hand, unwittingly created the economic conditions that lured private traders to China. The seemingly simple and innocuous act of drinking tea encouraged the development of a new global financial system that connected Britain, India, and China but predated dependence on Indian opium.

While the history of tea begins in China, we often associate tea with India. Since the middle of the nineteenth century, tea plantations in India have supplied much of the world's tea.[4] Tea plants are indigenous to Assam, and several local tribes used tea leaves to brew a medicinal beverage, but the plant was not cultivated until the 1830s and 1840s, when the British taste for tea stimulated its growth on a commercial scale.[5] Wild Assamese tea plants were considered too "jungly" for the refined palate of British tea drinkers, who were already long habituated to the flavors of Chinese tea. Chinese seeds and Chinese farmers (many of them Straits Chinese from Penang—an island off the coast of today's Malaysia—and Singapore) were brought to Assam during the 1830s to launch Britain's tea industry in India.[6]

British traders, plant hunters, and scientists had long been searching for ways to cultivate Chinese tea plants. In 1788, Sir Joseph Banks, president of the Royal Society and director of the Royal Botanic Gardens at Kew, recommended to the East India Company's directors that tea become "an object of cultivation and manufacture in the possessions of the East India Company."[7] According to Banks, Chinese teas were widely considered "superior in flavor" and were grown in the hills of Zhejiang and Fujian Provinces. "Merchantable teas" were grown between 26 and 35 degrees latitude, with 26 to 30 being most favorable for growing black teas and 30 to 34 for growing green teas. If the directors of the Company were to examine their territorial possessions in India, they would "find them, spread over a variety of climates, from the burning heat of the tropic, to the wholesome coolness . . . fertile in the extreme from one end to the other, peopled by a numerous race of frugal industrious and intelligent natives, accustomed to labor for lower wages, possibly [more] than any other men, and intersected in a multitude of directions by navigable rivers placed as if on purpose to bring the fruits of their industry at a cheap rate, to the center of commerce." Banks advised the Company's directors to bring Chinese tea plants to the northern parts of the province of Behar near the mountains of Bhutan. His plan depended on the cooperation of Chinese farmers, who he hoped could be induced to "embark [with] their tea shrubs and all their tools of culture and manufacture and migrate with them to Calcutta [today's Kolkata]," where they would receive twenty acres of land "which is already cleared and prepared for similar purposes and lying under very nearly the same latitude as Canton." Banks imagined that Chinese cultivators would then teach "the natives" in Behar the "culture and manufacture of the article."[8] Banks's vision was not realized until the middle of the nineteenth century. Until then, British consumers had to depend on China for their tea.

In China, tea had been cultivated and consumed for more than a millennium before Samuel Pepys, the famous London diarist, took his first sip of the "China drink" in 1660.[9] The words used around the world to name the drink all come from either Hokkien, a southern Chinese dialect (*tea, te*), or from Mandarin, a northern dialect (*chai, cha*).[10] Sometime before the Han dynasty (206 BCE–220 CE), Buddhist monks began cultivating tea in the mountains around their monasteries in Sichuan Province. By the time of the Tang dynasty (618–907), people "at all levels of society" were drinking tea.[11] It was considered one of the "'seven necessities' of life" during the Southern Song period (1127–79).[12]

Tea was processed and prepared in various ways in China. The cup or pot of tea with which we are familiar today, loose leaves steeped in hot water, was an innovation of the Ming dynasty. Before the fourteenth century, tea was roasted as cakes, ground into a powder, and then "whisked to a froth in very hot water," or it was boiled with ginger, citrus peels, and various condiments in a soup.[13] Various forms of black (oxidized) tea, or "red tea" in Chinese (紅茶), were developed in the sixteenth century, including souchong (小種茶), bohea (武夷茶), and congou (工夫). Oolong (烏龍茶) and pekoe (白毫茶) came later, in the eighteenth century.[14]

Developments in tea production and consumption brought "a total reorientation of Chinese culture," and "restructured social life."[15] Xu Guoqi, a Ming-dynasty scholar-official, described the importance of tea to Chinese state and society during the 1600s: "Tea is a divine herb. Profits are ample if one plants it. The spirit is purified if one drinks it . . . It is something esteemed by the noblemen and well-to-do which commoners and déclassé folks cannot do without. Truly it is a necessity in the daily lives of the people, and an asset for the fiscal prosperity of the state."[16] British writers would say the same about tea in their own society a century later.

As Chinese tea was being transformed into a British beverage, Chinese farmers and peasants in Fujian and Zhejiang Provinces responded to the new, ever-increasing demand from Europe.[17] Elaborate networks for the transport of tea from central China to Canton also emerged, requiring the joint efforts of inland merchants, middlemen, and tens of thousands of coolie laborers who "carried the tea for six days over the Bohea Mountains." From farm to market, it took between one and two months for tea to reach Canton, where it was sold to European merchants.[18]

Chinese tea made its appearance in England around the early seventeenth century with the help of Dutch traders.[19] But England was slower than its European neighbors to warm to the hot beverage. Although "small amounts" were available in the 1650s, tea did not start to become popular

than a duty on wine."[25] From the 1730s on, tea prices fell, making it, most particularly black tea, increasingly affordable to a wide swath of society.[26] Tea was no longer a luxury; as in China, it had become a necessity.

London served as the British emporium for imports, and as a result, Londoners became precocious tea consumers. In 1717, Thomas Twining opened the first teahouse in London.[27] But tea drinking was not confined to London and quickly spread to other parts of Britain and its expanding empire.[28] By the 1740s, "mass consumption certainly had taken hold throughout much of the country," with the English and the Welsh probably consuming one pound of tea per capita annually.[29] In the first decades of the eighteenth century the gentry of Northumberland and Durham, in northeastern England, drank tea frequently. By the 1740s, middle-class northerners regularly enjoyed a cup of tea.[30] The same was true in Scotland, where aristocratic elites were drinking tea as early as the 1690s. By 1745, Scottish society had developed "clear preferences and a definite awareness of varieties, price and quality."[31] In British North America, over half of urban dwellers leaving estates worth more than £50 possessed tea and tea services in the 1720s, and between 1745 and 1754, 40 percent of those with estates worth less than £50 also possessed tea and various tea accoutrements.[32] By the middle of the century, tea drinking had become a widespread social practice that also included the "lesser-sorts," who now "insisted on drinking tea" as well.[33]

Why did tea catch on in Britain and its Atlantic colonies? From a practical point of view, tea was a healthy and energizing beverage and easy to prepare at home. Boiled tea was safer and more interesting than plain water and, unlike coffee, was less likely to require elaborate or expensive equipment to brew. Its price also appears to have fallen relative to coffee during the first quarter of the eighteenth century.[34] In contrast to other British staples, such as beer and ale, caffeinated tea had an invigorating effect on mind and body and seems to have replaced alcoholic beverages in certain social contexts. As modern consumers well know, the caffeine in tea can make it addictive, and with the addition of sugar, it became even more so.[35]

Tea possessed several attractive qualities. It complemented social and cultural developments already under way in early modern England—

for example, social visits. Tea drinking created an occasion upon which people, particularly women, could socialize in their homes. This might mean lingering around the breakfast table with family or stopping by in the afternoon to take tea with friends and neighbors.[36] The tea table quickly became an important social institution. In 1749, George Vane revealed the source of his gossip regarding Lady Bowes. He reported: "By the addition in her bulk, the tea tables say she is going forward towards adding another to the family."[37] Tea accessories also supported a trend in early modern England toward more refined tableware and the accompanying etiquette, evidenced by the increasing popularity of forks, knives, and metal plates. Many welcomed the opportunity to invest more in their homes by buying and displaying new and exotic Chinese porcelain teacups and teapots.[38] Tea drinking may also have provided rituals and symbols to the rising middle class and nouveaux riches that they used to define a new social identity, one characterized by "respectability." These rituals and symbols "revealed the manners and social status of whole groups in society previously excluded from the visual image of what passed as genteel, respectable or polite."[39] Some families commissioned paintings, known as conversation pieces, depicting themselves drinking tea in their homes, perhaps with guests or while playing cards. This performance of a new middle-class identity could also take place outside the home—for instance, in coffeehouses, where patrons read newspapers or talked politics and business while sipping hot cups of tea.

In addition to social and cultural meanings, tea could signify different things to those who partook of it. For some, connecting with the elite of faraway lands by drinking the same drink "drank by the Mandarines, Milletarie, Literatie in China" may have been appealing. That is how tea was marketed to potential consumers in the *Newcastle Gazette* in 1752.[40] For others, tea drinking was a solitary ritual that provided personal enjoyment or marked the hours of one's day. Elizabeth Carter, a poet, scholar, and translator, described herself dining alone and reveling in cake and tea, "a kind of independent luxury in which one need very little apparatus, and no attendants; and is mightily consistent with loitering over a book."[41] For Ralph Grey of Backworth (near Durham), tea drinking was a way of struc-

Hubert-François Gravelot (1699–1773). *A Game of Quadrille,* 1740. Courtesy of the Yale Center for British Art.

turing his time. He recorded a typical day in his diary: "to drink tea the 3d hour from sitting down to dinner and from dinner to tea time to sit quiet in that the victuals may digest, after tea walk an hour then study till supper."[42] Tea drinking could have myriad meanings, reflecting the idiosyncrasies of those who drank it.

Tea did not escape the notice of British statesmen. After coming to power in 1783, Prime Minister Pitt (the Younger) and his close associate Henry Dundas quickly recognized tea's economic significance to the British state. The value of the tea trade was so obvious that they felt it was "unnecessary . . . to enlarge upon the great national importance of the trade" between Great Britain and China.[43] The end of the Seven Years' War in 1763 saw tea imports into Britain and Europe increase by 70 percent over the previous seven years. But the most important leap in East India Company tea sales occurred in the 1780s, specifically after 1784, when sales tripled. In 1783 the East India Company sold 5,858,000 pounds of tea to home and European markets, in 1785 it sold 15,082,000 pounds, and by 1794 the amount had reached 19,127,000 pounds.[44]

It was no accident that the Company's tea imports grew so dramatically over the course of one decade. Although domestic demand for tea was rising, this impressive growth owed much to a legislative measure, the Commutation Act, adopted by William Pitt in 1784 to halt the smuggling of tea into Britain. Before 1784, the British state heavily taxed the East India Company's tea imports with duties increasing the net cost by 65 to 110 percent.[45] The inflated cost of legal Company tea in Britain encouraged the development of a black market. Tea smuggling became acute during the 1770s, when tea imported into Europe by various competitor companies rose to 13,400,000 pounds, the vast majority of which was intended for the British market.[46] British consumers found smuggled tea attractive because it allowed them to evade the British government's heavy tax on tea, but black market tea threatened the British state's tea revenues, "variously estimated at £600,000 and £900,000," as well the finances of the East India Company. Both state and Company were suffering after the disastrous war with the American colonies (1776–83). The British state responded by passing the Commutation Act, which lowered the duty on tea to 12.5 percent.[47]

The Commutation Act of 1784 "put the smugglers out of business and placed the tea trade more thoroughly in the hands of the British state."[48] Prior to 1833, when the Company's monopoly on trade with China was abolished, the Commutation Act was, according to one historian, "the most important event in the history of Anglo-Chinese relations."[49] Henry Dundas claimed, ten years after its passage, "You cannot omit to take under your consideration how much the value of that trade has been augmented by the Commutation Act."[50] The legislation bound Britain and China's fates together. The Company's directors, Prime Minister Pitt, and Henry Dundas all understood that the survival of the East India Company depended on the tea trade with China. Although war and territorial conquests in India resulted in financial losses for the Company, the China trade remained profitable. It had become the Company's only profitable venture in the East Indies by the middle of the eighteenth century.[51] Tea was its caffeine-laced lifeblood.

The East India Company, however, could not find a product to sell in China to match tea's popularity in Britain. This trade deficit forced the Company to export American silver to China, a practice severely criticized by the British public. Reacting to pressure from home, the Company's directors sent very little silver to China around the time of the American Revolution and the Fourth Anglo-Dutch War, during the 1770s and early 1780s. They hoped that wealth generated in their new Indian territories would find its way to China. Since the Company had recently acquired *diwani* rights, the authority to collect taxes, in Bengal, the richest province in India, the Company's directors thought this a reasonable expectation. As a result, they pressured their three settlements in India, particularly the Bengal Presidency, to use their revenues to fund the tea trade. This strategy might have worked had Bengal tax revenues ever lived up to the expectations of those involved in the conquest of Bengal, and had the Company managed to stay out of wars in India. But this was not the case; military and administrative costs made it impossible for the Indian presidencies in Madras, Bombay, and Bengal to provide the silver necessary to finance the China trade. Lord Cornwallis, the governor-general of India between 1786 and 1793 (the same Cornwallis who surrendered to General George Washington in Yorktown, Virginia, several years earlier), was not alone in his sentiments when he complained to Henry Dundas privately: "I have few greater plagues than the remittances to China, and indeed I must be candid enough to acknowledge that I think I have not managed that business well."[52]

Financing the growing tea trade with China had been an ongoing struggle for several decades. As early as 1759, the Company's directors in London chastised the Bengal and Bombay Councils for making large drafts upon the Company's treasury in London. The Court of Directors explained, "We are under the almost indispensable necessity of starving the only profitable trade the Company has, we mean that to China." Two years later, the Court of Directors in London warned their employees in Bengal that it was of "the utmost importance to feed it [the China trade] with as plentiful remittances as circumstances will admit of" because it is "our principal resource for valuable returns." In 1761, the Company's directors reiterated the point: "As the China trade is a certain source of profit, and considering the present great demand for teas here, [it] will stand in need of as large supplies as can be afforded." In 1768, they explained to the Bengal Council, "The enlargement of the trade to China to its utmost extent, is an object we have greatly at heart, not only from the advantages in prospect, by gaining a superiority and thereby discouraging foreign Europeans from resorting to that market; but also from a national concern, wherein the revenue is very materially interested."[53] The directors' repeated instructions to the Indian presidencies to send silver to China reveal their anxiety about financing the tea trade.

While demand for silver was growing in Canton, capital was accumulating in private British hands in India. In the south, political instability in the region around Madras made it possible for the British and French East India companies to back rival political rulers and fight wars against each other through their respective Indian allies.[54] Ultimately, the British East India Company prevailed, becoming, according to S. Arasaratnam, the "real holder of political power along the coastal belt."[55] Territorial conquests and military victories in Bengal and Madras in the 1750s and 1760s paved the way for the post-Plassey plunder. The Battle of Plassey (1757) was a crucial victory for the British by which many Company employees—the most notorious being Robert Clive, founder of the British empire in India—enriched themselves through "gifts" and private contracts with local Indian rulers. With increased military and political power in the region, Company employees also intervened in the internal trade of Bengal. They could now access and, in some cases, monopolize the trade of India, including the trade in cotton, rice, indigo, saltpeter, and opium.[56] With all of the new commercial opportunities available, many got rich quick in this East Indian bonanza.[57] But what to do with their new wealth?

Depending on their tolerance for risk and desire for profit, the British nouveaux riches in India could choose from an array of investment options, including real estate in Britain and India, Indian diamonds, British government bonds and annuities, East India Company and Bank of England shares, Company bonds in India, East Indies commerce (known as "country trade"), marine insurance, and private loans to European and Asian merchants and rulers. When choosing among these options, British investors considered the risk, the potential return on investment, the amount of capital needed for the investment, and the amount of time their capital would be tied up. They also attempted to minimize their risk by diversifying their portfolios and distributing their assets among a variety of investments.

Those who sought large profits preferred to invest their money in ventures in Asia, where rates of return were significantly higher than in Britain. Some invested in the East India Company's growing debt in India by buying Company bonds and treasury notes, which yielded 8–12 percent interest and often much higher rates of return if bought at a discount.[58] Company employees and private traders could also lend money to European residents in India. By the mid-1770s, Europeans in Bengal generally paid 12 percent annual interest for private loans.[59] "Remember that Indian interest is high and that you never [have] money lying dead in your Chest" was Laurence Sullivan's advice to his son who was embarking for Madras in 1778.[60] Investors sometimes provided loans to maritime traders in the form of respondentia, or bottomry (marine insurance) bonds. Interest on these loans was high (18–50 percent per year) because they insured the cargo or the ship. Investors assumed the risk but stood to make a handsome profit if the voyage succeeded. Private loans to Indian merchants and rulers at interest rates as high as 25 percent per year were also attractive to many British investors.[61]

More risk-averse Company employees preferred, instead, to remit or transfer their wealth to Britain. George Vansittart, a Company servant in Bengal, voiced this sentiment to his friend and attorney, Robert Palk, former governor of Madras: "I hope by next April to be worth about five lacks [lakhs] of rupees and although I should like to double that sum, yet it will not be worth my while to stay to attempt it if I am to suffer a present loss and depend only on the prospect of future advantage." Once an investor's wealth had been transmitted to England, the most cautious and successful bought landed estates. Vansittart, for example, did not "like to have my money in the Funds. I am not of humour with their continual fluctuations. And I cannot even bring myself to have a perfect confidence in their security." He directed his agent instead to purchase an estate for him.[62] Investments in land in England at that time yielded returns between 3 and 4 percent. Those who could tolerate slightly more risk than Vansittart became fund holders by buying government annuities, or East India Company and Bank of England shares and bonds. Interest rates and dividends were relatively low but fluctuated between 3 and 6 percent during the second half of the eighteenth century.[63] Private loans in England were legally capped at 5 percent interest but probably obtained somewhat higher rates despite the usury laws.[64]

In the eighteenth century, transferring wealth from Asia to Europe was no easy task. To minimize risk, many relied on bills of exchange, a financial instrument developed by Italian and French merchants during the twelfth century, which allowed traders to "remit payments in foreign cities, to extend short-term credit, and to speculate on currency arbitrage."[65] Private traders made use of the East India Company's system of treasuries in India, Canton, and London, as well as its bills of exchange.[66] They shipped and managed cargoes of goods financed or consigned to them by their clients in India. After selling these cargoes in Southeast Asia and China, they deposited the profits into the Company's treasury in Canton and received bills of exchange, which their clients could cash at the Company's treasury in London, usually after one year's time.

Between 1761 and 1780, the East India Company identified over twenty unlicensed private traders doing business in Canton at different points in time, but there were probably more.[67] Many of these private traders, such as George Smith of Madras and John Crichton, first arrived in India and later established themselves in Canton without the Company's permission. Others, such as George Smith of Bombay and David Scott, remained in India but made regular voyages to China. While the Company enjoyed a legal monopoly on trade in the East Indies and China, it tended to look the other way as long as private traders quietly performed important financial services for the Company and its employees. There seems to have been a gentleman's agreement regarding interloping private traders. The official Company policy toward them was unambiguous: trading in the East Indies without a Company license was illegal. However, actual practice differed. Although the Court of Directors in London repeatedly instructed their supercargos in Canton to order interlopers to leave China, the Company was perfectly willing to do business with them. Supercargos, who held an official Company post, were responsible for the buying and selling of cargoes in Canton.[68] In 1774, George Smith of Canton requested preference from the Council of Supercargos in Canton to be granted Company bills of exchange for the 1776 season.[69] The Company's directors in London responded with instructions to the Council of Supercargos: "In consequence of our determination to continue to open the treasury in China for bills of exchange on us several gentlemen have desired to make use of that channel for remittances, you are therefore, if you want the whole of the sums set against their names, to give . . . their attorneys the preference in receiving the under mentioned sums for which you are to pass your drafts upon us etc." The Court of Directors later noted that "Mr. George Smith stands first in the list of persons to whom bills were to be given and his name [is] set down for £40,000."[70]

The commercial and financial services provided by private traders operating between India and China pumped much-needed silver into the Company's China trade. Indeed, "without this arrangement the China trade could not be financed."[71] George Smith of Canton claimed that were it not for private traders, "the yearly investment of the India Company could not have been supplied."[72] According to John Rogers, captain of an East Indiaman, a Company ship, the Company "ever looked to those private persons for their supplies of cash when their treasury was open . . . Their commanders of ships could not produce a sum equal to the Company's investment . . . I cannot suppose the East India Company have suffered" by the residence of unlicensed private traders in China.[73] This was not merely braggadocio. No private trade meant a substantially reduced tea trade. Between 1769 and 1792, private traders deposited $28,817,076 into the Company's Canton treasury. The cost of purchasing tea in China for the same period was $29,334,051.[74] Major Samuel Shaw, the first American consul in Canton, noted in his journal that the proceeds of private trade, much of which was deposited into the Canton treasury, had "for a number of years rendered it unnecessary for the Company to export from Europe any specie for carrying on their commerce with the Chinese."[75]

When the Company's directors in London asked their Canton supercargos, "What are the benefits which the Company derive in China from the remittances from India?" the responses were unanimous. "Infinite! The Company's funds would seldom or never be adequate to furnish their cargoes for Europe without them," replied Alexander Bruce, a supercargo appointed by the Company in the 1770s. His colleague William Fitzhugh, who also ran a private side business or agency house with two other Canton supercargos, David Lance and Henry Lane, added: "The benefits in which the Company receive from the remittances made from India, or the trade which produces them, whether considered in a political or commercial light, are of the utmost importance . . . these remittances have supported the China trade . . . without them the Company must have been forever discredited, or perhaps under the necessity of sending out fewer ships and giving up the market to other adventurers." Fitzhugh also extolled the industriousness of private traders, who, in his opinion, "owe everything to their own activity and exertion, and are of so much use in India as merit all the encouragement which the government of that country can possibly give them."[76]

In recognition of these benefits to its trade, Company officials coaxed their employees to remit their new wealth from India to Britain via the Company's treasury in Canton. This encouragement took numerous forms. For instance, the Court of Directors periodically altered the exchange rate of British pounds to Spanish silver dollars to attract private British capital. From 1769 on, "the Company offered bills on London at generous rates of exchange for private money from India presented at its factory at Canton."[77] The Bengal Presidency also experimented with several ways of inducing British residents in India to deposit their wealth in the Canton treasury, sometimes offering freight-free shipping on Company ships sailing between India and China and at other times taking up subscriptions for silver to be shipped to the Company's Canton treasury on the king's frigate at the Company's risk. Afterward, the subscribers received bills of exchange in Canton that they could cash at the Company's London treasury.

What kinds of goods and cargoes did British investors ship from India to Southeast Asia and China? In other words, in what form did they transmit their wealth to their Canton brokers? Although opium has received much attention as the cure for the East India Company's trade deficit, during the lifetimes of the three George Smiths, opium composed only a small part of private traders' diverse commercial portfolios. Company employees transferred their wealth from India to China through a variety of commodities, including food, spices, medicines, crafts, and curiosities. Cargoes shipped from India and Southeast Asia to China included an exotic-sounding hodgepodge of products, including tin, redwood, saltpeter, rattan, pepper, rice, sago, arrack (alcoholic drink), catch, sandalwood, nutmeg, "dragons' blood," ivory, sharks' fins, putchuk (a fragrant root), fish maws, seed pearls, coral, stick lack (to make shellac), yellow beads, black wood, cloves, snuff, camphor, handkerchiefs, long ells (of woolen cloth), palampores (cloth), bêche-de-mer (sea cucumber), moco stones, birds' nests, looking glasses, clocks, lead, plant cuttings, window glass, raisins, gold thread, amber, stone blue, watches, cloves, cardamom, cochineal (for red dye), and tortoiseshell.[78]

During the 1780s, Bombay cotton emerged as a particularly important commodity. Sending raw cotton from India to China solved the problem of paying for Chinese tea imports, whose cost European exports to China could not cover by themselves. The Chinese took cotton "in ever-increasing quantities," and the Bombay cotton trade was quickly captured by private traders.[79] Between 1774 and 1785, private traders shipped "almost 60 per cent of all of the cotton imported into Canton."[80] Bombay cotton helped keep the Canton tea trade flowing, and the growing commerce between these two port cities, in turn, ensured Bombay's survival as a British commercial and military settlement.[81]

Like cotton, opium imports to China grew during the second half of the eighteenth century. But because of the riskiness of the trade—it was illegal to sell opium in China—the East India Company, for the most part, abstained from directly participating. The Company did, however, actively encourage private individuals to buy opium at its auctions in India and then distribute the drug throughout Southeast Asia and China at their own discretion. In that way, "whatever opium might be in demand by the Chinese, that quantity would readily find its way thither, without the Company being exposed to the disgrace of engaging in an illicit commerce."[82] Or so the Company hoped. According to the Company's supercargos in China, "almost every country vessel that comes here [brings opium] and we imagine they will continue to bring it."[83] Some saw in opium a panacea for the East India Company's trade deficit in China. James Kerr, a surgeon's assistant in Bengal, informed the Court of Directors in 1773 that the "Chinese smoke opium with their tobacco as the greatest delicacy. After the ceremony of salutations, it is the first compliment payed to a visitor or stranger." He reported that the consumption of opium was annually increasing and "is now said to be double of what it was a few years ago."[84] In 1782, one of the Company's supercargos stationed in Canton, Thomas Fitzhugh, explained to the Court of Directors in London that opium "for a long course of time, has been annually carried to China, and often in large quantities both by our country vessels and those of the Portuguese. It is sometimes landed at Macao and sometimes at Whampo."[85] The Company's indirect opium trade with China, with private traders serving as intermediaries, seemed to some to be working very well. In 1781, a lieutenant colonel in the Company, Henry Watson, claimed that "by the best authority I find that the present yearly consumption in the South East provinces of China alone amounts to twelve hundred chests."[86]

The opium trade, however, had its skeptics. Only with hindsight do we know the important role opium would play in the nineteenth century. Traders like George Smith of Madras had no such certainty. Smith found the business extremely volatile: "We now have no certain market for that commodity, in my plan, though I took opium, I had a certain resource for the amount or for its deficiency."[87] When Thomas Fitzhugh was asked his "opinion, whether it would be proper to send opium from Bengal to China on the Companys account," he replied that it was "an article which of course fluctuates greatly in price according to the quantities brought, and the Chinese who buy it, and who are of the lower sort, will not venture on the purchase without a large profit, as the risk and difficulty are great after they are in possession of it. The price was so low in the year 1779, that a Captain of one of the country vessels (who had a good deal of his own) purchased of others on speculation; and, as his ship was obliged to return to India, he bought a small vessel at Macao—brought her up to Whampo—put all his opium into her, and remained there the whole year; selling it at several times in small parcels as he could find purchasers." Fitzhugh painted a picture of a trade fraught with risk and unpredictability, "liable to difficulty and disgrace." He closed his letter with a warning to the Company's directors: "The Chinese are very sensible of the difference between the country ships and those of the Company. Between the Companys mode of transacting business and that of all private traders. They look up to your servants as people conducting the affairs of a great Company; who at the same time that they endeavor to prevent impositions, act with candor, regularity and liberality. How must this opinion change when your servants are (on the Companys account) to deviate from the plain road of an honorable trade, to pursue the crooked path of smuggling?"[88]

Members of Parliament also had their doubts about opium. In response to Henry Dundas's prescient assertion that Bengal cotton and opium could balance Britain's trade with China, "Mr. Sheridan ridiculed very strongly the idea of paying £275,000 per annum with opium, which was a commodity only smuggled into China."[89] When asked by the Court of Directors whether the export trade from Europe or India to China could be augmented with either old or new articles, the Company's Canton supercargos pointed to cotton, lead, tin, pepper, sandalwood, and woolen goods. None mentioned opium.[90] According to William Fitzhugh, "the only articles of consequence are cotton, pepper, and sandal wood, of which a greater quantity has been brought for several years past by private people."[91]

In 1786, at least 2,000 chests of opium were smuggled into China.[92] These are small quantities when compared to amounts in later decades. In 1821, imports of the drug in China hovered around 4,500 chests per year. It was not until the late 1830s that opium imports skyrocketed to 40,000 chests per year.[93] The late eighteenth-century opium trade did not begin to approach the scope or scale of the nineteenth-century trade.

On the other side of the globe, Britain's encounter with a more innocuous drug, Chinese tea, brought about new social and cultural rituals at home and encouraged financial innovations abroad. As consumer demand for tea increased, the East India Company struggled to send enough silver to finance its tea trade in China, its only profitable commercial venture in Asia by the middle of the eighteenth century. British private traders came to the rescue. Basing themselves in Canton and Macao, they facilitated new intra-Asian financial networks that kept silver and tea flowing during the second half of the eighteenth century. With the help of private traders, Company employees could safely transfer their private fortunes from India to Britain, while the Company saw its Canton treasury filled with silver. Everyone was content, for a time. This financial system was so effective that the Company came "to rely increasingly heavily upon private country traders for the supply of liquid funds to the supercargoes at Canton." Private country traders played a crucial role in this new global economic system centered on Chinese tea.[94]

TWO

George Smith of Madras

IN THE MIDDLE OF THE EIGHTEENTH CENTURY, three George Smiths, all Scottish, learned of the lucrative business opportunities emerging in India and China and decided to act. They left their homes and families when they were in their early twenties and traveled halfway across the world to make their fortunes. They were not alone.

Many British youths like the George Smiths moved to the East Indies to try "to earn an independence." Most viewed their time in India, Southeast Asia, or China as a temporary exile from Britain. They hoped to earn "a competence" and come home to their friends and families "as quickly as possible."[1] Upon returning to Britain, the most successful East Indies traders, the "nabobs," bought large landed estates in England and Scotland and became members of Parliament and even directors of the East India Company.[2] While some looked forward to an early retirement in England or Scotland, others continued to run their businesses from London.

Frederic Davy, the son of an Anglican minister, set out for India in 1775 at the age of sixteen. He worked as a merchant apprentice with an agency house, the Bengal Commercial Society of Killican, Robinson, Croftes, Grant, and Fergusson of Calcutta.[3] Houses of agency began as "rudimentary banking businesses, receiving money on deposit and investing it," but their operations later came to include shipbuilding, trading in Company bills of exchange, shipping, remittances, insurance, sugar and indigo plantations, and opium trading.[4] While apprenticing at this house of agency, Davy aspired to become the supercargo of a private ship bound for China, which he believed to be the "most profitable of any business in India" and might earn him £3,000 in one voyage. While he dared not dream of great fortune and fame, he did hope for "enough to make my own life easy and happy" and a "humble though independent obscurity as soon as possible."[5] A savings of £20,000 seems to have been sufficient to earn a trader and his family retirement in Britain, while the more ambitious aimed to take home as much as £60,000.[6]

As an English trader, Davy was struck by the ubiquity of Scots in the East Indies and their loyalty to one another at the expense of other capable merchants like him: "In all Companies particularly amongst the Europe and Country captains, you seldom see more than five English to twenty Scotch; the poverty of their own country obliges them to go abroad and this is the reason every other part of the world is so stock'd with them; I have made it a rule, never to speak in prejudice of any body of Men, or Nation whatever; but their general Character is Pride and Self Conceit over bearing when in power, mean and submissive independence; and partiality to their own countrymen, is carried to so ridiculous a height, that no other however deserving has any chance of preferment with them."[7] Davy's observations, while hyperbolic and self-interested, highlight the ubiquity and conspicuousness of Scots in the East Indies. Many Scots obtained positions as supercargos (*taipan* 大班), the business managers of ships bound for India and China. According to Andrew Mackillop, between 1732 and 1750 approximately one-third of the Swedish East India Company's voyages "had a majority or large minority of Scottish supercargoes."[8] And probably many more young Scots, like the three George Smiths, found employment outside of the East India companies on private country ships.

Davy was correct to suggest that poverty drove many Scots (as well as English youths) to the East Indies. Poverty, however, was not the only force compelling young Scots to sail thousands of miles to make their fortunes. Sojourning and migration were deeply rooted in Scottish history and culture.[9] As far back as the Middle Ages, Scotland had been a "particularly outward-looking place, characterized by a 'culture of migration,'" particularly to Europe.[10] In the seventeenth century, "global adventuring became a way of life for Scots," and with the union of England and Scotland in 1707, "the traditional continental sojourning of Scots as soldiers and scholars was pressed into the service of the inchoate yet expanding eighteenth-

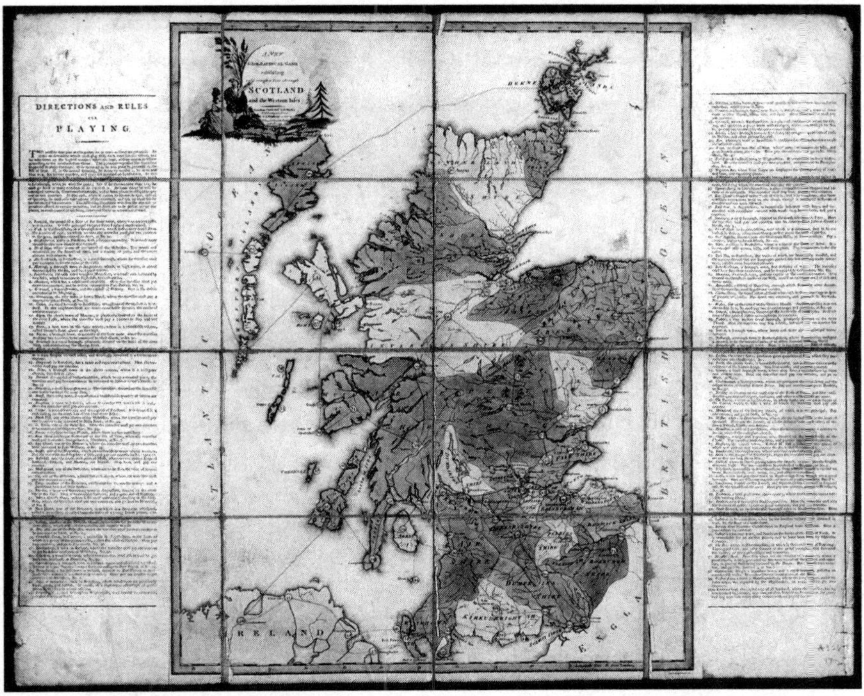

A New Geographical Game Exhibiting a Complete Tour through Scotland and the Western Isles (Neele Sc. London: J. Wallis & E. Newbery, 1792). Beinecke Rare Book and Manuscript Library, Yale University.

century British Empire."[11] The three George Smiths were participants in a long history of Scottish migration.

Beyond the Scottish culture of global adventuring, other more urgent push-factors encouraged Scottish youths, particularly Highland Scots, to leave their families and venture to the East Indies during the eighteenth century. In 1688, James II was deposed by his daughter, Mary, and her Dutch husband, William of Orange, in an event known as the Glorious Revolution. Almost six decades later, in 1745, Charles Edward Stuart, James II's grandson, landed on the western coast of Scotland and with the help of Highland clan leaders raised a small army. The second Jacobite uprising, or the '45, was fought to restore the Scottish Stuart line to the

British throne. The rebels met defeat "on a sleet-swept wasteland known as Drumossie Moor, near Culloden House." For many young Scots, the Jacobite defeat at Culloden "led them to seek their fortunes far away from the graves of the clansmen who died on that field."[12]

The Highlands of Scotland seemed to some British observers to resemble North America, "a place on the edge of the empire, where metropolitan standards of behavior, the rule of law, and the authority of the central government were weak."[13] The failed uprising provided the British state with an opportunity to subdue and "civilize" a region of Scotland that had long been perceived as primitive, savage, rebellious, violent, and dangerous. The British Army engaged in a violent punitive mission through the Highlands, looting and destroying private property and brutalizing local communities. The British government also began a longer-term imperial project that involved the restructuring and assimilating of Highland communities according to British economic, cultural, and political norms. Parliament's design was nothing short of the "destruction of the ancient Gaelic culture of the Scottish Highlands."[14] The Highlanders were disarmed, religious life was regulated, Jacobite estates were confiscated, the English language was promoted over Gaelic, and the authority of the clan chieftains and the barons' courts and clan councils was subverted.[15] It was in the aftermath of the '45 that the three George Smiths made their way to India and China.

Of the three George Smiths, it appears that only Smith of Madras obtained permission from the East India Company to reside and trade in the East Indies. In theory, the Company enjoyed a state-sanctioned monopoly on trade east of the Cape of Good Hope, but in reality, it did not control the flow of people to the East Indies. In particular, "there was no effective means of stopping enterprising individuals from going to India." Those who were too old or who lacked the influence or wealth needed to obtain appointment to the Company's civil or military service might apply to the Company for licenses to trade in India as free merchants. Upon payment of £1,000 in security, they were allowed to live and work in the Company's settlements in India and, rarely, in China for a limited period of time.[16] Some, however, attempted to bypass the Company entirely by joining one of the competing European East India companies. The Danish, Swedish, and Ostend companies all hired British supercargos, mariners, and officers in large numbers.[17] Private traders also found their way to the East Indies by other means—for instance, over land, by traveling east via the Levant. Others bypassed the Mediterranean route and obtained employment in the East India Company's army or on its ships to secure passage to India, only to quit the Company and start trading on their own.[18] By 1787, there were at least 175 Europeans in Madras who "had drifted to India in devious ways."[19] Seventy free merchants were living in Bengal during the 1760s, but this estimate does not include those without licenses from the Company.[20] The number in China—that is, in Canton and Macao, where the East India Company had no independent settlement of its own—was much lower, with probably fewer than ten British private traders permanently residing there in any given year.[21]

If commercial opportunities in the eighteenth-century Indian Ocean and South China Sea were numerous, so were the risks. The lure of wealth and future self-sufficiency was great, but private traders who ventured to the East Indies faced a host of obstacles, competitors, and dangers, both financial and physical. By sailing to India and China, they risked everything. Morbid reminders of the dangers at sea fill the logbooks of the East India Company's ships: "At 4am departed this life Thomas Francess invalid. at noon committed the body of the deceased to the deep."[22] If traders survived the six-month journey from England to India and avoided being "committed to the deep," they could expect to be struck down by any number of insect- and water-born diseases. William Hickey, who traveled to India in 1777 and served as an attorney at the supreme court in Calcutta, nearly died of a typhoidlike illness which he described as "a horrid dream, accompanied with sensations of agonies so complicated I cannot describe."[23] Lives in the East Indies often ended prematurely and painfully with fever and diarrhea. Forty-four percent of Company civil servants venturing to India at the same time as Hickey never returned to tell the tale.[24]

Physical survival was a struggle, but commercial survival was even more so. There were the normal hazards and difficulties of eighteenth-century business: insufficient capital, information asymmetries, principal-agent problems, shipwrecks, venal government officials, political instability, and war. But trade in the East Indies had heightened risks and also new ones. The drain of money from India was a constant concern. Silver, the primary currency of the Indian Ocean world, was often scarce, and interest rates in India and China could soar well over 12 percent per year. Linguistic, cultural, and political differences created formidable obstacles to long-distance trade. British private traders had to negotiate with a plethora of political elites and commercial mediators. In China, where teaching the Chinese language to foreigners was technically illegal, the linguistic barrier forced most British traders to depend on Chinese merchants and linguists to interpret for them. This dependence on Chinese translators, they believed, put them at a serious disadvantage relative to their Chinese trading partners.[25] British traders frequently complained about "harsh and unjust treatment which the Europeans meet with at Canton" and "the frauds and villainy of those mandarins."[26] The variety of business hazards and simple bad judgment made it all too easy to fail. Many careers began with youthful optimism (or greed) and ended in insolvency or bankruptcy. As we shall see, this was also true for two of our George Smiths.

Another obstacle for private traders in India and China at this time was the East India Company itself. From 1667 until 1784, Company employees in India were officially entitled to trade in the East Indies on their own account. Private trade was no mere side concern for them; it was the main attraction of Company employment. George Vansittart earned himself a private fortune while serving as chief of Patna for the Company. At the same time, he admitted that the Company should "increase the allowances of Counsellors and restrain them altogether from trading," since he believed "it must inevitably be a very destructive system for the rulers of a country, especially in a despotic government, to be the merchants of it."[27] Non-Company private traders were at a serious disadvantage. They were permitted to reside only in the Company's settlements and had trouble competing with Company employees for the inland trade in India.[28] It helped to have Company connections. "Unless you have very great interest amongst the gentlemen particularly of the new Council sent out by Parliament in whom all the power is centered little is to be obtained," Frederic

Davy complained. But for those less well-connected, maritime commerce, particularly trade with China, provided the most profitable opportunities available to them. Davy was elated in 1776 to learn he would be sailing to Bombay and China with another private trader, John Fergusson. Davy explained to his family back in England, "This affair gives me great spirits I assure you, as I know of nothing from which greater advantages are to be derived in a short time to one not in the company's service."[29]

In the 1780s, the Company decided to prohibit most of its employees in India from trading on their own account.[30] This prohibition paved the way for private traders, such as David Scott of Bombay and John Fergusson of Calcutta, to take "the initiative in opening up new avenues for trade."[31] While maritime trade between India, Southeast Asia, and China was nothing new, private traders accelerated the export of particular products from India, most notably raw cotton from Bombay and, later in the nineteenth century, opium from Bengal. Private British shipping could now create new Asian networks.[32]

Trading in the East Indies was not for the risk averse, but for many, the potential riches were simply too tempting to resist. As Davy wrote to his father, "We ought not to count our chickens before they are hatched, less we should be disappointed, yet still there is a pleasure in hopeful expectations."[33] The promise of fortunes lured traders eastward.

In 1754, George Smith of Madras, a native of Ross-shire in the Scottish Highlands, sailed to the East Indies. He was lucky to have connections to the Munro of Foulis clan, one of Scotland's leading gentry families with "strong electoral influence in Ross-Shire."[34] During the eighteenth century, many Scots found their way to India as Company civil servants, cadets, surgeons, and free merchants. That was no accident. The British government bestowed Company employment opportunities and residence permits upon influential Scottish families, such as the Munro of Foulis clan, as part of a deliberate plan to encourage Scottish loyalty and obedience to England during the politically precarious decades after the union between the two countries in 1707. The dispatch of many Scots to different parts of the British empire helped to keep the new British nation-state intact.[35]

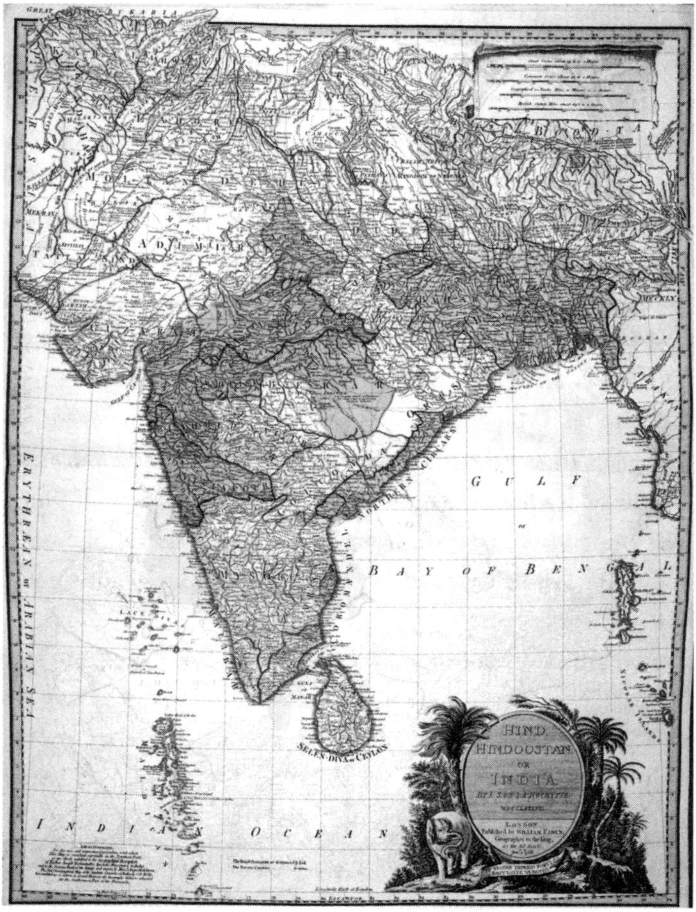

L. Delarochett and W. Palmer, *Hind, Hindoostan, or India* (London: Published by William Faden, 1788). Beinecke Rare Book and Manuscript Library, Yale University.

George Smith of Madras's relatives were part of this trend, making their way to India as Company surgeons. The Munro clan of Foulis was teeming with doctors, some of whom practiced at the renowned University of Edinburgh. The Munro doctors began moving to India in 1718, when Dr. Duncan Munro of Obsdale and, a few years later, his cousin Dr. Andrew Munro served as surgeons at Fort St. George, Madras, for the East

India Company. Between 1720 and 1757, every principal medical officer for the Company in Madras was a Scot; two of them were Munros.[36]

Dr. Andrew Munro was George Smith's uncle. As the Company's principal medical officer in Madras for several years, from 1742 to 1746 and from 1749 to 1757, Dr. Munro had the opportunity to treat none other than Robert Clive. Munro must have been considered a highly competent surgeon, although his bedside manner left something to be desired. He was, in fact, "renowned for his short temper and violent dislike of anything he thought might approach hypochondria" and received a reprimand from the Madras Presidency for his "notorious" behavior after a complaint from James Alexander, a Company employee. Alexander had "several times in vain applied to the surgeons for a few ingredients to compose a powder for the scurvy in his teeth." When Dr. Munro finally acceded to the request, he did not disguise his annoyance in his directions to the surgeon's mate: "Pray give that impudence what he wants, and let me not be plagued with his nonsense. Yours, A.M."[37]

George Smith's relatives, whatever their abilities as doctors, became fixtures of the Madras settlement. By the 1750s, two generations of Munros had experienced life in Madras. Dr. Andrew Munro and his wife, Francis Mary Munro, owned a house on Charles Street where they raised four children: Robert Duncan, Hugh John, Katherine, and Margaretta Aurora. Dr. Munro also served as mayor of Madras in 1754, was well connected to important people at the Company's settlement in Fort St. George, and chose Sir Robert Palk, a future governor of Fort St. George in Madras, and Thomas Saunders, Esq., the former governor of Fort St. George, as executors of his estate. Dr. Munro's private business concerns included trade with China; a certain amount of his money at the time of his death in 1757 was "now lying at Canton in China."[38] The Munro family's connections and influence in Madras undoubtedly made it possible for Dr. Munro's son Robert Duncan to obtain Company employment there.

Dr. Munro's influence, however, had limits. He could not obtain a Company position for his nephew, George Smith. In 1754, Smith set out for China, although he had a sojourn in India along the way. Undoubtedly through his uncle's influence, Smith was permitted by the East India Company to reside in Madras and trade in the East Indies. While free merchant licenses were highly prized, employment with the Company was an easier and more secure way of earning a fortune in India. As we shall see, Smith's inability to obtain employment with the Company proved a great source of regret as he grew older. Once he had his own son, also named George Smith, he would exert considerable time and energy in securing his nomination as an East India Company writer. That would give him an entry-level position in the civil service of one of the Company's Indian presidencies.

The Munro family network proved valuable to Smith in other ways. It provided him with a base and the resources to transform himself quickly into a well-connected private trader. Only three years after his arrival in India, Smith received the praise of his proud uncle for his proven "prudence and discretion." Dr. Munro rewarded Smith in his will by trusting him with "the sum of two thousand pagodas to be employed by him in his hands at the rate of twelve percent respondentia in India for the term of seven years." Dr. Munro also legally empowered his nephew to ensure that the money still lying in Canton would be remitted either in Smith's "hands or the greatest part of it at respondentia or in the best manner possible on the ships bound from Canton to Europe to the hands of my executors" in Culcairn, Ross-shire, north Britain, and London.[39]

The financial responsibility for 2,000 pagodas undoubtedly boosted Smith's commercial enterprise, which was already well under way by the 1750s. At the time of his uncle's death in 1757, George was no longer in Madras; he was plying his trade in China.[40] And the records suggest that he spent most of his time in Canton and Macao from 1754 until he permanently returned to India in 1765.

While we know a great deal about the Munro side of George Smith's family, nothing is known of the rest of his family. We can surmise, however, that Smith's parents were at least of professional or gentry status. In his letters, Smith is silent about his past, but the quality of his writing indicates that he received an excellent education. Not only did he write with facility and clarity, but his letters also demonstrate a basic knowledge of Latin as well as a fluency in written French. Smith frequently interspersed his arguments and observations with Latin commonplaces, such as *verbum sapienti* (a word to the wise) and *delenda est Carthago* (Carthage must be destroyed), drew parallels between the British and Roman empires by quoting a maxim of Manlius, *tenere pacem* (maintain peace), and occasionally broke into French prose in mid-sentence.[41] His knowledge of classical history, Latin, and French indicates a high level of education for the time. Smith of Madras later ensured that his own son was educated in London at the Harrow School.[42] This familial emphasis on education suggests that the Smiths enjoyed a parity of social standing with the Munros.

Smith's social background was comparable with that of Scottish employees of the East India Company. Scots who applied for Company employment in India tended to occupy a higher rung on the social ladder than their English counterparts. Of the Scots who listed their fathers' professions on their applications to the Company between 1750 and 1795, "nearly half were gentry, with the rest from commerce and the professions."[43] In this regard, George Smith of Madras typified Scottish traders in the East Indies.

Since Madras served as George Smith's home from 1765 to 1779, his contemporaries came to refer to him as "George Smith of Madras." But this title, which stuck even after he shifted his operations to Bengal in 1783, was something of a misnomer. Although Madras provided Smith with a base, the real focal point of his business from 1754 until 1765 was China. Later in his life, Smith would claim to have "a long established acquaintance and connection, with the first mercantile Chinese houses of Canton."[44] We know from British, Swedish, and Danish records that he spent the first twelve years of his career as a commission merchant and broker illegally residing and running a business in China.

Smith's presence in China was first documented in 1757, the year his uncle Dr. Andrew Munro died. Munro's will designated Smith the manager of his remaining estate in Canton. Smith's letters to the executors of his uncle's will reveal how he managed his deceased uncle's money and ran his own business as a commission merchant in Canton. Smith loaned 11,000 taels of his uncle's money at interest in Canton. He also received 2,000 Spanish dollars from Manila and 2,073 Spanish dollars from a

William Daniell (1769–1837). *The European Factories at Canton in China,* 1806. Courtesy of the Yale Center for British Art.

Mr. William Elliott, formerly of Canton, for Dr. Munro's children "Bob" (Robert Duncan) and Kitty (Katherine). The larger amount Smith subsequently placed in the hands of a merchant in Canton, where he believed it would be safe. He also directed "Messrs Cliff, Walpole and Clark bankers in London to pay Thomas Saunders Esq. the sum of £3,450 pounds sterling" on behalf of the estate of Mr. Andrew Munro. Smith was sure they would do it as soon as they received cash from the East India Company bills of exchange that he had "sent them toward this payment."[45] Smith planned to lend the remainder of Dr. Munro's estate at interest in Canton for one more year, when he would remit the whole amount to England. However, one part of Dr. Munro's estate, which had been loaned to the Chinese Hong merchant known as Beaukiqua (黎開觀) could not be recovered. A native of Fujian Province, Beaukiqua was a prominent Hong merchant who earned a reputation for his high-quality silks. He owned a pawnshop in Fujian Province and several pieces of real estate in Canton and was considered by European traders to be one of the most important Hong merchants during the 1750s. It thus came as a surprise to many when he died insolvent in 1758.[46] Smith lamented, "I am sorry to certify to you that no part of Beaukiqua's debt to that estate can be recovered, he having left no effects; I have used every possible means in my power to recover any part of the money, but all in vain."[47] Beaukiqua's "was the first large-scale failure that had occurred in Canton," and it hinted at a larger financial crisis looming on the horizon.[48]

Smith appears in the records of the Danish Asiatic and Swedish East India companies as having conducted a considerable amount of business with them. According to Danish records, between 1759 and 1764 Smith helped to finance the Danish company's operations in Canton. In 1759, he loaned £5,000 at a 15 percent premium for ninety days, after which £5,750 was to be repaid him "or his order at the House of Messrs. Henry and Peter Miulman in London." In 1761, he paid 3,052 taels at 30 percent interest on behalf of his client George Baker of Madras to insure the return voyage of the Danish ship *The Queen of Denmark Juliana Maria* from Canton to Copenhagen. Smith seems to have made a practice of financing and insuring Danish ships against "dangers of the seas, fires, enemies, hindrances, or other troubles whatsoever." He loaned 9,900 taels in 1763 and £1,666 in 1764 as marine insurance for two of *Prince Friderick of Danmarc*'s return voyages to Europe. Smith also paid money into the Danish Asiatic Company's treasury in Canton for bills of exchange that could be cashed in London sixty to ninety days later.[49]

Swedish records provide a further window into Smith's business affairs in Canton during the early 1760s. The letters of Swedish East India Company supercargos reveal that Smith did business with the Swedes and transported hundreds of bottles of Madeira wine, liquor, cloth, and opium between Madras and China. He worked with Señor Arutum, an Armenian merchant, and probably formed a business partnership with a Captain Robert Jackson. The Swedish records suggest that Smith worked closely with Thomas Arnot, a British East India Company surgeon, as well as Monqua (蔡世文), a prominent Hong merchant who operated his business in the red for many decades after having been compelled by Canton officials to take over the debts of his father and other failed colleagues. Plagued by debt and prohibited from resigning his position as a Hong merchant (Hong merchants could not quit the trade without government approval), death was his only escape. "He was found lying dead in his bed" in 1790, having overdosed on opium.[50]

Smith of Madras surfaces frequently in the records of the British East India Company, though not for routine transactions. From the point of view of the Company, he was an interloper. By trading in China without Company permission, he was infringing upon the Company's legal monopoly on trade in the East Indies. The Company's supercargos in Canton noted that George Smith "is also one of those traders, the Honble Court have ordered off the place for these four years past."[51] The supercargos also wrote that "Mr. George Smith is known to have had every year affairs of his own to transact there [Macao]." They described Smith as someone who was "particularly well acquainted with all the merchants" of Macao and had "a more extraordinary intimacy and influence with the Portuguese merchants."[52] By 1764, legally or not, Smith had become a fixture of the Macao and Canton commercial communities.

The Company's supercargos in Canton formally protested Smith of Madras's continued residence in China while tacitly tolerating him. It probably did not hurt that Smith represented the commercial interests of Henry Vansittart, the governor of Bengal from 1759 to 1764.[53] From time to time, the Company even made use of Smith's financial services. His reputation as an experienced China trader, with particularly strong connections to Macao, made him an obvious choice when the Company's supercargos were planning secret negotiations with several Portuguese merchants in Macao for a loan. With a vote of five-to-four, the supercargos resolved to send Smith of Madras to Macao "to borrow what money we could get at Macao" without raising the suspicion of French and Swedish competitors. The Company's supercargos hoped Smith's trip to Macao would go unnoticed by the other Europeans "who make a common practice of borrowing money" from the Portuguese and might attempt to frustrate the scheme.[54] In August 1764, Smith of Madras was dispatched to Macao, where he was directed to procure another year's loan worth $72,000 and to borrow as much additional money as possible at 12 percent interest per annum or less.[55]

The East India Company's relationship with Portuguese Macao was a complicated one. In 1557, the Portuguese received permission from the

Chinese government to create a settlement in Macao where they enjoyed the privilege of self-government.[56] Macao became part of the Estado da Índia, Portuguese India, with its capital in Goa. The governors in Goa banned foreign trade in Macao and prohibited foreign traders from settling there. But these prohibitions were regularly ignored by the Macao municipal council, Senado da Câmara, and Portuguese merchants who had a strong commercial interest in opening Macao to foreign commerce, including opium smuggling.[57] Within this context, the East India Company developed a symbiotic commercial relationship with the Portuguese in Macao but chafed under their authority. Power struggles and conflicts frequently arose. The bottom line for traders, however, whether Portuguese or British, was profit. In Macao, profit trumped politics.

After arriving in Macao, Smith reported that four merchants, Lewis Coeilho (treasurer of the city), Manuel Peireira De Fonceca, Antonio Joza de Costa, and Simon Vicente De Rosa (procurador of the city), had agreed to renew their loans to the East India Company for one year longer and that Joaquim Lopez de Silva would lend the Company $16,000 at 12 percent interest per year. Smith believed he could procure "a considerable amount" of money from several other merchants.[58] After negotiating for a couple of weeks, Smith concluded, "I have done all I could in this affair, as I shall in any other wherein the Company's interest, or your pleasure may happen to be concerned." He reiterated his commitment to helping the Company, adding, "I shall account myself fortunate if any endeavors to serve the Company at Macao, have in any manner proved of utility to them, or of satisfaction to you, being on all occasions, ready to approve myself."[59]

The Company's supercargos were "much obliged" to Smith of Madras "for the trouble" he had taken.[60] Yet not long after, and for reasons that are unclear, the Company demonstrated its gratitude by expelling him from China. "I left that country to my very great detriment in obedience to the Company's orders . . . having large concerns in China unsettled," Smith would later lament.[61]

In 1765, Smith returned to Madras, making it his permanent residence. By the time he relocated there, the East India Company's political position in Madras was beginning to stabilize, but war was a regular feature of life in southern India during the second half of the eighteenth century. The British and French East India companies frequently fought wars by supporting rival local leaders, but a provisional peace between the two European powers was agreed to in 1754.[62] Life in Madras did not remain peaceful for long. The spread of the Seven Years' War (1756–63) to India encouraged the French to attempt overtaking Madras again in 1758; they had already done so once before, in 1746. But the East India Company's troops along with two royal regiments successfully repelled them. Between 1767 and 1769, war came again to Madras when the Company's council there attempted to consolidate its control over a coastal territory, the Northern Circars, by attacking the formidable political power, Mysore. In retaliation Mysore's raiding parties broke "past the British armies, cut off their supplies," and ravaged the region, creating "panic in Madras itself." In 1780, panic broke out once again in Madras, when Mysore attacked the region around Madras with a force said to be 80,000 strong. The Mysore army nearly reached Madras, but the Company's settlement was rescued by a "dispatch of troops and money from Bengal and by the arrival of royal regiments and warships from Britain."[63]

Within this chaotic and precarious context George Smith of Madras set out to make his livelihood and build a life in Madras. He wrote, "We still continue in a state of tranquility on this coast, how long it may continue, I am not politician sufficient to determine."[64] Despite the constant uncertainty, Smith of Madras threw himself into the civic life of his new community. He served as mayor of Madraspatnam, assisted the Board of Police, and was a judge of His Majesty's Court of Record.[65] The civic duties could be burdensome: "The sessions are sitting, and I have pleaded indisposition in excuse of my absence, the truth is, that I shun this piece of necessary duty, because [it is] now more troublesome than formerly."[66] But he clearly felt a strong sense of civic responsibility and undoubtedly enjoyed the prestige that accompanied these administrative roles. Just as he had done in China, Smith established himself as a well-respected and prominent member of Madras commercial and civic life.

Unlike many of his contemporaries, Smith of Madras did not defer marriage until his return to Great Britain. Although the majority of residents were men, Madras was home to a relatively large number of European women, so Smith did not have to search very far for his bride.[67] In fact, he looked no further than his own family: to his first cousin Margaretta Aurora Munro, Dr. Andrew Munro's daughter. Margaretta Aurora, known as Aurora, was the younger sister of Katherine, called Kitty. Kitty married Colonel James Kirkpatrick of the Madras Cavalry and gave birth to a son, James Achilles Kirkpatrick, who is the subject of William Dalrymple's biography, *White Mughals.* Margaretta Aurora was the aunt of this now famous "white Mughal."[68] She was born in Madras but spent several years in Britain between 1760 and 1768.[69] It was extremely common for British families in India to send their young children back home to receive an education. Not long after her return to Madras, Margaretta Aurora and George Smith were married.[70] Smith was probably in his early thirties at the time, a sensible age for a young trader who had likely been advised to "postpone marriage until he had secured his economic position."[71] The marriage seems to have been a happy one, at least during the honeymoon years, when Smith of Madras thanked a close family friend for his congratulatory compliments "on our union, which hither to has been perfect and will I hope continue so."[72] During the Smith family's residence in Madras, this perfect union was also a productive one. The births of four of their children were recorded in the Madras parish register: Aurora Catherine (baptized December 24, 1772), Catherine Frances (baptized May 25, 1775), George (baptized August 27, 1776), and Jemima Claudia (baptized December 1777).[73] A fifth child, Henrietta Christiana, was born at the Cape of Good Hope in 1780.

In Madras, British residents lived in the East India Company's settlement at Fort St. George. Many of them also bought country homes outside the settlement.[74] During the eighteenth century, according to Søren Mentz, "wealthy Englishmen began to settle outside the walls of Fort St. George in villas beyond 'White Town.'"[75] The Smith family leased eleven acres of land in Egmore, outside Madras. They also appear to have resided in the Luz, an area southeast of Madras, not far from the coast, in 1778.[76]

In Egmore, their neighbors included Margaretta Aurora's brother, Robert Duncan, and her future second husband, William Petrie.[77] One can imagine the Smiths raising their family in one of the Georgian-style mansions "suitable for large households with many servants," an arrangement that was common for wealthy Madras merchants at the time.[78] Perhaps they enjoyed rides through the countryside, which was decorated by "a number of elegant country-seats." Living close to the ocean in the Luz, the Smiths could experience the healing power of the "sea breeze, emphatically called *the Doctor,* which regularly comes in about ten o'clock in the morning."[79]

Despite the distance from the home country and the vulnerability to deadly fevers and disease, life in Madras was comfortable for the Smith family. A prosperous merchant family could afford to employ numerous servants and slaves, an "excess" that often drew criticism from newly arrived Europeans. The Smiths employed at least several female servants or slaves.[80] Despite the opulent lifestyle they probably still longed for many of the creature comforts of home. One wonders if they were as lucky as Charles Smith (no known relation), a Company civil servant in Madras, whose brother, Culling, made sure to send various items from Britain that Charles desired. In 1767, having received a care package from his brother, Charles Smith expressed his gratitude "for the wine, shoes, and spectacles all of which came safe to hand, but the shoes are useless, as I fancy the shoe maker made them for your foot instead of mine, I will see and send a shoe as a master by this Ship." Charles had several additional requests as well: "The spectacles are very neat and good, I have given away one pair, so beg you will send me another of the same sight, together with some spare glasses, let it be mounted the same as the others. Always send the wine and pray let me have the magazines and any newspapers by the first ships to the Coast."[81] If George Smith and his family did not have a relative back in Britain who was willing to send them current reading materials and spectacles with which to read them, perhaps they borrowed some of these highly prized items from their circle of friends in India.

The Smith family enjoyed the company of prominent Madras residents, such as Lord George Pigot, the settlement's governor, who dined frequently with them. They were very close to the Pigot family; two of Smith's trading partners, Claud Russel and Edward Monckton, married Governor Pigot's daughters. The Smiths undoubtedly attended the numerous dinner parties and balls that the British residents of Madras organized for their own entertainment. A contemporary and acquaintance of Smith of Madras, William Hickey, "found the inhabitants of the settlement exceedingly gay . . . There was scarce an evening without some great entertainment, public or private, a weekly concert of a superior kind, many of the performers being of a description that would have created admiration in any part of Europe."[82] The residents of Madras did their utmost to recreate the lives they had left behind in Britain. Families such as the Smiths "formed the spinal cord in the social life of Madras."[83]

To support this lifestyle Smith of Madras worked as a merchant and broker, representing the commercial and financial interests of his clients in India. He earned a living by investing his clients' capital in commercial ventures in the Indian Ocean and South China Sea and by remitting their fortunes to England. Shortly after settling in Madras, Smith "launched out greatly into trade jointly with M. Russell and others, and took up large sums payable in London."[84] One of Smith's clients included Robert Palk, the governor of Madras between 1763 and 1767 and a member of Parliament from 1767 to 1787. Smith helped Palk remit some of his Indian earnings to England.[85] In 1765, Governor Palk advanced a bond of £2,400 to Smith.[86] He also put 64,634 rupees into a cargo that Smith sent to China on the Portuguese ship *Nostra Senhora de Carmo*.[87] Three years later, Smith was still busy managing Palk's "moneys in China" and hoping to remit his fortune to England as soon as possible.[88]

China was at the center of Smith's remittance business. He regularly contracted with the Fort St. George Presidency in Madras to ship goods, particularly cotton and tin, freight free on Company ships to China. The proceeds of the sales were deposited in the Company's treasury in China. During the 1760s and 1770s, Smith of Madras shipped hundreds of thousands of British pounds' worth of sandalwood, tin, cotton, and pepper to Canton on East India Company ships. In 1769, he sent 1,000 bales of cotton freight free to Canton.[89] Smith also leased an East India Company ship, the *Huntingdon*, upon condition that the ship would be delivered to the Council of Supercargos in Canton before the end of October 1774.

Smith frequently collaborated with Sir Edward Monckton, a Company civil servant who had worked in Madras since 1762.[90] Commercial partnerships between private traders and Company employees were not unusual in Madras.[91] In 1769, Smith and Monckton's proposal to send cotton, pepper, and sandalwood to China on several of the Company ships was accepted.[92] Two years later, they loaded 50,000 pagodas worth of tin and cotton on Company ships destined for Canton. The cotton was purchased on the west coast of India; the tin was probably obtained in the Malay Peninsula, probably at Kedah, or from Palembang, Sumatra. In 1772, Smith and Monckton engaged to pay $150,000 into the Company's Canton treasury "in consequence of their having consented that they should send 2500 bales of cotton" on the Company's ships freight free.[93] Smith and Monckton's agent in Canton sold the Indian cotton and then deposited silver into the Company's Canton treasury. Their agent deposited a further $112,500 into the Canton treasury for Company bills of exchange.[94]

Who were Smith and Monckton's Canton agents? John Crichton and William Dalrymple, both Scots, resided for several years in Canton without the Company's permission and managed Smith and Monckton's business concerns in China.[95] In 1769, Crichton ruffled feathers in Canton when he tried to sell 511 bales of woolen cloth shipped to him by Smith of Madras. The sale of wool in China was a sensitive issue for the Company, which had been trying unsuccessfully for decades to reduce its trade deficit in China by exporting woolen cloth from Britain. Demand for the traditional British export product was low, and the Company often sold it at a loss. Smith and Crichton's interference in the wool trade was particularly irritating to the Company's Canton supercargos. They explained to the Company's directors in London: "The [Chinese] merchants as observed before, complain of the great quantity of woolens sent yearly from Europe, and wish to lower the prices, and therefore if the importation of woolens be permitted from any of the presidencies it must greatly affect our investment from Europe."[96] Crichton assured the Canton Council that the importation of Smith's woolens was not an "illegal or clandestine affair." He did "not think my Constituent, Mr. George Smith, or myself answerable for any damages whatever, the Honble Company may sustain, by the importation of the said five hundred and eleven bales of woolens, which were purchased at their sales."[97] But the Company's Canton supercargos nearly unanimously agreed that

George Smith of Madras must be held accountable for any damage to the East India Company resulting from his shipping woolens to China.[98]

After Crichton returned to England in 1774, Smith of Madras began working with a new agent in Canton. He was—yes—George Smith of Canton. In 1775, Smith of Canton received a cargo of tin and cotton that had been shipped on board an East India Company ship, the *Morse,* and consigned to him by Smith of Madras and Edward Monckton.[99]

The volume and extent of Smith of Madras's trade in China was impressive. He claimed to have already remitted £100,000 from India to London by 1770. The scarcity of silver in Canton, however, could make the remittance business unpredictable at times. Commerce in Canton depended on Spanish galleons arriving from South America via Manila and pumping large quantities of American silver into China. In 1771, Smith's agents in Canton could not make payments into the Company's Canton treasury as promised because of "the late arrival of the ships [carrying silver] from Manila." Chinese merchants often did not have enough silver on hand to pay immediately for the goods they bought from Smith's agents. These types of liquidity problems could delay remittances and lead to major conflicts with clients. According to P. J. Marshall, "No relationship was more corrosive of friendship than that of the returned Nabob, expecting installments of his fortune by every ship, with his harassed former colleague who was trying to disentangle his affairs."[100] Smith complained that one of his clients, Colonel Campbell, had used him "ungenteelly," although Smith had "informed him of the unavoidable accidents which retarded his payment." Smith of Madras blamed trade conditions at the time: "It hurts me exceedingly to think that I have not been able to be punctual in my payment at home, notwithstanding my unceasing efforts for the due performance of any engagements. Had trade been on the footing even on which it was when you was last here, I should have made a handsome fortune by it, but such are the terms now, that I have nothing but anxiety and trouble for my pains."[101]

Some of the more successful nabobs, however, showed more patience. Smith's close friend and client, Sir Robert Palk, settled Smith's debts to him in a "friendly manner." Despite a few disappointments, Smith still boasted that his many engagements for the payment of large sums into the Canton treasury were "always discharged with punctuality."[102] While "slow sales [and] the loss of ships passages" meant that business had become a struggle, Smith managed for the most part to move large sums of his clients' money around the globe.[103]

Smith of Madras's clientele was not limited to British East India Company personnel. He also partnered with Michael Grubb, a supercargo of the Swedish East India Company, who arrived in 1750 and "became one of the first Swedes to stay in Canton for several years."[104] Smith served as Grubb's agent in Madras and arranged for the shipment of goods from India to China, such as snuff, piece goods (cloth), chintzes, clouded gingham (including some purple), long cloths, and very good blue cotton handkerchiefs. Grubb also requested that Smith sell 440 bottles of very good claret that had been shipped to their mutual friend Jacob Hahr but was also addressed to George Smith in case of Hahr's absence.[105]

Smith of Madras also did business with Indian rulers, including Muhammad Ali Khan Wallajah, the nawab of Arcot, who required large amounts of money to maintain and expand his power base in southeast India. Owing to the weakening and fragmentation of the Mughal empire, whose rule had not been particularly strong or long-lived there, the region was extremely unstable by the middle of the eighteenth century. Within this chaotic political context the nawab of Arcot borrowed extensively from the East India Company in Madras to expand and defend his new territories. He also turned to individual members of the East India Company's civil and military establishment in addition to the British mercantile community to borrow funds. Smith of Madras was one of many private investors who loaned money to the nawab of Arcot in the 1760s. Smith also sold pearls to him "to the amount of 32,000 pagodas [$48,000] for which the Nabob [nawab] gave him an order or tankah on the country of Tanjore, payable in six months, without interest."[106]

But Smith's economic relationship with the nawab was closer than most. He even served as the nawab's commercial agent, sailing on the nawab's behalf to Manila on the *Sultanissa Begam* in 1767 to sell his goods worth "not much short of a lakh sterling," or £100,000.[107] We know this because the ship encountered trouble in Manila, where the Spanish detained it, held Smith and his crew prisoner on board, and extorted presents from Smith. The matter not only concerned George Smith of Madras but also another Smith, the future acting governor of Madras, Charles Smith, who had "about a thousand pounds at risk on her, not in the stock and block, but at respondentia, and insurance." According to Charles Smith, the ship, which was "worth not much short of a Lack [lakh] Sterling, is prevented doing business there [Manila] and the supracargo of her, George Smith and co., are prisoners on board; how this matter will terminate is not as yet known, but it is thought it will be accommodated on paying some money."[108] When the affair was finally resolved, George Smith of Madras reported to the nawab that the losses amounted to $144,650. The nawab also eventually received a letter from the governor of Manila explaining that what was done to Smith "proceeded from suspicions of English property being under" Smith's management.[109]

Manila was a regular port of call for Smith of Madras and an important source of silver for trade in the East Indies. Although trade with European nations (except Portugal) was officially forbidden in the Spanish colony, British traders evaded this policy and obtained Spanish silver brought from America by Spanish galleons in return for Indian manufactures.[110] The creation of the Royal Philippines Company in 1785, however, liberalized commerce in Manila, and, according to W. E. Cheong, Smith of Madras had a share in the Spanish contracts obtained by Graham and Mowbray, a British trading house.[111] Private traders who sold Indian goods in Manila brought back much-needed silver to India and China. "And if this [silver] is not imported from Manila or Europe," Smith of Madras warned, "all the rupees in the country [India] will be drained for China, and in a short time [there will be] none to be had, which would be attended with very serious consequences unless they [the East India Company] send silver from Canton to England, which they have not done for some years past."[112]

In addition to Manila, Smith's business brought him to modern-day Indonesia and other parts of the Philippines. He may have been a member of a corporation of Madras merchants trading to Aceh in Sumatra.[113] The activities of this Madras corporation, referred to by its members as "the concern," raised concern back in London. In 1772, the Court of Directors ordered the Madras Council to dispatch an investigatory mission to Aceh after hearing allegations that "the concern" had established a trade monopoly there and was intervening militarily against the local population with the help of approximately seventy to eighty hired Indian sepoys, or mercenary soldiers.[114] We can only speculate as to Smith's role, if any, in all of this. In addition to Aceh, Smith also traded in Jakarta, known at the time as Dutch Batavia. In 1767, he obtained a cargo in Batavia worth 70,000 rix dollars, which included several "curious pieces of Japan ware and china."[115] (Ten rix dollars were worth two pounds five shillings.)

While the Smith family made the most of their time in Madras, the goal was always to return to Britain, either north or south of the Tweed River, the historic boundary between Scotland and England. Like other merchants, Smith of Madras saw the time in India as nothing more than "a temporary exile" until retirement.[116] Just several years after arriving in Madras, Smith hoped to have saved enough money to retire, but unexpected commercial losses encountered in Manila in 1767 meant that "I must labour some years more . . . so have dropt my thoughts of seeing England so soon as I hoped; and now I have my hands at the oar I must even pull away until I have got my vessel into port."[117]

After twelve years with his hands at the oar, Smith was finally ready to enjoy his retirement in England. On October 16, 1779, the Smith family left Madras for good, setting sail for England on the *Nassau,* a 723-ton ship built in 1771 and commanded by Captain Arthur Gore.[118] Most of what we know of their voyage home comes from the colorful memoirs of William Hickey, a lawyer who lived in India almost continuously from 1777 until 1808. In 1779, Hickey returned to London briefly to help manage a petition to Parliament, and it was during this journey on board the *Nassau* that his life became briefly entangled with the Smiths'.[119]

Hickey's memories of their voyage from Madras to England provide a glimpse into the lives and personalities of George and Margaretta Aurora Smith and their brood. The voyage home did not get off to a good start. When Hickey embarked on the *Nassau,* he found the ship's captain in a violent rage:

> The quarter-deck [was] covered and the passage blocked up by trunks, chests, bandboxes, and packages of every description, belonging to Mrs. Smith, who he swore had sent on board *one hundred and twenty* different parcels . . . I strove to console him, though rather unsuccessfully, for he continued to curse and swear outrageously at the unreasonable and shameful quantity of baggage with which the Smith's had encumbered the ship, declaring that in case bad weather came on, which might be expected every hour, the whole must and would be thrown overboard.
>
> In the midst of the bustle Mr. Smith and his family came alongside in the Government boat, Captain Gore instantly attacking poor Mr. Smith with uncommon vehemence, for whom I felt great compassion, the poor man being already sufficiently tormented in attending to the complaints of his wife and children. Mrs. Smith was quite as furious as Captain Gore, whom she honoured with the epithets of brute, sea monster, and savage, vowing she would not stay on board the Nassau. "As to you, George," she said, turning to her husband, "you may do as you please, stay or go I care not, but for myself, proceed in this abominable pigsty I will not."
>
> Mrs. Smith's intemperate behaviour quite silenced Captain Gore, and Mr. Larkins just then coming forward and endeavouring to pacify the lady, succeeded.[120]

Was Mrs. Smith the strong-willed curmudgeon Hickey portrayed her to be? Was Mr. Smith the even-keeled peacemaker? The reluctance to give up one's possessions is understandable, and preparing for a long ocean voyage in the heat of the Indian summer while almost six months pregnant would have tried anyone's patience. Perhaps Hickey was being unfair to Margaretta Aurora Smith.

The Smiths encountered more difficulties along the way. During their stay in Ceylon (Sri Lanka), they suffered in "a miserable residence" on the shore. They were "in woeful plight, their apartments being deluged, the rain pouring in through apertures innumerable, so that they had not a dry spot in the house, nor a single change of clothes to put on, all being completely soaked. During two entire nights they had been obliged to sit up, the children having thereby all got severe colds." But it was not all misery on the island of Ceylon around the Dutch fort of Trincomalee. Hickey and the Smiths amused themselves with various recreations, such as fishing, "rowing about various inlets and small bays where we found innumerable guanas, an animal of the lizard kind, but very much larger," and hunting "guanas" and wild hogs, which they got plenty of and enjoyed the "high-flavoured, delicious meat."[121]

The stop in Ceylon provided a brief respite, but a number of passengers did not live to see the shores of England. At least twenty unfortunate people died between December 19, 1779, and February 1, 1780, before the *Nassau* had even reached the Cape of Good Hope. Scurvy seems to have struck down many of the ship's crew.[122] The *Nassau* also encountered some extremely rough weather between Ceylon and the cape, during which time Hickey made it his daily business to console Mrs. Smith:

> One day when the motion of the ship was extremely violent I went into the round-house to Mrs. Smith. I had taken her eldest child, George, upon my knee as I sat upon the deck, having just advised her to let the rest come by me, as being safer than where they then were, when a sea broke over the ship that for a time quite overwhelmed her. Down she went upon her beam ends. The shock was so violent and sudden everything yielded to it. Mrs. Smith, who was sitting on her bed with a child on each side, came, cot and all, bodily over to leeward, as did chests, trunks and every article in the cabin. How George and myself escaped being maimed, if not killed, was marvelous. Although for some moments I actually thought the ship had upset, I could not help smiling at the scene that presented itself, the female servants floundering about in all positions, Mrs. Smith screeching to them to cover

> their nakedness, whilst she herself was employed in gathering up curls, toupees, and various articles of her toilette she would not upon any consideration have exhibited to profane eyes.

Mrs. Smith was not the only one unnerved by the bad weather. Hickey described what happened to Mr. Smith.

> [He] had just come in from deck, and was comforting his family by telling them the officers thought the fury of the gale was spent, when the ship took the desperate heel I have above mentioned. He was then standing by the side of his wife's cot, when the violence of the jerk made him lose hold. Finding himself going bodily to leeward, and being apprehensive of falling upon the children, he by an extraordinary exertion stopped himself by laying hold of a cot-hook fixed in one of the beams, but in so doing swung round with such force as to put his shoulder out of joint. The pain attending it was so acute as to occasion his fainting. His namesake [the ship surgeon] instantly attending, put the arm into its place again before he recovered. These united accidents were the more distressing and serious from Mrs. Smith's being in hourly expectation of laying in. Apprehensions were therefore entertained that the consequences might be fatal to her. Happily, however, no evil attended.[123]

Luckily for the Smiths, the night they landed in Cape Town, "Mrs. Smith was delivered of a daughter," whom they named Henrietta Christiana Smith. The Smith family remained in Cape Town for some time while Mrs. Smith recuperated. Hickey did not continue on the *Nassau* with the Smiths but sailed to England on an earlier ship.[124]

Back in England, the Smiths made their new home in the parish of St. Marylebone in the county of Middlesex, London, surpassing Smith's earlier prediction that he might only earn enough to retire to his "own country north of the Tweed."[125] Despite being far from Scotland, the Smiths probably felt at home on Upper Harley Street, which seems to have become a kind of diasporic community for East Indies traders and former East India Company employees. With neighbors such as Thomas Bevan, the East India Company's only Chinese-speaking Canton supercargo, Smith probably felt right at home.[126]

Smith's successful retirement was short-lived. In February 1782, his name appeared in the Saturday issue of the *London Gazette.* He was bankrupt.[127] Smith of Madras's bankruptcy may have been tied to the financial failure of his namesake and former business agent in China, George Smith of Canton.

THREE

George Smith of Canton

HOW GEORGE SMITH OF CANTON found his way to China remains somewhat of a mystery. The East India Company's Court of Directors got word that in 1770 "a Mr. George Smith and other persons were going to India by different ways" and that "George Smith also arrived at Basra the 30th July last [1769] intending to proceed to Bengal, but continued at the former place as clerk to Mr. Garden . . . Whether Mr. George Smith proceeded to any of the Company's settlements in the East Indies and proceeded from thence to China, or how else he got there," the directors of the Company could not be sure. They were certain, however, "that he got to China in 1771" without their permission.[1] Close examination of Smith of Canton's life during his decade-long residence in Canton and Macao reveals the crucial role he and other private traders played in financing the East India Company's tea trade in China. It also sheds light on the place of women and families in British outposts in maritime Asia.

Like his namesake, George Smith of Madras, George Smith of Canton did not leave many records behind. We know much more about Smith of Canton's wife, Charlotte née Peche. Charlotte was born to John and Anne Peche and baptized in the parish of St. Mary in Guildford, Surrey, England, in 1757. She was the fifth of six children: John, Anne, James, Betsy, Charlotte, and Onslow.[2] The Peches' grocery business must have been fairly profitable because in 1810 John Peche (the father) bequeathed to his children and grandchildren the proceeds of "his long annuities" as well as over £2,500 in cash. He also left his daughter Charlotte "all the remainder of my property . . . to purchase as much permanent Stock as will add Six pounds a week to the Widows in Mr Parson's Hospital."[3]

Charlotte's three brothers all served in the East India Company's army. Charlotte was probably too young to join her brother John and his "black servant" (perhaps in actuality a slave) "named Mungo" on their way to India in the early 1770s. But she may have accompanied another brother, James, on his voyage to Bombay on board the *Latham* in 1776, when she was nineteen years old.[4]

Very shortly after arriving in Bombay she married her first husband, Joseph Smith, Esq., an officer in the East India Company's army. Charlotte and Joseph's marriage was cut short by his untimely death, but he left half of his estate to her. According to Company records, she received £6,000, no small sum considering that £20,000 was thought sufficient to retire from the East Indies trade and return to Britain. Joseph also left her a small collection of diamonds, pearls, jewels, as well as his slaves. These slaves were to receive their liberty "on the departure from this country or the death of their mistress."[5]

Not long after Joseph Smith's death in 1777, George Smith of Canton sailed from China to Bombay to purchase a ship, the *Eliza,* from David Scott, a prominent Scottish private trader. In Bombay, George Smith not only obtained a ship but also a wife. He married the recently widowed Charlotte Smith—now Charlotte Peche Smith Smith—in 1778. The newlyweds moved back to China shortly after their wedding, and in 1779 Charlotte gave birth to their first daughter, Charlotte Eleanora, in Macao.[6]

We know little about George Smith's life before he went to China. The most important clue regarding Smith's origins comes not from a document or written record but from a coat of arms at the bottom of a plaque hanging on a wall in St. John's Stoke Church in Guildford, Surrey. The memorial plaque, which still can be seen today, was commissioned at some point between 1857 and 1866 by George and Charlotte Smith's two surviving sons, Henry Browne Smith and David Scott Smith. From the text on the plaque we discover that their father was born around 1746, so he would have been in his mid-twenties when he first arrived in China. Charlotte, who was twelve years his junior, was only twenty years old when she married George Smith of Canton. George and Charlotte had eleven children, of whom three died in infancy. Two others, George Fordyce Smith and George Moubray Smith, died while serving as lieutenants in the East India Company's cavalry in Madras.

St. John's Stoke Church in Guildford, Surrey, UK. Photograph by the author.

Below the text on the plaque is a coat of arms: the crest, the top part of the coat of arms, contains a golden dolphin haurient (upright); the shield is azure or blue and displays a crowned lion rampant with a forked tail on one side of the shield and a burning cup between two chess rooks on the other side. The motto at the bottom reads: "*mediis tranquillus in undis,*" or "calm in the midst of waves." Henry Browne Smith and David Scott Smith appear to have creatively combined two different coats of arms to commemorate their family: one from their father's side and one from their mother's. The coat of arms for the Peachey family—that is an alternative spelling for Peche—also shows a crowned double-tailed lion rampant on an azure background.[7] The two Smith sons seem to have modeled the rest of

Smith family coat of arms on the family memorial hanging on an interior wall of St. John's Stoke Church in Guildford, Surrey, UK. Photograph by the author.

their family's commemorative coat of arms on that of David Smith of Methven Castle in Perthshire, Scotland. David Smith's coat of arms contained a dolphin haurient on the crest, a burning cup between two chess rooks on a blue shield, and the motto *mediis tranquillus in undis.*[8] It is difficult to confirm whether George Smith of Canton was a direct descendent of the Scottish Smiths of Methven Castle, but this coat of arms firmly connects him with Scotland. The name of Smith's eldest child, George Fordyce, also intimates that Smith had Scottish origins.

From 1779 until 1782, George and Charlotte Smith made their home in Macao. Because the Chinese government did not allow foreign women to enter Canton, Macao was the only family-friendly residential option for foreigners in China. Those caught breaking the rules could pay a heavy price. When a Company ship captain's female companion from Madras was discovered in Canton by Chinese authorities (despite being dressed as a servant boy), she was sent off to a Macao prison.[9] The Smiths abided by Chinese laws, and Charlotte seems to have stayed put in Macao. The Smiths' first two children, Charlotte Eleanora and Harriet Ann, were both born there, in 1779 and 1781 respectively. The Smith family was probably "well accommodated" and may have enjoyed a "very pleasant" residence in Macao, as the first American consul in Canton described life there. Foreigners "not being suffered to hold any real estate" by the Portuguese government, the housing situation could be a nuisance. Still, the Smiths would have enjoyed strolling by the handsome brick-and-stone buildings, such as the hospital, senate house, prison, and courthouse, and the "large and commodious" private houses "painted white or washed with lime." Fresh fish, pork, poultry, and an abundance of vegetables could be bought at the market, and in the evenings the "society," which included various East India Company employees and some private traders, was "not bad." Residents could participate in various forms of entertainment: billiards,

Pupil of George Chinnery (1774–1852). *East End of the Preya Grande, Macao.* Courtesy of the Yale Center for British Art.

pleasure boating, social parties, dinners, and balls.[10] Charlotte and George probably enjoyed the best that Macao's European expatriate community had to offer.

While the Smiths were based in Macao, their network of friends, family, and business associates spanned the Indian Ocean and the South China Sea. The names of George and Charlotte Smith's children shed some light on the extensive network. Three of their children were named after David Scott and his wife, Louisa. When the first David Scott Smith died in infancy in 1791, George and Charlotte gave another one of their sons, born in 1796, the same name. A daughter born in 1793 was named Louisa Scott Smith. The children's apparent namesakes were most likely the Smith children's godparents.

Scott, the most influential trader in Bombay during the 1770s and 1780s, claimed that in 1784 the Company's Bombay settlement "owed him on his private account £191,254 and on the accounts of his constituents £208,870."[11] After returning to Britain, his financial success continued. Scott became a member of Parliament as well as a member of the East India Company's Court of Directors. The Scotts and Smiths remained friends for decades. David Scott not only managed several trust funds for Charlotte Smith but also helped the Smith sons obtain employment in the East India Company. Scott considered himself to be "the most attached and at the same time the most useful friend that the family had had" since their marriage in 1778.[12]

Two Smith children, George Moubray Smith (born in 1792) and Caroline Moubray Smith (born in 1782), were named after George Moubray, a cousin of George Smith's. George Smith and George Moubray may have set out for India together. They were the same age and appear to have arrived in the East Indies at the same time (around 1769). In contrast to his cousin, however, Moubray managed to obtain employment with the East India Company in Madras and served as a Company accountant, member of the Grain Committee, and member of the Board of Revenue at Fort St. George. He also held the titles of sheriff and mayor of Madraspatnam. Mowbray Road and Moubray's Gardens (Moubray's Cupola), his residence in Madras, which can still be seen today in modern-day Chennai, are named after him.[13] Moubray returned to London in the 1790s after making a great fortune in Madras and upon his death in 1825 left a large sum of money to the Smith family. He bequeathed £2,000 to "my cousin David Scott Smith," one of George and Charlotte's sons. He left £2,000 to Charlotte Smith and £1,500 to the children of his deceased godson, George Moubray Smith. To George and Charlotte's four daughters he provided "an annuity of fifty pounds" to be paid "during their respective lives . . . half yearly."[14]

A fourth child of the Smiths, Henry Browne Smith (b. 1789), was named after Henry Browne, the former head of the East India Company's Council of Supercargos in Canton. In the Anglican parish register for Woking, Surrey, Henry Browne is named as one of the godparents of Henry Browne Smith.[15]

When the Smith family resided in Macao, George Smith plied his trade in Canton. The commute by ship up the Pearl River from Macao to Canton, roughly eighty-three miles, took several days depending on the currents and weather conditions.[16] Smith probably sailed with various European trading vessels or hired private Chinese sampans to travel back and forth between Macao and Canton.[17] There were many interesting sights on the Pearl River. Smith could not have missed the boat people who lived year round on their sampans or the prostitutes, some of whom were probably slaves, on "flower boats" near "Lob Lob creek" (perhaps Pidgin English for "love love") who provided their services to both Chinese and foreign sailors passing by Whampoa.[18] Upon approaching Canton, Smith must also have been struck by the "scene upon the water," which was "as busy a one as [on] the Thames below London Bridge, with this difference, that instead of our square rigged vessels of different dimensions, you there have junks."[19] Another contemporary of Smith's felt that any description he could give "will convey but a faint idea of this place. The river for a mile or two below Canton is covered with boats of various sizes from those of 100 tons down to a ferry boat all in motion and so close that it is with the utmost difficulty you can get past them."[20] Smith may also have admired the various factory houses of the different European East India companies—Danish, Swedish, Dutch, French, British—lining the waterfront outside the city of Canton, each with its flag flying "on a lofty ensign staff."[21]

Foreigners were not allowed within the city walls, but if they dared to force their way through the city gates, it was "ten to one" that they would "get out again with a whole skin or without having your bones broke," one British trader reported.[22] Smith's life in Canton was confined to a narrow waterfront area outside the city walls. He probably rented accommodation from a Chinese merchant and lived in one of the buildings described by another British trader as "good houses but very confined being one at the back of the other for six or eight on."[23] While in Canton, he certainly encountered many of the things that his contemporaries described in their journals with fascination and awe: "extremes of opulence and wretchedness" in Chinese society; the "shoes of iron" and bound feet of women who "are of course cripples and can scarce walk"; the unique experience of Chinese massage, involving "cracking different joints and rubbing every part of the body with instruments made for the purpose," which was "odd and not unpleasant"; the chanting of Buddhist prayers and the burning of incense

Thomas Allom (1804–1872). *The House of a Chinese Merchant near Canton.* Courtesy of the Yale Center for British Art.

in "a niche" inside people's homes and boats, activities that appeared "quite incomprehensible" to the foreign observer; and the lavish homes and parties of Hong merchants.[24] John Adolphus Pope, an officer working on board the private country ship *Princess Royal* during the 1780s, was struck by the Hong merchants' estates, which, according to his estimates, occupied "ten times as much ground as [that of] a man of equal rank does in Europe." He found their gardens, through which the Hong merchants displayed their wealth and status, particularly impressive.[25] According to Pope, Puankequa, one of the wealthiest and most successful Hong merchants at the time, had a brother who had collected "10,000 Koofas, a kind of small sun flower which were calculated to be worth 3000 dollars."[26]

William Hickey, the same person who sailed with George Smith of Madras's family back to England in 1779, provides a vivid account of one of Puankequa's galas. This politically influential and prominent Hong merchant held two back-to-back parties that creatively played on the cultural diversity of the participants.[27] The first of the parties was

> a dinner, dressed and served à la mode Anglaise, the Chinamen on that occasion using, and awkwardly enough, knives and forks, and in every respect conforming to the European fashion. The best wines of all sorts were amply supplied. In the evening a play was performed, the subject warlike, where most capital fighting was exhibited, with better dancing and music than I could have expected. In one of the scenes an English naval officer, in full uniform and fierce cocked hat, was introduced, who strutted across the stage, saying "Maskee can do! God damn!" whereon a loud and universal laugh ensued, the Chinese quite in an ecstacy, crying out "Truly have much ee like Englishman." The second day, on the contrary, every thing was Chinese, all the European guests eating, or endeavouring to eat, with chop sticks, no knives or forks being at table. The entertainment was splendid, the victuals supremely good, the Chinese loving high dishes and keeping the best of cooks. At night brilliant fire works (in which they also excel) were let off

> in a garden magnificently lighted by coloured lamps, which we viewed from a temporary building erected for the occasion and wherein there was exhibited slight of hand tricks, tight and slack rope dancing, followed by one of the cleverest pantomimes I ever saw. This continued until a late hour.

Hickey was "much gratified with the liberality and taste displayed by our Chinese host."[28] It is very likely that Smith of Canton also had opportunities to attend these kinds of elaborate celebrations at the homes of the Hong merchants.

In his spare time Smith of Canton may have explored two shopping streets around the European factories, Hog Lane and China Street, where he could have wandered up and down in search of gifts for family and friends.[29] According to Maria Mok, "One of the highlights of shopping in Canton was

Thomas Allom (1804–1872). *Dinner Party at a Mandarin's House.* Courtesy of the Yale Center for British Art.

no doubt the stupefying experience of finding oneself in a treasure trove of ingeniously designed and finely executed products." In many of the Canton shops, Smith would have had the opportunity to observe various kinds of Chinese artists and craftworkers producing items specifically designed for the European export market. The shopping list of one Benjamin Shreve of Salem, for instance, included "one lady's parasol, six mother-of-pearl spoons," and "two 'teeth' brush cases with covers," in addition to "silverware, tortoiseshell combs, lacquerware, silks, china and nankeens." This list gives an idea of the kinds of crafts sought by European traders. Like many of his contemporaries, Smith of Canton might have commissioned souvenirs from local Chinese artists—for instance, a painting of the trading factories of Canton along the waterfront. Such paintings were a "type of historical record" that represented foreign traders' lived experiences in China. Smith may have hung one of these paintings in his home as a memento of his family's "bold and precarious existence on the China coast."[30]

Chinese artist. Folding fan, c. 1795. Paper, bone, gouache. China. 10 1/2 × 18 1/4 × 3/4 inches (26.67 × 46.355 × 1.905 cm). Peabody Essex Museum, Gift of Mr. and Mrs. John E. Rogerson, 1977. E80202. Courtesy of the Peabody Essex Museum, Salem, Mass. Photography by Jeffrey R. Dykes.

Tingqua, studio (Chinese, active dates 1840–70). *Shop of Tinqua, The Painter,* c. 1830. Gouache, paper. Asia, China. Image 7 1/16 × 10 1/4 inches (18 × 26 cm). Peabody Essex Museum, Gift of Leo A. and Doris C. Hodroff, 1998. AE85592. Courtesy of the Peabody Essex Museum, Salem, Mass. Photograph by Mark Sexton.

There were several amusing ways to pass the time in Canton, but Smith went to China for business, not pleasure. In Canton, he served as an agent and broker for his clients in India. He received cargoes of goods and silver consigned to him by his clients. After selling these goods, he deposited silver into the Company's Canton treasury in return for East India Company bills of exchange, which could be cashed in London. The diaries of the Company's supercargos in Canton record nineteen occasions between 1772 and 1779—ten of which were in 1777—when Smith and several business partners, John Crichton, Hugh Mackay, and Abraham Leslie, deposited silver into the Company's treasury on behalf of twenty-plus clients. The smallest deposit was for $408 and the largest for $28,000. Between 1772 and 1779, Smith and his colleagues deposited more than $167,736, or £41,934, into the Company's Canton treasury.[31]

Some of Smith of Canton's more notable clients included Sir Eyre Coote (commander in chief of the East India Company's military forces in India), Sir Robert Palk (a governor of Madras), David Scott and John Hunter (prominent private traders), and the Calcutta commercial society—David Killican, John Robinson, Charles Croftes, Charles Grant, and John Fergusson—for which the young Frederic Davy worked. Erye Coote, Robert Palk, David Scott, and John Hunter all became members of Parliament; David Scott, Charles Grant, and John Hunter also served as members of the Court of Directors of the East India Company.

Smith of Canton provided a variety of commercial services to his clients. He managed cargoes of cotton, tin, and redwood shipped and consigned to him by his clients and agents in India. Redwood may have been imported from the Philippines, Malaysia, or many of the islands in present-day Indonesia. Smith also purchased Chinese products for his clients, which included the East India Company. In 1779, he informed the Company's supercargos that he could provide them with "170 to 250 peculs of nankeen silk at the price of 270 taels per pecul." In exchange, Smith requested 20,000 taels immediately upon delivery of the silk and bills of exchange on the balance owed him.[32]

Like Smith of Madras, Smith of Canton used the East India Company's network of treasuries, located in its settlements in India, Southeast Asia, China, and London, to move his clients' money around the globe. But the scarcity of silver, the lifeblood of the Canton tea trade, could make for tense relations between private traders and the Company's supercargos. In 1774, the Company's officers in Canton refused to honor immediately two bills of exchange presented by Smith of Canton. The bills had been written by the Company's council in Fort Marlborough, Bencoolen, on the west coast of Sumatra, to draw $3,651.38 cash on the Company's Canton treasury. When Smith presented these bills to the Council of Supercargos in Canton, they "were this afternoon returned to me unaccepted." Smith attempted to evoke the supercargos' sympathy and convince them of his urgent need for the silver: "Sorry I am from the disappointments I have met with, and other circumstances needless to trouble you with."[33]

One of these disappointments was most likely the loss of a Company ship, the *Huntingdon,* which had been leased in 1774 to Smith's client in India, George Smith of Madras, "upon condition that she should be delivered" to the Canton government "on or before the end of September 1774." After the *Huntingdon* was lost at sea, Smith of Canton had no choice but to pay into the Canton treasury the $19,849.50 in freight costs drawn on him by Smith of Madras.[34]

If the Company's supercargos refused to pay the $3,651.38 they owed him immediately, Smith demanded that they offer him 18 percent annual interest, which was, according to him, "the accustomary rate of interest at Canton, betwixt Europeans and Chinese." The Company's supercargos had only offered 1 percent per month. He threatened to take his business elsewhere if they did not cooperate. He would no longer remit his clients' funds through their treasury but would instead use other means (probably the Dutch or Swedish East India Company's treasuries), thereby starving the East India Company of badly needed silver for their tea investments.[35]

Smith of Canton received payment from the Company in 1775, but it was a Pyrrhic victory. Later that year the Company's supercargos showed little sympathy when the tables were turned, and Smith's silver was not sufficient to obtain the bills of exchange he required. Smith requested Company bills worth a remarkably large sum: $480,000. But instead of paying silver into the Canton treasury, Smith proposed providing the Council of Supercargos with "chops," or contracts from several Chinese merchants, as security. He would also arrange for several Chinese merchants to provide goods directly to the Company on his account, in a triangular balancing of credits and debts commonly practiced in Canton among Chinese merchants, private traders, and the Company, known as transferences. The Company's supercargos, however, insisted on silver. Smith complained that they had not given him "a just or the smallest share in the transferences you have taken upon the merchants, which for various cogent and evident reasons in such a place as Canton I ought to have had." Out of desperation, he pleaded with the Company's supercargos to delay the departure of the Company ship that would carry the bills of exchange to England until he had enough time to procure silver. Smith promised to compensate the

Company by paying the ship's demurrage, the cost of delaying its departure. This was Smith's last resort: "Should you refuse me both of these offers I have then only left me the consolation which I hope ever to maintain that of having done my utmost for the benefit of my constituents and in support of the honor of my own credit." The Company's supercargos reiterated that they could not "comply in granting bills in any mode whatever for any sums of money that we are not in actual possession of."[36]

By the end of 1775, Smith of Canton had developed a reputation as someone "desirous to cavil." The Company's supercargos noted that "in contrast to all the other bill holders," who had accepted their proposal to pay the Fort Marlborough bills of exchange as "it suited our convenience," only George Smith "insisted on 1½ percent per month." He had also threatened "in case of our non-compliance with his terms to protest the bills . . . declaring it would influence him in regard to paying money into the Honble Company's treasury." As a result, "we were obliged to procure an advance from a China merchant to pay them." Smith had embarrassed the Company in this affair, and they were "in dread of worse consequences" in the future. The Company's directors in London also expressed their displeasure at Smith's behavior: "We have duly considered your representation on consultation 24th August 1775 of the litigious behavior of Mr. George Smith, and cannot avoid expressing our surprise at his endeavors to distress our affairs by not accepting the offers you made him for the discharge of his bills although we do not dispute his right of demand yet when he was made acquainted with the state of your cash and still persisted in having them accepted so evidently detrimental to our interest, we cannot but censure his conduct and esteem him very ungrateful, considering the advantages he has reaped by remaining in China in direct contradiction to the Company's regulations."[37]

George Smith of Canton and others like him were wearing out their welcome. The Company's supercargos could "not help taking notice on the occasion, that this gentleman is one of those individuals, who has remained in this country contrary to the express commands of the Court of Directors, and to whom we have several seasons delivered a protest of so doing." As early as 1771, not long after his arrival, the Company's supercargos acquainted "Mess. George Smith Junr. Wm Dalrymple and Walter Goadie . . . with the Company's orders relative" to residing illegally in China. It seemed at first that Smith might comply: "I have received your letter of 22nd ult. communicating to me the Honorable Company's orders, I beg leave to inform you it is my intention to proceed to Madras by the way of Bengal on board the ship Vansittart." Smith probably never left Canton, or he did so only briefly, because on November 11, 1772, the Council of Supercargos warned him again. This time Smith complained that he "found the Chinese so very dilatory in their payments to him he was afraid he could not possibly leave China this season." In 1773, he again explained "that the state of my affairs in China would not permit me to leave it this season."[38]

Smith did leave Canton briefly in 1778 to pursue a new commercial opportunity. He sailed to Bombay, where he bought the ship *Eliza* from his friend and agent David Scott of Bombay. That same year, the *Eliza* made a round-trip voyage between Bombay and Canton. The ship's large crew was racially hierarchical. The British commander, Robert Smith (perhaps a relative of George Smith of Canton), received eighty rupees per month for his work. Several British shipmates were paid thirty to fifty rupees per month. Twelve Eurasian "serangs," the heads of the lascar crew, with Portuguese names such as Joquin, Lazarus, Domingo, Joze Antonio, Antonio Dias, and Pedro de Silva, received twelve rupees per month. And the Indian lascars at the bottom of the hierarchy—there were at least sixty of them—earned the meager wage of five rupees per month. The *Eliza* was most likely transporting Bombay cotton to China. A Dutch source reported that on its return voyage to India the "private English ship *Eliza* of George Smith . . . is being freighted by Armenian merchants here [Canton]." The well-armed ship stopped at various ports between Bombay and Canton, including Goa, Cochin, Tellicherry, and Malacca, and returned to Bombay with "sapon wood," candles, and other unspecified goods.[39]

Smith of Canton took the lead in this commercial venture, but the *Eliza*'s voyage was financed by at least twenty different lenders, among them John Fergusson, John Hunter, and Patrick Crawfurd Bruce, who together invested over 40,000 rupees.[40] This was typical practice for private traders who did not own their own ships. According to Ann Bulley, most "captain-owners," like Smith of Canton, "took their chance wherever the market seemed best." In Bombay, they typically owned "only one ship and did so for only one season." Their ventures were often financed by respondentia loans, which paid for and insured the cargo. Sadly for Smith of Canton, the *Eliza* venture was a complete failure. In 1779, he was forced to sell the *Eliza* and everything on it to pay the ship's crew and compensate the many investors who sponsored the voyage. The *Eliza* was eventually repossessed by David Scott of Bombay, and it changed hands several times over the next three decades.[41]

After Smith's brief and unsuccessful stint in Bombay, he and his new bride, Charlotte, relocated to Canton in 1779. Unfortunately for the new couple, their move coincided with a much bolder initiative on the part of the East India Company to expel unlicensed British private traders from Canton. By 1783, only John Henry Cox, a clock merchant, remained.

George Smith of Canton, however, proved uniquely obstinate. When the Company's Canton supercargos pressed him to leave, he responded with a scathing letter disputing the Company's monopoly rights in China and its claim to authority over him: "I have received your letter of yesterdays date, it is a general maxim where protection is offered power is implied, every year brings you fresh and most mortifying instances of the total want of the latter, of course the former is not in your power to grant from an inability to enforce it, the instructions of the Honorable Court of Directors to you carries with it an appearance of power without its essential reality, I never admitted the authority of the Honorable Company or their Court of Directors in China, in any one shape whatever over me a British subject. I trust for protection to a power capable to enforce it, whose duty it is, and who will not permit its subjects to be oppressed." Smith of Canton warned: "The Chinese know perfectly well your situation and mine, they are too good politicians ever to deviate so far from sound policy, to withdraw their protection from me an old resident in this place, to whom their merchants appointed by government stand so deeply indebted."[42] Smith of Canton was right. While the East India Company sought to uphold its monopoly and stop unlicensed British merchants from doing business in China, the

Chinese government's free-trade policies welcomed all traders, regardless of affiliation, to the port of Canton.

When the Company's directors in London learned of Smith of Canton's audacious letter, they became determined to expel him from China, even if it meant using physical force to extradite him back to England. In 1780, they consulted George Rous, counsel to the Company, and James Wallace, the solicitor-general, about the legality of removing Smith forcibly from the East Indies. Both concurred that Company servants could legally "seize and arrest and send home the person of Mr. Smith if he shall be found within the limits of the Company's charter."[43] So the orders went out from London, and on February 3, 1781, the Company's supercargos notified Smith that unless he left China immediately, they would make use of a special commission under the seal of the Company to seize him and send him on the next Company ship back to Europe.[44]

Smith found help in Macao. With the complicity of Don Francisco Xavier De Castro, the Portuguese governor of Macao, he managed to extend his stay in China by a year. The Company's supercargos requested that the governor withdraw his protection from George Smith of Canton, but he refused.[45] Governor De Castro "had some time ago granted this gentleman protection, and therefore as the Council of Supercargos could not pretend to any jurisdiction in Macao, he should not suffer them to molest him."[46]

The Company's supercargos decided it was "out of their power to enforce the Honorable Court's orders," so Smith of Canton succeeded in buying himself another year in China. If he dared to leave Macao and set foot in Canton, however, the Company's supercargos vowed to the Company's directors in London that they would seize him by force and ship him back to Europe.[47] That never happened. In November 1781, Smith notified them that he would be stopping in Canton for a short business trip and begged to be informed whether he could "go there and return again" to his family unmolested upon giving his "word of honor" and pledging to proceed to Europe in the same season.[48] Smith's word of honor satisfied the Company's supercargos, and they reassured him he could remain in Canton unmolested "whilst your business renders your stay here necessary."[49] They did, however, keep an eye on him, noting his movements in their consultation: on November 26, 1781, they recorded that "Mr. George Smith arrived from Macao," and on January 2, 1782, that "Mr. Smith went to Macao."[50]

Smith of Canton and his family eventually returned to Britain. The extra time in Macao was important, though, for the Smith family. Early in 1781, Smith's wife, Charlotte, was about to "lay in" and give birth. She was clearly unfit for "so long a voyage with an infant at the breast, and another not twenty months old."[51] An extra year in Macao bought Charlotte time to give birth on dry land; a daughter, Harriet Ann, was safely delivered in Macao on February 18, 1781.[52]

A year later, George, Charlotte, and their two little girls, two-and-a-half-year-old Charlotte Eleanora and one-year-old Harriet Ann, began a nine-month voyage to England on the 137.5-foot-long, 777-ton East India Company ship *Contractor,* with Captain James Baldwin in command.[53] Their journey was mostly uneventful, although on the way from St. Helena to Portsmouth, the *Contractor* encountered strong gales, heavy squalls, and high seas that split the foresail "up to the head" and caused the ship to take on "a good deal of water."[54] The Smith family was no doubt relieved three weeks later when they spotted "the extremity of the land" on their approach to the entrance to Portsmouth.[55]

But rough seas also awaited them in England. Smith of Canton continued to work as a merchant in London, although the nature of his business is unclear. The family settled in Charlotte's home parish of Stoke-next-Guildford, where her father, John Peche, still lived. Smith claimed that he returned to England "to meet his creditors as an honest man, [and] to do them every justice in his power."[56] In the eighteenth century, creditors who failed to meet their obligations were subject to bankruptcy. According to one explanation, "bankruptcy was used because it treated all creditors alike and gave full access to a debtor's estate."[57] Smith's creditors were numerous and dispersed, yet almost all of them preferred to settle Smith's debts amicably out of court. Perhaps also out of sympathy for or trust in Smith of Canton, who was "in habits of intimacy with a great many of them," his creditors had been "friendly towards him, and some in a very

George Chinnery (1774–1852). *An English Family in Macao,* 1835. Courtesy of the Yale Center for British Art.

eminent degree."[58] Smith met with them and provided a statement and balance sheet for his affairs upon leaving China, according to which he owed £128,514 to British investors and was himself owed £73,224, being "the honest fruits of many years industry."[59] The creditors jointly decided upon an assignment of his property and agreed to release Smith from his debts as long as he "rendered a fair and honorable account and delivery of all his property."[60] For reasons that are unclear, John Hunter, Smith's largest and most "inimical" creditor, was dissatisfied. Hunter, a member of Parliament and director of the East India Company, wasted little time in paying the required £200 bond to the lord chancellor to issue a commission of bankruptcy against Smith.[61]

Several years earlier, Smith of Canton's former business partner, John Crichton, had explained the English bankruptcy process to the Hoppo, the emperor-appointed superintendent of customs in Canton: "When a man stops payment, he takes out a statute of bankruptcy from the judges appointed for this purpose, delivers over everything he has in the world to his creditors, meets with lawyers appointed, his books and papers respecting his affairs are delivered into their hands for inspection—they are examined by them from time to time as the nature of them requires and resolutions are taken not only with respect to them, but that a just and equal division be made to each creditor, according to the demand he has on the estate of the bankrupt."[62] Crichton perhaps depicted the English bankruptcy process a little too generously. He neglected to mention that the potential bankrupt had no right to defend himself while being investigated. Nor did he mention that "when the commissioners made their declaration of bankruptcy they notified the bankrupt . . . by placing an advertisement in the *London Gazette,* ordering him to surrender himself and his property. His house would be searched and his immediate effects seized."[63] To declare Smith of Canton a bankrupt, it first had to be determined that he had "committed an act of bankruptcy, which amounted to the unreasonable evasion of his creditors' just demands for repayment."[64] According to Crichton, "If it appears to the creditors the merchant has conducted his affairs with prudence and honesty, and that it has been really through misfortunes that he stopped payment, he is not only discharged, but even assisted with money by his creditors and often by their friends."[65]

Smith of Canton's "misfortunes" did not result from his "imprudence, misconduct, or extravagance," or so he claimed. Rather, according to Smith, his inability to discharge his debts "proceeded solely from the injustice of the officers of the Chinese government at Canton in conjunction with the Hong merchants."[66] John Hunter, who initiated bankruptcy proceedings against him, was unmoved by Smith's misfortune. Smith of Canton felt betrayed; his situation was "totally contrary to the intention and spirit of the laws."[67]

Smith of Canton's bankruptcy appeared in various London newspapers during the 1780s. In 1782, the *London Chronicle* advertised that "George Smith, late of Canton in China, but now of London, merchant (copartner with John Crichton, late of Canton aforesaid, but now of London, merchant) to surrender Dec. 31, Jan. 11, Feb. 1 at Guildhall."[68] Not long after, the *Public Advertiser, London Chronicle,* and *Morning Chronicle and London Advertiser* announced that Smith's creditors had met at the Guildhall to discuss his debts to them.[69] In 1783, it was official. The *London Gazette* reported that a commission of bankruptcy "was awarded and issued forth against George Smith."[70] Smith's creditors split dividends of £2,600 from Smith's estate and effects among themselves. This ritual took place again in 1785, twice in 1786, and once every year between 1787 and 1791.[71] During these trying times the Smith family may have sought strength in their family motto: *mediis tranquillus in undis.*

Why did George Smith of Canton, like his namesake and business partner, George Smith of Madras, go bankrupt around the same time? Expulsion from China undoubtedly exacerbated his financial situation. What, then, prompted the East India Company to force British private traders out of China so suddenly? The answer lies in a financial crisis in Canton.

FOUR

Financial Crisis

GEORGE SMITH OF CANTON helped his clients to remit their private fortunes from India to Britain via the East India Company's treasury in Canton. In the process, he also helped to finance the Company's tea trade in China, ensuring that the Company had enough silver in Canton to pay for its seasonal tea purchases. If that were all Smith of Canton did, though, he would never have appeared so frequently in the records of the East India Company, despite being a freelance trader interloping in Company territory.

Smith of Canton's financial dealings extended well beyond the straightforward remittance business. During the 1760s and 1770s, Smith, along with several other private brokers, loaned large sums of money to Chinese merchants at extremely high interest rates. Although cash-strapped Chinese merchants eagerly sought these foreign loans, which at 18–22 percent annual interest stood well below the Chinese legal limit of 36 percent per year, many of them were eventually ruined by the loans. When insolvent Chinese merchants could not repay the $4,296,650 demanded of them, British investors bribed a British Navy admiral and rear admiral to send warships from India to China, thus instigating a major financial and political crisis in Canton.

This crisis sheds light on the development of a new commercial system that increasingly depended on risky high-interest loans to Chinese borrowers. The system also extended far beyond the geographical boundaries of the British empire in Asia by connecting capital markets in India and China. Most of the British investors involved in the Canton financial crisis worked and lived in India.

Following the money trail and tracing the machinations of private British capital in India and China reveals the financial fragility and

Chinese artist. *View of Guangzhou (Canton),* c. 1800. Watercolor and gouache on paper. China. 24 1/2 × 47 inches (62.23 × 119.38 cm). Peabody Essex Museum, Museum purchase with funds donated anonymously, 1975. E79708. Courtesy of the Peabody Essex Museum, Salem, Mass. Photograph by Jeffrey R. Dykes.

instability at the heart of Britain's trade with China. It also shows how imperial engagement on the geographical edges of Britain's empire could be amplified and intensified by seemingly marginal actors. When economic experimentation on the ground failed, when crisis struck, the complexity of the financial interdependence and the sheer audacity of private traders

meant that imperial stakes were suddenly raised. Faced with personal ruin, private traders and their clients devised increasingly aggressive strategies for enforcing their contracts and protecting their interests in China.

If financing the Canton tea trade was a struggle for the East India Company, it was perhaps even more so for the Chinese Hong merchants, who required large amounts of silver to pay tea merchants, upcountry growers, suppliers, and manufacturers.[1] According to economic historians working on China, "much of the demand for credit in the early modern

Chinese economy could be satisfied within social institutions and networks that did not require new specialized institutions with particular efforts to document credit transactions."[2] However, as the tumultuous interplay between the Hong merchants and European traders in Canton indicates, domestic credit markets and social institutions alone did not satisfy the capital requirements of the eighteenth-century tea trade. British traders on the ground, in fact, justified their risky financial dealings by suggesting that "the total want of banks, and the no less want of confidence between the China merchants" made their lending practices a necessity.[3] Without the infusion of foreign silver, the Hong merchants would have had tremendous difficulty financing their end of the tea trade.

Compounding this issue was the fact that most Hong merchants had trouble obtaining loans in China as they often lacked the collateral with which to secure capital. As a result, pawnshops and other better-capitalized Hong merchants would not lend them money. The debt adjudication system available to Chinese subjects also seems to have discouraged them from extending credit to each other; it may have been so onerous and unreliable that it "discouraged risk taking in the form of the general extension of credit." The result was that local institutions, money markets, and lenders did not supply Canton merchants with sufficient capital for the growing tea trade. "The lack of affordable domestic credit was a severe problem."[4]

Lacking domestic credit, Chinese merchant houses turned to foreign credit and were "intensely focused on procuring foreign capital." European and Armenian lenders appeared to be the best source of short-term loans and "liquid credit (silver coin)" in Canton. The Chinese viceroy and the Hoppo, the superintendent of customs, observed that "the foolishness and craftiness of the Hong Merchants is owing to the fact that at present they only want to borrow money." They demonstrated concern that Hong merchants aimed to develop "close relationships with the foreigners who stay and do business in their factories . . . They sell the foreigners' goods for them at higher prices than other merchants, and they buy goods for the foreigners at cheaper prices than the other merchants. They do this hoping they gain more business with the foreigners."[5]

Centuries of piracy and political volatility on the southeast coast of China made Chinese rulers in Peking wary of long-term financial entanglements between natives and foreigners. Since the beginning of the eighteenth century, all accrued foreign debts were supposed to be settled by the end of each trading season. In 1760, the Qianlong emperor reemphasized this expectation by declaring it illegal for outstanding debts to remain between European and Chinese merchants at the end of the trading season. According to Canton officials, that "order is put up and fixed in the most public places when the European ships yearly arrive." Yet when the debt crisis occurred nineteen years later, Company and private merchants proclaimed their innocence; the edict "seems not to have been known among the English." The captain of an East India Company ship claimed ignorance of the maximum legal interest rate in China (it was 3 percent per month), yet he was adamant about the legality of credit transactions between Chinese subjects and foreign traders: "Formerly many gentlemen received payment of such bonds . . . by petitioning the Hoppo. This is an absolute fact and in my humble opinion incontrovertible proof of the legality."[6]

Despite the illegality of these long-term credit relationships, Chinese officials in Canton tacitly accepted and at times supported them over the course of more than half a century. Everyone recognized the importance of European credit to the Canton trade. Local officials understood that credit facilitated trade and increased state revenues, and they intervened only when Chinese merchants failed. British lenders were willing to make long-term loans to Chinese merchants because they knew the loans would ultimately be repaid.[7] According to the supercargos of the East India Company, British investors believed they could enjoy the "great additional security of trading under the sanction of the Chinese government."[8] There was "no person who ever lent to a Cohong merchant that did not conceive the government of China as their ultimate security," claimed a captain of a Company ship.[9] Foreigners could actually enforce their contracts in China more easily than Chinese creditors could. In contrast to Chinese plaintiffs who sought legal redress through the Qing courts, Europeans were not beaten and "interrogated" (tortured) by magistrates, were not required to kneel during hearings and trials, and were not punished if their claims were falsified. Chinese officials typically assumed the veracity of foreigners' claims. They only disputed the amount of unpaid debts.[10] As a result, "foreign creditors were always able to recover something from the Chinese."[11]

As it transpired, British investors probably had too much faith that the Chinese government would enforce their contracts. "There were no facts to support" this belief, according to the Company's supercargos.[12] British traders in Canton often found it difficult to access the governor and the superintendent of customs. By the second half of the eighteenth century, audiences were granted "only under special circumstances."[13] Canton officials preferred that Hong merchants and Chinese "linguists" serve as translators and intermediaries between foreigners and themselves, a practice that forced British traders to depend on the very people about whom they were complaining.[14] Foreigners in Canton were at a linguistic disadvantage because the Chinese government strictly prohibited natives from teaching the Chinese language to them. (Despite the ban, however, two Company servants were furtively attempting to study with a native tutor in 1755.)[15] Canton officials also exercised considerable discretion in reporting problems to the emperor. According to Paul Van Dyke, the "tedious process of settling debts" played a part in the collapse of the Canton system of trade.[16] The limits of Chinese arbitration should perhaps have been more obvious to British lenders. Motivated by greed and overconfidence in the debt adjudication system available to them, private traders provided extensive long-term credit on behalf of their clients to Chinese merchants.

By the late 1770s, "almost all of the European inhabitants of any long standing ha[d] large debts due them in China."[17] Company directors, governors, administrative employees, and ship captains were all implicated. Their loans to Chinese merchants were rolled over from year to year and resold in a rapidly growing secondary market for Chinese debt. The Company's supercargos in Canton attempted with great difficulty to trace the origins and lineage of the merchants' debts. They followed the trail of several bonds, including one which began its life with George Smith of Canton, passed through several hands, including those of an Armenian merchant, and ended up in the possession of a Company supercargo. In another case, the supercargos reported that "Doctor Gordon had originally a small sum, at interest. Then it became a bond to Mess. Hutton and Gordon and last year it was . . . made over to Mr. Sealy [at] 20 percent interest due the end of this year."[18] Two indebted merchants, Yngshaw (顏時瑛) and Kewshaw (張天球), testified to the governor of Guangdong and the superintendent of customs in Canton about the loans they took from British lenders: "Because for a short time we could not pay back the money, and the foreigners also did not force us to repay, the interest on the loans was added to the principal and new bonds were written . . . The foreigners did not come and these bonds were passed through many hands and exchanged. These other foreigners also added compound interest according to the new bonds, and increased and rewrote the bonds. Interest piled up for more than twenty years. Thus, [the debt] accumulated so tremendously."[19]

Yngshaw and Kewshaw's testimony confirms that a market for Chinese debt had emerged in Canton.[20] Of the eighty-nine bonds that Kewshaw and Yngshaw reported to the East India Company's supercargos, as many as sixty-two had been refinanced, making them very difficult to analyze: "The bonds of money lent have been so often renewed, and blended with principal and interest, likewise bonds for large sums in one name divided into smaller, in the names of two or three persons, that it is impossible to be quite right."[21] By 1781, there were at least 248 bonds amounting to $4,296,650 (slightly less than the amount owed to British subjects by Virginians after the American Revolutionary War). In 1792 the East India Company's Court of Directors estimated from the best information they could obtain that "the Chinese never received in money or goods more than $1,078,976."[22] The rest was accumulated interest.

Brokers in Canton made loans to Chinese merchants at "various values of interest from 16 to 24 percent per annum," although most loans appear to have been at interest rates between 18 and 20 percent.[23] Such high premiums reduced the probability that the borrowers could repay their loans. According to W. E. Cheong, after 1740, Hong merchants' indebtedness had become chronic, and by 1760, there were "all the ingredients for a financial crisis."[24] "Our country traders are unreasonable. We are very ashamed," the most senior Company supercargos in Canton supposedly admitted to Governor Li Zhiying and Customs Superintendent Tu Ming'a about the lending practices of British traders.[25] John Crichton, a Canton broker, instead blamed the Chinese government for setting the legal interest rate so high. He proposed that the annual maximum permissible interest rate in China be lowered from 36 percent to 12 percent. As things stood, Crichton was fairly certain that the Hong merchant "will be ever incapable of discharging the demand, while such a heavy interest is running on against them."[26]

Did brokers like George Smith of Canton and John Crichton fully disclose the true situation of their clients' investments? Or had their brokerages in Canton turned into Ponzi schemes? Were they paying old clients' dividends with new investors' money? And if so, for how many years? Unfortunately, the letter books of the Canton brokers do not survive. Letters relating to two lenders in India, George Vansittart and George Graham, however, shed some light on the relationship between investors in India and their brokers in Canton. George Vansittart, a Company employee who later served as a member of Parliament and director of the East India Company, claimed that he never intended for his money to be invested with Chinese merchants. When he and Ewan Law, another Company employee, shipped a cargo of goods on Captain Shaw's country (non-Company) ship in 1774, the Company's Canton treasury was closed and was not issuing bills of exchange that year. As a result, Shaw loaned $106,000, which he had previously wished to convert to an East India Company bill of exchange, to George Smith of Canton, who then loaned the money to Chinese merchants in Canton.[27] This enabled Vansittart to "remit" his money home via a bond, but in reality it merely added him to the confused financial web of Canton debt. The records do not reveal whether Vansittart, Law, and Smith of Canton communicated between 1774 and the outbreak of the crisis five years later.[28]

In contrast to Vansittart, George Graham, a private trader in Bengal, instructed Charles Crommelin, a Canton broker, to lend his money to Chinese merchants. Although the initial amount of the loan is unclear, it was probably substantial, for Crommelin eventually remitted to Graham the sum of £12,000.[29] After making a quick fortune in India, Graham returned to Britain and left it to his agent in Bengal, David Killican, to continue handling his financial affairs in Asia.[30] Graham, Killican, and Philip Milner Dacres, the head of the Board of Trade in Bengal, who also happened to be Crommelin's close relative and business partner, corresponded over the Chinese debts for at least the years between 1776 and 1784.[31] In September 1777, Killican made an unfortunate discovery: "As Mr. Crommelin could not get his money from the Chinese it was out of his power to make good his engagement with those gentlemen in Bengal whose money he had received and there was no other alternative but to accept of interest on the bonds he had granted." The year 1779 brought even worse news: "The accounts from China are really dreadful, there is not a Chinese merchant [who] can be trusted, and they owe immense sums to the English; The English who reside there and have transacted money affairs for some years past, have lost all credit, indeed not without too much reason." Crommelin corresponded regularly with Dacres, who transmitted information to Killican and others concerned with Crommelin's affairs in China. Killican attempted to allay Graham's fears of further losses: "I think you are in no danger of having any new concerns there, which I am very glad of as there is no knowing whom to trust." According to Dacres, Crommelin had "left in China the bonds locked up in an iron chest, and given no one authority to open it to receive the dividends that have been made by the Chinese."[32] All Crommelin's clients could do was wait for events to play out in Canton.

By 1774, there were already hints of the looming crisis. According to one source, when a Hong merchant known as Seunqua became insolvent in 1773, British investors panicked, "refused to lend or to extend the maturity of existing loans, and tried to collect amounts then due."[33] An anonymous correspondent of Warren Hastings, then governor of the presidency of Fort William (Bengal), reported that in 1775, "large demands were made upon them [the Chinese merchants] on behalf of gentlemen in England and going thither who wanted their money home and sent orders for its being paid into the treasury at Canton for Bills on the Court of Directors."[34] George Smith of Canton confirmed that the sums demanded from Chinese merchants in 1775 were "far greater than at any anterior period" and this state of affairs "renders them unable to pay large sums in the course of a year."[35] Matthew Raper, a Company supercargo, suggested that the problem arose because Chinese merchants borrowed money from India at very high interest rates during the 1760s. They paid off their debts by continuing to borrow money "till the influx of bullion was in great measure stopped" and they could no longer keep up with their payments. "The demands of the country merchants became very pressing whereby they lost in great measure their confidence."[36] John Crichton, the Canton broker, provided yet another explanation, suggesting that some of the Hong merchants' businesses were ruined because the superintendent of customs suddenly forced them to pay large amounts of overdue taxes. Crichton blamed him for the Hong merchants' misfortunes: "Your excellency cannot be a stranger that a merchant in any part of the world, must be ruined if his ready money is all at once paid into the treasury for arrears of a long standing."[37] In 1779, John McIntyre, a private trader who had served as purser for the East India Company in the *Gatton* on a voyage to China between 1771 and 1773, complained to his wife in Scotland about the dreadful mercantile conditions in Canton: "Just about the time Mr. Gordon left this place last year for Europe, I found one of the houses in which the half of my money that I left when with Captain Money had failed for about half a million Sterling, my sum the Principal and Interest amounted to Spanish dollars 994—which is a great loss as nothing will be recovered, the whole of the partners are in prison on account of debts they owe the Europeans."[38] Whatever the cause of the panic, there was no doubt that by the late 1770s, half of the Chinese merchants licensed to trade with foreigners were in deep trouble.

All three George Smiths loaned money at high interest rates to Chinese merchants.[39] While managing Andrew Munro's estate in China during the late 1750s, Smith of Madras invested some of his uncle's money with the Chinese at interest.[40] About ten years later, he reported that "a little sum of £20,000 which thank God I can still call my own, is accumulating in China in good hands."[41] The East India Company's records also reveal that in 1779, Yngshaw owed Smith of Madras $9,665 at a 15 percent rate of annual interest while Seunqua owed him $3,412. After Seunqua became insolvent, "it was agreed on all sides that the debt amounting to 266,672 dollars should be paid in ten years from that time without interest." Smith of Madras recovered some of his money from Seunqua, but he would see only a small fraction of the money he demanded from Yngshaw.[42]

Smith of Madras was implicated in the debt crisis, but George Smith of Canton was the true ringleader. Of the $4,296,650 in debts claimed by British lenders in 1780, Smith of Canton was owed $763,111, or roughly 18 percent of the total amount.[43] He and five other Canton brokers—Abraham Leslie, Charles Gordon, Thomas Hutton, Charles Crommelin, and John Crichton—possessed "merchants bonds to near three fourths of the whole debt."[44] All but Crommelin were Scots. Private Scottish brokers (several of them retired surgeons) were disproportionately involved in the emerging financial market in Canton.

Abraham Leslie came to India to work as a Company surgeon in Madras, but in 1773 private business brought him to China. When the Company's supercargos ordered him to leave Canton, he responded that his "own concerns with that of my connections brought me to China this year for the first time." He promised that as soon as his work in China was finished, he would return to Madras on a Portuguese ship. Leslie must have kept his word and not caused further trouble because he offered his services as a temporary surgeon four years later to the Canton supercargos "until the gentleman appointed in Europe arrives, with full assurance that I will use my best endeavor to discharge the duty incumbent on me in that station." The Company's supercargos had "a very good opinion" of his "knowledge and experience" and happily accepted his offer. Leslie seems to have been a competent surgeon and served the Company's employees well. When he retired from the post a year later, they expressed appreciation of his "care and attention to the gentlemen of the factory while in the Honorable Companies employ."[45]

Like Leslie, Charles Gordon's brother Robert also worked as a Company surgeon in Canton. While providing medical care to the Company's staff in China, he engaged extensively in private trade.[46] "My letter book, cash book, day book, and ledger will show what sums I have borrowed at interest and what sums I have at interest with the Chinese for the amount of other persons," he explained to the executors of his estate. More specifically, he mentioned outstanding loans to Monqua and Puankequa and estimated his net worth just before his death to total £16,000. After Robert Gordon's death in 1771, Charles Gordon traveled to China and continued his brother's business with the help of Thomas Hutton. Their firm became known as Hutton and Gordon.[47]

Thomas Hutton began his career in the East India Company as a ship surgeon, working aboard the *Devonshire* from 1765 to 1766 and the *Duke of Kingston* from 1768 to 1769. He was appointed surgeon in Canton in 1771, after Robert Gordon's death, serving until 1776, when failing health forced him to resign from his post and take up residence at the Cape of Good Hope. The following season he returned to Canton, and "from that time, to the year 1782 did the duty of his former station without any emolument whatever, his successor Mr. Dewar being incapable thereof from indisposition."[48]

Charles Crommelin, the non-Scot in the group (he was of Huguenot descent), was born in Bombay in 1717. As the son of a Company employee, he rose steadily in the Company's ranks to become governor of Bombay from 1760 to 1769. He then moved to England, but poor finances forced his return to India, where he worked as a licensed private trader in 1772. He later moved again, this time to Canton, where he served as a broker for George Graham and John Hunter.[49]

John Crichton ventured to India in 1755, when he was just sixteen years old. He began his career as a Company writer but later shifted into full-time private trade. In 1765 and 1767 he served as supercargo for two country ships, the *Chesterfield* and the *Pocock,* respectively. Finally, in 1768, he moved to Canton with the "resolution" to reside there permanently. During his long residence as a private trader and broker in China, Crichton developed business relationships and friendships with many British and Chinese merchants. He worked for several years in partnership with George Smith of Canton; served as a broker for clients in Madras, including Edward Monckton and George Smith of Madras; and became the executor of Robert Gordon's estate. Gordon bequeathed to Crichton a ring "as the grateful offer of a heart that warmly felt the ties of friendship." Gordon also left his horse, his dog (Prince), and a boy named Lorenzo in Crichton's care.

Crichton developed business relationships with many Chinese merchants, including Yngshaw, Tinqua, Teyqua, Monqua, Chowqua, Kewshaw, Teoqua, and Keyqua, and had "extensive concerns both in goods and money" with his "very worthy friend" Shy Kinqua. He formed a connection to the successful Hong merchant Puankequa, whom he described as a "very good friend." In 1774, after a long residence in Asia, Crichton decided to retire to England to pass the remainder of his days with family and friends, including his seventy-five-year-old mother, from whom he had been absent all those years. But having been disappointed by recovering only two-thirds of his fortune from Chinese borrowers, he was compelled to return to the East Indies during the late 1770s to settle his affairs.[50]

Smith, Leslie, Hutton, Gordon, Crommelin, and Crichton first turned to Canton officials for help. Abraham Leslie claimed he had already "used all possible means to present his request to your majesty's mandarins but without effect." He decided to approach the superintendent of customs' assistant regarding "the merchants' obligations and his request regarding the sum owing him by the Honnists [Hong merchants]." Leslie claimed that the superintendent never responded, and after waiting "for near the space of twelve months," he attempted to enter the city of Canton (which was off limits to foreigners) to present his request directly to the Chinese officials. After being beaten by soldiers at the city gate, he finally gave up.[51]

John Crichton and George Smith of Canton both suggested that the linguists and Hong merchants who acted as mediators had deceived and bribed officials to impede arbitration. In 1780, Li Zhiying, the governor of Guangdong Province, claimed complete ignorance of the debts.[52] Fearing severe punishment (which could include imprisonment, torture, and banishment), Chinese merchants and linguists had a strong incentive to prevent the government's intervention. Perhaps they succeeded temporarily, perhaps not, but even if Canton officials knew about the debts, they may have feared for their own reputations. A serious credit crisis would have to be reported to the emperor in Peking and would undoubtedly reflect badly upon their ability to govern Canton. Perhaps Canton officials hesitated to act, hoping that the debts could be settled without government interference.[53]

Smith of Canton and the other five brokers eventually decided to bypass local and provincial officials and contact the Qianlong emperor directly. They reasoned that if the emperor were aware of the gross injustices committed in Canton, he would administer justice. They knew better than to attempt a voyage to Peking to present their grievances in person, as supercargo James Flint had done in 1759. Flint languished in a Chinese prison for several years as punishment for this bold gesture.[54] But there was little harm in writing a petition. How the brokers planned to get it into the emperor's hands is unclear. They complained to the emperor that they had "used all possible means to enter our petitions to the mandarins your majesty's justices but by no method or mode possible could we succeed by reason that the merchants always found methods to obstruct us so that we could not make our complaints known to the Mandareens." The brokers tried to appeal to the Qianlong emperor's sense of compassion for their situation as strangers in a strange land: "We come here from a great distance with much danger and trouble by sea even to the risk of our lives only to establish trade and to preserve an union and friendship among nations." They requested that the emperor send his own personnel to Canton to whom they could confidently present their grievances and "all the chops and obligations we have of these merchants indebted." The brokers' petition probably never reached the emperor. It only survives today in the papers of Britain's first ambassador to China, Lord George Macartney.[55]

British creditors and their agents clearly would have to find another means of recovering their money. War in America gave them the perfect opportunity. As the American Revolutionary War (1776–83) spread to India, Rear Admiral Edward Vernon was dispatched to Madras to protect British interests in Asia. It was Vernon, when he arrived in Madras, who served as the deus ex machina for which the creditors had been waiting. Thinking it "my duty to pay respects to him," John Crichton met with Vernon and "asked him if he had heard anything respecting the great demands the English had on the Chinese merchants." When Vernon answered affirmatively, Crichton eagerly requested permission to send him some papers he had written on the subject. Taking "a day or two" to consider Crichton's case, Vernon replied that "he should in consequence . . . take it up in his public character." He asked only that Crichton "address him a letter in his public character as representative of the King his Master."[56]

The pact between Rear Admiral Vernon and Crichton did not go unnoticed in Madras. Not long after their meeting, "creditors and attorneys of creditors of the Chinese merchants at Canton" also requested meetings with the rear admiral. They hoped he would represent to Governor Li Zhiying and Superintendent of Customs Tu Ming'a the hardships under which they labored. They also requested that he deliver John Crichton's memorial to the superintendent of customs, which contained "a plan for the payment of their debts at a future period, on terms advantageous to the Chinese merchants." As a reward for Vernon's intervention, the Madras creditors "engaged to give Sir Edward a tenth part of the amount recovered."[57]

British creditors portrayed the crisis in Canton as a matter of national concern. As Crichton explained to Vernon, "It is sir a national affair as it will not only be rendering the East India Company essential service, but the means of saving a number of families from utter ruin and misery."[58] Luckily for the creditors, Vernon agreed. Without waiting for permission from the Madras government and without consulting the Canton supercargos, Vernon came to "the resolution of sending his Majesty's frigate the *Sea Horse* to China" and ordered the commander of the vessel, Captain Alexander Panton, to deliver personally to the superintendent of customs the representations of the British creditors. Vernon explained in his letter to the governor of Guangdong Province, Li Zhiying, that he was "the representative of my most gracious sovereign the King of Great Britain, by whose commission I have the honor to serve in this country, as an Admiral and Commander in Chief of his squadron and of armed vessels, of the English East India Company," a role in which he could not "consistently with my duty to my sovereign and to my country see his subjects oppressed and distressed."[59]

This was not the only time Captain Panton sailed to Canton on account of the British creditors. Almost a year later, in 1780, they decided to solicit the help of another admiral, this time Admiral Edward Hughes. They had been encouraged by the impression of some gentlemen residing in Canton "that the Mandarins and merchants were much afraid, on hearing the business with which Captain Panton was charged; which gave sufficient proof that if proper spirited measures should be pursued the recovery of the China debts, may be easily accomplished." The creditors believed that a "more than ordinary interposition" was necessary to "forward the success of the national object" and so decided again to address "the Commander of his Majesty's Squadron requesting the continuance of his good offices, on the behalf of the creditors." On June 2, 1780, a group of creditors in Madras (including George Smith's first cousin George Moubray) requested that Admiral Hughes "give such further instructions to Capt. Panton to procure the best, speediest, and most secure arrangements for the payment of the creditors, that can be obtained." Admiral Hughes thus dispatched Captain Panton to Canton again. In doing so, he claimed to have "yielded to the national impulse of every well wisher to his country, who is ever ready to relieve the distress of his fellow subjects." Although Hughes spoke of moderation, he warned the Chinese officials: "The King of Great Britain my Royal Master, whose justice and magnanimity, is known to all the world, has been pleased to send me to the East Indies, with a strong squadron of His ships of War, to protect His own dominions and subjects."[60]

John Crichton, George Smith of Canton, and Thomas Hutton expressed their gratitude to Admiral Hughes for his intervention in Canton, but they had hoped for an even greater show of British power in China. After Panton's arrival in Canton, there was talk on board several British ships in China that "a proper remonstrance should have been made." If Admiral Hughes would spare "a proper force" to be sent to Canton, Crichton, Smith, and Hutton were certain it "would have the desired effect."

As it turned out, George Smith of Canton reported, "His Majesty's service in India, at this period, did not permit the Commander in Chief of His Majesty's fleet to pursue further measures for the relief of the unfortunate British subjects in China." Smith of Canton and his colleagues were disappointed that "the affairs on the Coast of Coromandel would not permit the Admiral to take the necessary steps, to convince the Chinese he had been in earnest in his application for Justice in behalf of British subjects."[61]

Despite their disappointment, Captain Panton's arrival in Canton in September 1779, and again in 1780, sent shock waves through the Canton mercantile community. This was a serious breach of the rules of the Canton trade. Ships without goods or silver, especially warships, were not welcome in Canton. No one, except the British creditors and their brokers, was glad to see British warships in Canton. It was in everyone's interest (the creditors excepted) to keep Peking ignorant of the financial crisis. The Company's supercargos worried that the Company's trade would be taxed to repay the debts; Chinese merchants feared imprisonment and banishment; and local government officials worried about imperial censure for perceived mismanagement and incompetence in governing Canton. The Company's supercargos noted repeatedly that "the [Chinese] merchants were greatly distressed," and that Seunqua "seemed frightened and confused." They also heard reports that Li Zhiying, the governor of Guangdong Province, seemed extremely anxious, declaring he would "run no risks" on account of the merchants.[62]

At first, everyone in Canton scrambled to prevent Panton from presenting Edward Vernon's letters to the governor and the superintendent of customs. The Company's supercargos wrote a letter to Panton protesting his interfering in Canton, but Panton replied that "he was not authorized to hold a correspondence with us." The Hong merchants offered Captain Panton a $40,000 bribe "if he would go back without executing his commission, and say that he could not be indulged with an audience." The Chinese merchants were fearful that the government's involvement "must cause an edict from Pekin; and by which, some of them will probably be ordered into banishment." Panton, however, persisted and eventually met with Governor Li Zhiying and Superintendent of Customs Tu Ming'a, in October 1779.[63]

The Company's supercargos, the Hong merchants, and the local Chinese government could no longer ignore the crisis, but they hoped to manage it quickly and discreetly and, if possible, without informing the central government in Peking. Their motives differed, but the goal was the same: to settle the debts without the emperor's knowledge. Governor Li and Superintendent Tu encouraged the debtors and creditors to solve their financial disputes privately. The two officials met frequently with the Hong merchants and continually pressured them to provide proposals to liquidate their debts. Governor Li oscillated between leniency and strictness, at one time declaring "that if an account of their debts was not speedily delivered in, he would proceed with rigour," but at other times showing "an inclination to accommodate the business as much as possible."[64] Li and Tu also worked with the Company's supercargos to investigate and settle the debts privately. According to Chinese sources, two senior Company supercargos, including Thomas Bevan (Bevan had the unique ability among Company servants to communicate in Chinese), told Chinese officials that the East India Company was not involved in the crisis "because we follow our King's instructions forbidding us from lending money, which goes against the Qing dynasty." But they supposedly did admit the possibility "that country traders, foolish foreigners from our own and other nations brought foreign silver on their ships to Canton and privately lent it in secret."[65] The Dutch, Danes, Swedes, and Imperialists (Hungarians) "all declared no private debts were owing from the Chinese merchants to individuals of their respective nations." According to the Company's supercargos, however, their claims were spurious: "The servants of the Dutch, Danish, and Swedish Companies are greatly involved." The French and the Dutch were also owed money, although much less than the British.[66] Governor Li was befuddled: "How comes it that the English merchants did not settle their accounts in the same manner as the other nations, what is the reason the English alone are not entirely satisfied?" The Canton supercargos volunteered to send a small boat to Madras "to go investigate the names of the people involved and the amounts of silver owed." They were instructed by the governor and the superintendent of customs to dispatch the ship quickly.[67]

In March 1780, the Company's supercargos received an order from Governor Li and Superintendent Tu ordering the "English President" and British brokers to examine the details of the money owed them and to make an agreement with the Chinese merchants about the mode of repayment. Li and Tu also requested that "in making the account of interest they act with moderation and humanity." The Company's supercargos should then deliver their agreement to the governor. Once all was settled "as well on the English side as the Chinese," Governor Li would "take care to have justice done."[68] The Wooyuern, a military officer attached to the superintendent of customs' office, came to the British factory with all the Hong merchants to inform the Company's supercargos that the governor and the superintendent of customs "found the management of the debts owing from the Chinese to the English of a very difficult nature" because if the strictness of the law were enforced, the Europeans as well as the Chinese would be punished. That said, he emphasized their willingness to overlook the law prohibiting money lending between Chinese and foreigners. The Wooyuern reassured the Company's supercargos that Governor Li and Superintendent Tu "wished very much to accommodate the affair, and had directed him to desire us to consider some way of settling it."[69]

Canton officials did not wait long to propose a settlement, but the brokers were not satisfied. It amounted to only 10 percent of the claims and did not include interest during the proposed ten-year period of amortization. Smith of Canton, Hutton, and Gordon expressed their disappointment: "In consequence of Sir Edward Vernon's application to your excellencies, we flattered ourselves we should obtain from your excellencies, better terms, than the merchants would have been disposed to grant us—and it is with the greatest astonishment and disappointment, we experience the contrary."[70] In contrast to the Chinese officials' proposal, Smith of Canton, Hutton, and Crichton expected "the whole debts of the Chinese merchants made up with interest . . . to be paid in a course of years not exceeding ten in yearly dividends together with an interest of five percent per annum on the principal till the whole should be paid." According to Smith of Canton's ideal plan, the entire body of Hong merchants would repay the private debts of the indebted Chinese merchants annually by dipping into the $700,000 he estimated they were earning annually from trade with the British alone.[71]

The Company's supercargos had never been optimistic that such a diverse body of investors could come to terms agreeable to all. As two of them pointed out, the "business goes on with different opinions, and with a

William Alexander (1767–1816). *A Mandarin in His Court Dress.* Courtesy of the Yale Center for British Art.

divided interest." The investors, they said, were a motley crew, consisting of, firstly, those who "made it their profession to gain from the difference between a large interest which they gave to others and a still larger they received from the merchants. 2ndly those who were agents for persons they did not know. And 3rdly those who [were] acting for their friends and connections."[72] The Company's supercargos believed that "the bondholders, being no collective body, bound to act together, might reasonably be led to act for the good of their several constituents" but not for the whole. Even if "the mandarins [had] been just and indulgent to foreigners instead of being venal, and holding us in detestation," the terms they offered would nevertheless have been rejected by the most considerable creditors.[73]

When Smith of Canton, Hutton, and Crichton rejected the Chinese officials' proposal, Superintendent Tu pressured the British harder. "Being of the same nation," Tu expected the East India Company's Council of Supercargos in Canton to "take care to restrain them [the private British traders]." If they failed to do so, and continued "to consent to the private people committing irregularities, we shall find no difficulty in attending to reason and the Emperor's decree, and if any money be lent such money shall be forfeited, and the Company of Merchants likewise may be involved in difficulty." Superintendent Tu addressed the brokers directly: "It is necessary for you to submit, as you yourselves are to blame." He reminded them that outstanding debts between Chinese subjects and foreigners (with or without interest) were illegal, so according to the Chinese law, their money should be confiscated and they should be punished. If Smith of Canton, Hutton, and Crichton did not accept the Chinese settlement, they would "have no reason to complain if in future, we should not attend to or decide on your representation in any other way and you should not receive any part of the money lent."[74]

In a last-ditch effort to persuade the British brokers to accept the government's settlement proposal, the magistrates of Guangzhou prefecture and Nanhai county went in person to the East India Company's factory where Smith and Hutton were also staying. During the meeting with the supercargos, the magistrate of Guangzhou prefecture claimed that it was unreasonable for the creditors to insist they "be paid with accumulated interest to the end of the 44th year." He claimed that "the province of Canton would not answer to such a demand." The magistrate then turned the conversation to a comparison of law in China and Britain, "spoke much of the unjustness of accumulated interest, said it was not allowed in China," and asked if it was legal in the supercargos' native country. The Company's supercargos replied "that every country had its customs," and if it were not allowed in China, "the merchants had acted dishonestly, in tempting the English with profits, which they knew, when they offered them, were contrary to their own laws." Unimpressed by this line of reasoning, the magistrate turned the blame on the British: "Your people . . . tempted the merchants with large sums of money."[75] According to Smith of Canton's account of the meeting, the magistrate tried "to intimidate the creditors to relax from their just demands," but they held firm. The Company's supercargos also recorded that the magistrate "behaved rudely, and in an overbearing manner. He was certainly not well pleased for he went away without taking any notice of anybody and to show his authority, called out in the middle of the factory, to the linguists, to see that those people meaning the Bondholders, went to Macao immediately." Negotiations had failed. Several days later, Smith of Canton and Hutton returned to their homes in Macao.[76]

While this experiment in gunboat diplomacy was under way, Abraham Leslie tried another method, employing his own private Indian army to pry money from Chinese hands. The Company's supercargos were shocked to learn from Superintendent Tu that Leslie had "violently entered and seized a warehouse, formerly belonging to Coqua [陳科官], and had taken possession of the same, with sundry goods in it, the property of other people—that he had hung Lanthorns [燈籠] with Chinese characters on them, describing the warehouse to be an English House . . . and that he still kept possession by force of arms." The lantern he hung over the door proclaimed in English and Chinese characters: "Leslie, an English merchant, has taken possession of this factory until he is paid." Leslie ignored the warnings of the Chinese officials and Company supercargos, insisting "that no degree of hardships or threats will in any wise affect or deter me from pursuing all proper measures in my present undertaking for to come at my just right." Nor was he interested in cooperating any longer with George Smith of Canton and the other brokers in their negotiations with the Chinese: "What the other creditors do, is no rule to me," exclaimed Leslie.[77]

In addition to Coqua's factory, Leslie also "took possession of Yngshaw's warehouse, and put some of his Black people into it." It was reported that Leslie had "broken open the doors" and set up "a guard of two or three lascars with pistols and cutlasses to defend what he calls, his right to the premises." In the meantime, he capitalized on his new Canton real estate by renting out rooms in Yngshaw's warehouse at a reasonable price; "remuneration from the rent would be applied to Ingsia's [Yngshaw's] debt. An English Captain from a private ship soon rented a room." Leslie intimated that he might use further violence to recover his clients' property: "I have as yet, used no force, but mild measures to come at my just right, and if force is used to me, I am bound to see it, for my property in these merchants hands if denied or refused by government is the same to me as my life at the years I have arrived to." Amazingly, Canton officials were willing to negotiate with Leslie, but his recalcitrance eventually landed him in a Macao prison, where he was held for several months.[78]

Observers of the Canton crisis in London could not ignore the disturbing political implications of the creditors' actions. The directors of the East India Company expressed alarm that the "creditors found means first to induce Sir Edward Vernon and afterwards Sir Edward Hughes to interpose the authority of His Majesty's flag" in the recovery of their private debts. They warned their employees in China: "However careful the Captain of the Man of War sent to China at different times upon this business may have been not to give offence to the Chinese government, by any intimation of hostility, the appearance of sending a Man of War to a Chinese port upon such an occasion, is too plain an intimation of threat to admit of a double construction."[79] King George III also communicated his displeasure to Rear Admiral Edward Hughes through a letter from the secretary of state ordering "that no ship should be sent there [to Canton] again."[80]

The arrival of British warships in Canton also troubled Governor Li Zhiying to the extent that he felt the need to lie to the emperor about them. In his memorial to the Qianlong emperor, he reported that Captain Panton had come to Canton as a private trader on a country ship to deliver silver to the East India Company, not as a British Navy admiral in a warship to threaten the Chinese government. He also conveniently omitted Abraham Leslie's remarkable transgressions.[81] To avoid censure and keep commerce going, Governor Li made sure that the full truth about the Canton crisis never reached the emperor's eyes.

The Canton tea trade was simply too lucrative; the truth about its fragile financial foundations could not be revealed. And for the most part, no one in London, Peking, or Canton gave the matter much thought as long as peaceful commerce continued. But in the British empire, cross-cultural credit could quickly morph into colonial debt, fundamentally altering power relations between borrowers and lenders. That is precisely what happened in Madras, where the indebtedness of the nawab of Arcot to private British creditors eventually led to the East India Company's annexation of his state in 1801.[82] In contrast to other British settlements and trading posts in maritime Asia, in late eighteenth-century Canton there was no coup, annexation, or coloring Canton in red on the British imperial map. But there was at least an attempt, a considerable effort made by private traders and their clients, to devise increasingly aggressive strategies and to demand a stronger intercession on the part of the British state in order to impose the terms of economic exchange upon their Chinese trading partners.

FIVE

George Smith of Bombay and the Lady Hughes *Affair*

IN 1768, THE THIRD GEORGE SMITH of this book made his way to Bombay, where he lived and worked as a private trader. Of the three George Smiths, Smith of Bombay was the most commercially successful. He alone left a will, because unlike Smith of Madras and Smith of Canton, Smith of Bombay died solvent and left property to distribute to his family and friends. Despite his commercial prominence, Smith of Bombay does not appear to have formed connections with Henry Dundas or Edmund Burke, as his two namesakes had done. Burke, a politician and author of Irish origin, is perhaps best known for penning his *Reflections on the Revolution in France,* a prescient critique of the French Revolution of 1789, in addition to advocating and directing the impeachment of Warren Hastings, who served as governor as well as governor-general of Bengal between 1772 and 1785. Even without connections to important British statesmen, Smith of Bombay managed to leave his mark on British imperial policy. His involvement in a violent clash with the Chinese government in Canton in 1784, known as the *Lady Hughes* Affair, made the British government acutely aware of the vulnerability and instability of Britain's lucrative China trade. The Affair also fueled the development of a hostile and condescending discourse about China that emphasized the barbarism of China's legal system and, more broadly, the backwardness of its civilization. George Smith of Bombay's misadventures in Canton show how obscure actors and random events in China could have ripple effects across the British empire, informing the creation of new imperial policies in London and contributing to a new "Orientalist" way of conceptualizing and representing China.

George Smith of Bombay was born on the northern coast of Scotland, in Fordyce, Banffshire, in 1737 to James Smith and Elspet Fergusson. He was the youngest of eight children, six girls and two boys: Margaret, Cecilia, James, May, Mary, Elspet, Jean, and George. In 1740, when George was only three years old, the Smith children lost their mother, Elspet. Her untimely death may have been related to a devastating famine in Scotland that year. Seventeen years later, in 1757, the Smith family disbanded.[1]

Like many other Scottish families at the time, the Smiths of Fordyce found themselves scattered across Britain's global empire and beyond. George's older brother, James, ventured to Jamaica, where he may have worked as a merchant or steward on a sugar plantation. The oldest sister, Margaret, set off for London to work as a servant for the family of James Abercromby of Glassaugh, a member of Parliament, while another sister, Jean, made her way to Gothenburg, Sweden, where a Scottish community had existed since the mid-seventeenth century.[2] Many Scottish merchants and Jacobite exiles made this port town their home.[3] In Gothenburg, Jean worked as housekeeper "to George Carnegie, a cadet of the Southesk Family" who had served as captain of Prince Charlie's Life Guards during the second Jacobite uprising in 1745.[4] Perhaps the Smith family also had Jacobite connections or was at least sympathetic to the cause of Bonny Prince Charlie, the grandson of James II, the Stuart king who had been deposed in the Glorious Revolution of 1688. In 1757, the Smiths of Fordyce decided to join the many Scots who fled Scotland's Highlands after the '45 uprising to find opportunities and build new lives in Britain's expanding empire.

Like his sister Jean, George Smith also moved to Europe, settling in Holland, where he worked as a clerk. His choice of Holland was not atypical. Over the course of the late sixteenth and seventeenth centuries Scotland and the Low Countries developed a "special relationship."[5] Scottish students and merchants flocked to the Netherlands and established communities in Dieppe, Middleburg, Bergen op Zoom, Zeeland, and Rotterdam.[6] The Netherlands "hosted Scottish business networks that had originally serviced the North Sea trade system" and provided a springboard for significant Scottish participation in the Ostend Company and the Dutch Asiatic and Swedish East India companies. Perhaps Smith of Bombay served as a clerk for a Scotch-Dutch business, a type of dual-nationality partnership that was used to "negate Dutch mercantilism" and "transcend national borders."[7] He may also have been involved in smuggling tea into Britain, which has been "strongly linked" to the Dutch Republic.[8]

Ten years working in Europe as a clerk and bookkeeper (perhaps with connections to Asian commerce) prepared Smith of Bombay for his next career, as a supercargo in the East Indies. After spending some time in Paris, he made his way to Aleppo, Syria, then traveled "overland via the Euphrates Valley and down the Persian Gulf in 1768 to Bombay."[9] It appears that Smith of Bombay, like many others, ventured to India without the East India Company's permission and earned a living through maritime trade.[10]

Why Smith of Bombay, or any other British trader in the 1760s, would choose Bombay as a base is a bit of a mystery. Bombay had long held a reputation as "'the unhealthiest, the poorest, and the most despised' of all the English settlements" in India.[11] According to historian Pamela Nightingale, western India held "no prospects" for the East India Company "but those of defeat and gloom."[12] This "impoverished backwater" had come into British hands through the marriage of Catherine of Braganza of Portugal to Charles II in 1662, but it proved a troublesome gift.[13] Bombay was reputed to kill off its European population (estimated at about 1,000 people) "more quickly than any other settlement." The high rate of mortality may have been boosted by malarial swamps on the island and the custom of "manuring the cocoanut trees with decaying fish," which tainted the well water and produced "a most unsavory smell."[14] During its first decades as a Company town, "Bombay showed few signs of becoming a great entrepôt." Commerce was "sluggish" for many years.[15]

Bombay and its subordinate trading factories along the Malabar coast were also extremely vulnerable to two powerful kingdoms surrounding it, the Marathas in the north and Mysore in the south.[16] During the second half of the eighteenth century, its future looked grim: "Crushed between two great military powers, and with possessions which made its title of a presidency only pathetic, Bombay could hope for little from the future. Whether the Company would retain any hold at all in western India was, in 1784, much in doubt."[17] After its defeat by the Mysore army led by the Tipu Sultan, known as the Tiger of Mysore, Bombay was confined to several "small and practically defenseless trading posts on the Malabar coast."[18]

George Smith of Madras, who, like his Bombay namesake, did a lot of business on the Malabar coast, provided an account of the difficulties British traders encountered as a result of the Tipu Sultan's influence: "I touched at Calicut, one of Tippoo Saheb's sea ports, and after waiting on his governor, who received me with Oriental Courtesy, was told, that I was at liberty to dispose of any part of my cargo, but not to carry off pepper, sandal wood, cardamoms, or plants, and timbers, an embargo being laid on all these articles by the sovereign, which nearly amounts to a prohibition on trade with him."[19] George Smith of Bombay ran into similar trouble in 1785. On his voyage from Bombay to Calcutta he was unable to buy a cargo of goods in Tellicherry or Cochin on the western coast of India.[20] Between 1785 and 1789, British traders "were effectively cut out of the pepper trade."[21]

Despite these formidable obstacles, the East India Company's Bombay settlement survived. During the 1770s and 1780s, Bombay cotton emerged as one of the few products with a growing market in China. The East India Company had finally found an export product that could pay for its tea imports and balance its trade deficit with China. Private traders took the initiative in this quickly expanding trade. Of the 68,000 bales of cotton exported from India in 1787, it was estimated that "only 4,500 bales had gone on the Company's account."[22] Over a decade earlier, the young private trader, Frederic Davy proudly reported to his father that he would be working as the purser on a private ship carrying Bombay cotton to China.[23]

Private traders were quick to recognize the value of Bombay. George Smith of Madras, David Scott, and David Cuming all urged Henry Dundas, as de facto head of the Board of Control for Indian Affairs back in London, to maintain and support the Company's settlement in Bombay. They showed Dundas how Bombay cotton could finance Britain's tea trade.[24] In the end, Dundas decided to commit Company resources to saving the

Bombay Presidency precisely for that reason, as well as because of its military value. The same considerations led to the acquisition of other parts of the Malabar coast.[25] In 1792, Bombay's future in the British empire seemed much more secure than it had just a few decades earlier.

Little is known about private traders in Bombay during this period, but the story of George Smith of Bombay lets us explore their commercial and social world.[26] Smith does not appear to have married in Bombay, but if he did, his wife must have predeceased him. Later in life, Smith of Bombay formed a relationship with a woman from Goa, probably of Eurasian descent, named Esperanza Gaspar D'Almina. Romantic relationships between British men and local women were common during the eighteenth

George Morland (1763–1804). *Indian Girl,* 1793. Courtesy of the Yale Center for British Art.

century, and the children of these unions frequently appear in the wills of their fathers. Smith of Bombay and D'Almina had a daughter, Felicia, who was just an infant when Smith decided to return to Scotland in 1789 without them.[27]

Was Smith and D'Almina's relationship characterized by "ties of great affection and loyalty"? Did their cohabitation lead to cultural sharing? Did Smith learn to bathe or "shampoo" (the Hindi word for massage) from D'Almina? Did he think of her when he finally left Bombay for good? We can only speculate.[28]

Smith of Bombay also developed a close friendship with David Scott of Bombay, the same David Scott who was godfather to George Smith of Canton's son. This friendship was significant because Scott had become the most influential trader in Bombay.[29] Smith of Bombay chose Scott as an executor to his will. He also left Scott his stopwatch and bequeathed a pair of shawls and a piece of white cloth to Scott's wife, Louisa, as a token of his "respect and esteem" for them.[30]

Though based in Bombay, Smith had major commercial and financial concerns in China. Like the other two George Smiths, he invested large sums of money in Canton with the help of his Canton agents and attorneys, Hugh Parkin and George Smith Junior—a fourth George Smith with no apparent relationship to the three George Smiths of this book! These Company supercargos moonlighted as private brokers and managed two large bonds on Smith of Bombay's behalf. One was a loan to Geowqua (伍喬官), a Hong merchant, worth £12,423, and the other to Pinqua (楊丙官), another Hong merchant, worth £10,000. Both loans were made on December 1, 1787, at 18 percent interest per year. Even after the disastrous financial crisis in Canton in 1779, British traders like Smith of Bombay continued to lend money at high rates of interest to Chinese merchants. On the eve of the First Opium War, the Chinese debt to British investors stood at $3,000,000.[31]

In 1784, when George Smith of Bombay was forty-seven years old, he served as supercargo of the Bombay country ship the *Lady Hughes*. What should have been a routine voyage to China turned into a nightmare.

How do we know that it was Smith of Bombay, and not Smith of Canton or Smith of Madras (or any other George Smiths for that matter), who sailed to China in 1784 as supercargo of the *Lady Hughes?* Although many historians have discussed or referred to the *Lady Hughes* Affair, no one has ever made the distinction or tried to establish the identity of the hapless supercargo with the frustratingly common name.[32] Primary sources such as East India Company records, private journals, Chinese government records, and newspapers all fail to identify precisely who the supercargo of the *Lady Hughes* was.

George Smith of Canton can be eliminated as a possibility because he was no longer living in Asia. That leaves Smith of Madras, who, after sailing from Madras to England on the same ship as William Hickey in 1779, returned to India in 1783, this time to Calcutta, to try to build his fortune once more and repay his creditors. But Smith of Madras could not have been the supercargo of the *Lady Hughes* for several reasons. First, the ship's port of origin was Bombay, not Calcutta, where Smith of Madras then lived. Second, Smith of Madras never once mentioned the incident in his hundreds of pages of letters to Henry Dundas. Third, a letter written by Smith of Madras to the Company's Bengal Council places him in Calcutta on December 20, 1784, but the *Lady Hughes* remained in China until December 9, 1784, when it departed for Bombay. This would have given Smith of Madras just eleven days to return from Canton to Calcutta. According to William Hickey, "the shortest voyage that had then ever been made by an East Indiaman" between India and China was thirty-three days, so it is extremely unlikely that Smith of Madras was the supercargo of the *Lady Hughes.*[33] Fourth, in 1784 and 1785 the Company's Bengal Council received letters from two different George Smiths. One was from George Smith of Madras, who simply signed as "George Smith."[34] The other was written by George Smith, a private trader who had sailed from Bombay to Calcutta and offered to carry Company saltpeter back to Bombay on his return voyage. He signed his letter "George Smith Super cargo of the ship Lady Hughes."[35]

We can be reasonably confident, then, that George Smith of Bombay was the supercargo of the *Lady Hughes,* yet none of his private records has survived. We must rely instead on records produced by the Chinese government, the East India Company, and several eyewitnesses. Not surprisingly, they do not always agree. The Company's Canton supercargos wrote detailed accounts of the dramatic events that unfolded in Canton during the last week of November 1784. According to them, on November 24, 1784, the gunner of the *Lady Hughes* fired a cannon to salute a European ship passing by and accidentally struck a Chinese customs vessel lying alongside.[36] This maritime salutation resulted in the death of one person according to the English records and two Chinese sailors according to the Chinese records, named Wu Yake (吳亞科) and Wang Yunfa (王運發).[37] British sources never named the gunner responsible for firing the fatal shots.

The Chinese records, in contrast, gave him a name, "Di Xiehua" (的些華); they also gave him a voice in the story.[38] His testimony was recorded in a memorial written by Sun Shiyi (孫士毅), the governor of Guangdong Province:

> I am an English person. This year 35 years old. All along in [Captain] Williams's boat served as the gunner. In my country [Captain] Williams loaded goods and came to Guangzhou to trade. The ship was tied up at Yellow wharf on the river. This year on the 11th month 12th day from 3–5pm there was a [連國] Danish ship which was leaving the port. I was in the cabin window and fired the cannon to bid the ship farewell. At that time the [Chinese] skiff sailors hired by my ship were transporting goods nearby the ship. Because I was inside the cabin, I did not see them, I did not tell them to get out of the way. This resulted in the sailors of the skiff being hit by the cannon and injured. Two people, one after another died. During that day, the person who fired the cannon and injured the people was truly me. Why would I be willing to substitute [for the real killer] and suffer the punishment? Please have mercy on me.[39]

Other witnesses, however, described Di Xiehua differently. One claimed that he was a short elderly man with a dark complexion typical of Eurasians from Goa in India, while another thought he was Filipino.[40] But in the testimony above, Di Xiehua claimed to be an English national and only thirty-five years old. Were Canton officials misleading the emperor? If they had reported that Di Xiehua was Eurasian or Filipino, perhaps the emperor would have suspected the prisoner was a substitute for the real "English" gunner. The emperor was, in fact, skeptical that Di Xiehua was the murderer and expressed his concerns in an edict to Governor Sun.[41] These doubts may have been warranted because "two other contemporary accounts published in a major English newspaper based in India . . . claimed that this prisoner was a substitute for the British gunner."[42]

Before Chinese officials could arrest Di Xiehua, he went into hiding.[43] At first, Governor Sun suggested leaving the matter to the British government. They could punish the gunner as they saw fit. He was clearly attempting to avoid open conflict with the British. As provincial governor, he had a responsibility to the central government in Peking to maintain law and order in Guangdong Province, but to keep the Canton trade flowing he also needed to accommodate foreign merchants.[44]

Governor Sun's conciliatory attitude enraged the Qianlong emperor. He had been too lenient with the British in Canton. In an imperial edict the emperor chastised and threatened Governor Sun. How could Governor Sun be certain that the British would handle the matter properly? This case was too serious, in the emperor's view, to be treated so casually. The emperor had also recently received reports that at least eleven Catholic missionaries had secretly entered China through Canton and were residing illegally in central China. He blamed the disorder in Guangdong province on Governor Sun.[45] Governor Sun, who happened to be on his way to Peking to attend a large banquet, was ordered by the emperor to return immediately to Canton to apprehend the gunner and execute him in the presence of all the principal European merchants. Governor Sun would be given a second chance to bring order to Canton, but if he failed, he would be punished twice as harshly. The emperor wanted to make it clear to everyone in Canton that the Chinese government would enforce its laws with the utmost rigor.[46]

In fear of his career (and perhaps his life) Governor Sun responded to the emperor's edict remorsefully: "How could I have requested that the criminal be sent back to his country just because the murder was unintentional? All of my mistakes are unforgivable." Governor Sun had no choice but to apprehend the prisoner and execute him.[47]

The Company's supercargos initially refused to cooperate with Canton authorities. When several officials and merchants came to the British factory, the Company's supercargos recommended that they speak with the supercargo of the *Lady Hughes,* George Smith of Bombay. He was better qualified to provide information about the incident. It was agreed that Smith would be interviewed in the East India Company's factory by a Chinese government official accompanied by his usual retinue but without any soldiers.[48] According to Governor Sun's memorial to the Qianlong emperor, however, he sent two military officers: Wang Lin and Zhang Chaolong as well as the acting Guangzhou prefectural magistrate, Zhang Daoyuan, to arrest Smith and bring him into the city.[49] The word Sun used in his memorial to describe the arrest, "鎖拏," indicates that Smith of Bombay might have been physically restrained or chained.[50] But perhaps Sun was exaggerating to impress the emperor with his strict handling of the affair.

The emperor doubted the veracity of Governor Sun's report: "It is not certain that you sent an official to arrest the English Taipan Smith [士蔑] and bring him into the city."[51] British East India Company records confirm that Smith of Bombay had been lured from his factory by a "pretended message from Puan Khequa [Puankequa, the Chinese Hong merchant]; seized and conveyed . . . into the city under a guard of soldiers with drawn swords."[52] Smith of Bombay had been taken prisoner.

The Company's supercargos expressed outrage at the abduction of a British trader, an act they perceived as "contrary to every idea of reason and justice." They also feared for the safety of all those involved in the affair: "An act of violence towards an European unconvicted and not even charged with any crime so contrary to every idea of reason and justice has an appearance too alarming to have any doubt that some uncommonly harsh measures were intended to be pursued . . . the circumstances which followed the seizure of Mr. Smith were such as plainly indicated that our personal safety was not altogether free from danger."[53] Together with the heads of the other European East India companies they signed a collective petition against the Chinese government's abduction of Smith of Bombay. According to Governor Sun, they also came to his office to protest.[54]

While Smith was sitting in a Canton prison, the conflict escalated. The avenues leading to the quays were barricaded and filled with Chinese soldiers, and the Chinese merchants and linguists fled, deserting their factories. Meanwhile, the supercargos of the British and other European East India companies (including the Dutch, French, Danish, and Americans) banded together to retaliate. They "came to a resolution to order up the boats of the several ships staffed and armed as a guard to our persons in case any violence should be intended as well as to manifest in the strongest manner the very alarming view in which we considered their precedence."[55] Since "the present was not thought a time for punctilios," they did not request permission from Chinese officials (as was normally required) to dispatch two boats and some seamen to Whampoa with orders for all the ships of the British, European, and American companies to sail directly to Canton with their pinnaces "manned and armed."[56] The pinnaces and other foreign service boats were normally allowed to sail to Canton without restriction so long as they were manned with captains or supercargos and displayed their national flag.[57] Under these extraordinary circumstances, however, ships with armed British and European soldiers would have raised serious concerns. Although the ship commanders were ordered to avoid open conflict with Chinese officials, violence in this situation was almost unavoidable:

> The tide not being favorable it was dark before they approached the city, no notice was taken of them till near the first Hoppo House, when the headmost boats were hailed by one of their armed vessels, and ordered to return to Whampoa. No attention being paid to this injunction they retired and the boats proceeded to the factories—but the next that approached were attacked with repeated volleys of musketry from the fort near the Hoppos house and the armed vessels lying in the river which was continued as the boats approached

> from 8 till past 11 at night, when all except those hereafter mentioned arrived at the factory without having returned a single shot, or received any injury other than a Quarter Master of the Sulivan being lightly wounded on the breast, and a man in the Calcutta's boat in the back: this boat being far astern of the rest was almost surrounded by the Chinese vessels one of which boarded them, when the officer seeing his men were likely to be in a situation in which they could not avoid using their arms, with very commendable presence, ordered them to be thrown overboard, the Chinese after a short scuffle left the boat.[58]

The Chinese also fired on a Dutch ship, so it decided to anchor for the night where it stood. The British East India Company's supercargos surmised that their ships were attacked because Canton authorities suspected "our preparations had a more dangerous tendency than mere self defense."[59]

Governor Sun warned the British that if they continued resisting, he would send troops with muskets and artillery to cut off their retreat. "Reflect therefore," he said, "and see what is your force and your ability if you dare in our country to disobey and infringe our law. Consider well that you may not repent when it is too late." The following morning, Governor Sun fulfilled his threat by sending armed boats and galleys to blockade the factories. Troops were posted in the rear, and junks were moored across the river. According to an American observer, "ships of war, in number upwards of forty, lay opposite the factories."[60] Every means had been taken to "cut off communication with the ships and enforce obedience to the mandate."[61]

After several days of aggressive naval posturing, Governor Sun requested an audience with a representative of every European nation involved in the conflict except Britain. They met at a temple in the suburbs of Canton where Sun again warned that he could "easily destroy" them all "but was loath to hurt so many good men." If the East India Company's supercargos did not cooperate, trade would be stopped, provisions would no longer be supplied, and the East India Company's ships would not be suffered to return to England. Governor Sun prevailed on the European merchants to "desert" their British allies. He promised to overlook their provocations and free George Smith of Bombay if the gunner was delivered to him. It seemed to European witnesses that Governor Sun "was much agitated. That it was visible the measures we had pursued had thrown him into great perplexity." They had no doubt "he would be very glad to get handsomely clear of the business."[62]

The French, Dutch, and Danes all accepted Sun's offer and abandoned their British colleagues. On November 29, after almost a week of threats and brief naval skirmishes, and with George Smith of Bombay still confined in the city of Canton, the Company's supercargos also backed down and agreed to deliver the gunner of the *Lady Hughes* to Chinese authorities. At first, when the Company's supercargos suggested that the gunner might have escaped, Canton officials "answered that if it was so Mr. Smith was in their power; but advised us, as we seemed much interested about that gentleman, to substitute a servant or some person of less consequence in his place."[63] George Smith of Bombay's fate was hanging in the balance. The Company's supercargos decided to spare Smith of Bombay and requested that Captain Williams, commander of the *Lady Hughes,* deliver the accused gunner to the Chinese government immediately. Failure to comply would not only endanger the life of Smith of Bombay but also the lives of the other British traders in Canton.

Perhaps Smith of Bombay's urgent letter to Captain Williams helped to persuade the Company's supercargos to deliver the gunner to the Chinese: "I wrote to you yesterday that I had been forcibly carried away to the City. I am still in durance and must remain till the gunner or some other man to personate him is sent up. I desired you would send up such person if the gunner is not to be found. This will be forwarded to you by Mr. Pigou to whom this unlucky affair has given likewise much trouble. I must now insist that you send the gunner or some other person who is better acquainted with the circumstances of the business than I am, in order to answer the queries of the mandarins at the English Factory. I must likewise desire you not to go off with the ship at your peril till something definite is settled in this unfortunate accident. I cannot help observing that there must have been gross misconduct on board the Lady Hughes."[64]

According to Governor Sun, George Smith of Bombay was willing to be swapped for the gunner.[65] A prisoner exchange took place, and the gunner or perhaps some substitute was brought into Chinese custody. Recognizing Di Xiehua's unfortunate situation, the commander of the *Lady Hughes,* Captain Williams, sent a note to Smith of Bombay requesting him to leave a subsistence allowance with Monqua, a Hong merchant, for the gunner if the gunner was detained. Captain Williams worried for the gunner's safety: "I hope the Chinese will not do harm to the poor old man, as it was only a misfortune."[66] Chinese officials found this same letter on Di Xiehua's person when they took him into custody and had it immediately translated into Chinese. The Chinese version reads: "Di Xiehua is a poor barbarian, it was truly accidental that he killed someone by firing the cannon, now [he] has already been handed over [to the Chinese], he begs Smith to consider helping him pay his expenses."[67]

An hour after his release, Smith of Bombay reported to the Company's supercargos that he had received satisfactory treatment and that many Chinese officials had visited and sent him presents during his incarceration. Smith was fortunate.[68] Even short confinement in prison could prove fatal. As a foreigner, Smith was at least spared from "interrogation" by physical torture, including finger and leg presses, which frequently led to infections or permanent disfigurement, and sometimes to death.[69] In fact, he seems to have received unusually good treatment because of his status as a well-known and prominent private trader.

Smith of Bombay quickly resumed business. The Company's supercargos recorded in their books that "Mr. Smith Supracargo of the Lady Hughes country ship having tendered us 14000 Head Dollars upon bond at 10 percent per annum payable next year, we determined to accept the same."[70] On December 9, 1784, just fifteen days after the fateful cannon salute that resulted in the deaths of two Chinese men, George Smith of Bombay, Captain Williams, and the crew of the *Lady Hughes* departed from Canton. We can only imagine the complicated mix of emotions they experienced as the *Lady Hughes* sailed away.

Di Xiehua, the gunner of the *Lady Hughes,* would not be joining them. He was left behind in Canton to pay with his life for two Chinese deaths. He must have appeared despondent when he was taken into custody, because Chinese officials feared he would commit suicide in prison. He was interrogated and was determined to be the "true killer." Governor Sun sent an edict to the foreign traders in Canton explaining his decision to execute Di Xiehua: "Our Great Emperor is extremely kind. Every year you make a lot of money and when you are occasionally owed money, a fixed amount of time has been set for you to be repaid etc. His generosity goes on and on without end. Now, Williams's boat fired a cannon salute. And did not take care to inform the neighboring ship which resulted in two deaths. This crime is very serious. According to the laws of the empire, not only should we punish the murder, but we should also seriously punish the head of the ship, who failed to manage the ship strictly. For the moment, considering you come from a remote place, you are not familiar with our laws. Now we only take the gunner, Di Xiehua, and punish one man. This is truly the Emperor's exception[al] generosity. From this, now you should know [the Emperor's generosity] even more and feel grateful."[71]

Di Xiehua was strangled on January 8, 1785, as required by the emperor.[72] Governor Sun reported that in compliance with the emperor's decree he would hold the execution "in a place where all the English traders are gathered in a circle to watch."[73] But having realized that such a spectacle would only encourage further violence and unrest in Canton, Governor Sun instead had Di Xiehua strangled behind closed doors.[74] The Company's supercargos were enraged when they discovered that "the Chinese got this man and strangled him upon the spot, without form of trial or any circumstance, that could distinguish this act of their justice, from the summary executions of the Malays or other barbarous nations."[75] As far as the emperor knew, however, the British had accepted this outcome with contrition. According to Governor Sun's memorial to the emperor, the heads of each country promised to be more careful. They would not dare to make trouble again and offend Chinese laws.[76] From the Chinese government's perspective, the *Lady Hughes* saga had come to a close.

From the British perspective, though, this event marked an important point in a long struggle to escape Chinese legal jurisdiction and obtain extraterritoriality rights in China. The British and other foreign traders already enjoyed some degree of legal independence in China. The Chinese government insisted on adjudicating infractions when they involved both Chinese and Europeans, but they left it to the European supercargos to arbitrate disputes in cases concerning only European nationals. For example, in 1754, after a French officer shot and killed a British sailor, the Chinese viceroy tried to persuade French and British supercargos to settle their dispute "by a friendly arbitration." Several cases involving Dutch sailors during the 1750s and 1760s further demonstrate that Europeans actually did enjoy extraterritorial rights when no Chinese subjects or interests were involved.[77] But this did not satisfy their desire for legal independence; they wanted more.

The *Lady Hughes* Affair also fueled an increasingly disparaging and "Orientalist" discourse taking shape in late eighteenth-century Britain that portrayed Chinese law and society as barbaric and inferior.[78] An example of this language and thinking can be found in the letters of Company supercargos in which they complained vehemently about the tyranny and injustice of the Chinese legal system and the "exposed" situation of the Europeans in the port of Canton. Complying with Chinese laws "seems to us so contrary to what Europeans deem humanity or justice, and if we voluntarily submitted to it, must appear to all, that we gave up every moral and manly principle to our interest." Other examples appeared in the *India Gazette*, where writers complained that recent events in Canton were not only humiliating to Englishmen "but shocking even to human nature."[79]

The "Canton War," as it came to be known in Britain, and the execution of the unfortunate gunner, Di Xiehua, sent shock waves through British communities across the empire.[80] Newspapers and magazines in Calcutta and, half a year later, in London spread the news of a "Riot at China."[81] Calcutta, which was about one month's sailing time from Canton, received first wind of the events. On January 15, 1785, writers at the *India Gazette* were still hopeful: "When the Chinese cool a little, and are convinced, that the death of their countryman was accidental, the matter may be amicably settled."[82] When news of the *Lady Hughes* Affair reached Britain, it became a major topic of interest. The August 1785 edition of the *Gentleman's Magazine* devoted two pages to the story. The *Times* in London reported that its first article regarding "The riot at China" had "excited much curiosity and alarm." The editors therefore "thought it incumbent on us to enquire into the particulars" and followed up with a second narrative that "our readers may depend on as authentic."[83] Addressed in the *Public Advertiser* were the Chinese officials' motives for kidnapping Mr. George Smith.[84]

The Canton War not only concerned the general reading public but also worried Henry Dundas. He received letters from East Indiaman captain William Mackintosh, who knew firsthand about the *Lady Hughes* Affair because he had been in Canton at the time and had helped to hand over Di Xiehua to Chinese authorities. Captain Mackintosh warned that if the *Lady Hughes* Affair had not been settled at the time and in the manner it was, the Company's ships "would have gone without teas . . . much time would elapse before a proper understanding would have been established with the Chinese, and as it happened, in the very year of the Commutation Act [1784], when in addition to the Company's importation [of tea], the gleanings of Europe was scarcely sufficient to answer the increased demand [for tea], and quiet the murmurs occasioned by that measure, would not the consequences have reached even White Hall?"[85] Captain Mackintosh pointed to an unfortunate and potentially catastrophic coincidence: the same year that the British government decided to lower the tea tax (which would triple the East India Company's tea imports into Britain), a murder in Canton brought trade to a halt. The *Lady Hughes* Affair revealed the precariousness of Britain's tea trade. Random mishaps involving obscure individuals halfway across the globe could completely undermine Britain's commercial policies in China. At stake were not only Britain's lucrative tea trade but also future markets for its manufacturers. Private British traders and statesmen would not sit idly by. Together they determined that Britain must establish a settlement in China totally free from the legal jurisdiction and interference of the Chinese government. They hoped that an embassy to China, Britain's first ever, would convince the Qianlong emperor to grant extraterritorial rights to British subjects on Chinese soil.

SIX

Mission to China

TWO AND A HALF YEARS before Chinese officials threw George Smith of Bombay into prison, the East India Company expelled George Smith of Canton from China. In 1782, Smith of Canton, his wife, Charlotte, and their two small daughters had no choice but to pack up their lives and sail to England on board the East India Company ship *Contractor.* Not long after making their new home in Surrey, Smith of Canton began corresponding with Henry Dundas, right-hand man to Prime Minister William Pitt the Younger and de facto head of the Board of Control for Indian affairs. One of the major topics of their discussions was a British embassy to China. Several private traders, including George Smith of Madras, also corresponded with Dundas and helped to convince him of the necessity of sending an embassy to China despite the East India Company's strong objections. The embassy's stated goals—securing Britain's tea trade after the incredibly successful Commutation Act of 1784, opening new markets in China to British exports, and learning more about Chinese manufactures, technology, military and naval capacity, and botanical resources—are well known to historians. But other motives and interests lay behind Britain's first embassy to China.

During the 1770s and 1780s, Henry Dundas fashioned himself as the go-to man for issues relating to the East Indies. According to his biographer Holden Furber, none of Dundas's political contemporaries, with the exception of Edmund Burke and Richard Sheridan, took a serious interest in Britain's burgeoning Asian empire. Dundas, in contrast, not only enjoyed "wading through the masses of Indian documents" but "probably spent more of his time on Indian affairs than on anything else in his long public career. Not even Scotland or the management of the war against Napoleon occupied more of his working hours."[1] Dundas distinguished himself in 1781, when he served as head of a committee to investigate the cause of a war in southeastern India and the dubious conduct of various Company servants in the Madras Presidency.[2] His success in that position led to rumors that he would soon be appointed by Prime Minister Lord North as the first secretary of state for India, a position he would have welcomed.[3] But war with the American colonies caused significant political turbulence in the early 1780s. Between 1780 and 1783, four different administrations came and went. Dundas had to wait until William Pitt the Younger ascended to power at the end of 1783 for his own political star to rise. After only a few months, Parliament passed Pitt's India Act, the content of which owed much to a bill proposed by Dundas the previous year.[4] The act created a Board of Control to be staffed by six privy councilors appointed by the Crown. The Board of Control would oversee the political aspects of the East India Company's involvement in India, seek to prevent Company employees from engaging in reckless and expensive wars, and try to place loyal and trustworthy people in charge of the Company's Indian presidencies. While Dundas did not become the board's official president until 1793, "for all practical purposes until 1801," wrote Furber, "the Board of Control for India meant Dundas, or at most, Dundas and Pitt."[5] As a member of the board, Dundas oversaw the East India Company's affairs and acted as a liaison between the Company and Parliament. For instance, in 1787, he "introduced the practice of bringing annually before a Committee of the House of Commons, a statement of the situation of the affairs of the Provinces of India."[6]

At some point in 1785, Dundas began planning an embassy to China. To ensure its success he went to great lengths to gather accurate information about China's government, economy, and commercial conditions. Until the nineteenth century, the main sources of information about China were Catholic missionaries and European diplomats. According to James Cobb, a playwright who served as secretary of the East India Company, "All the information respecting China" since the medieval period "is derived either from the embassies sent thither from Europe, or from the accounts of the missionaries, most of which were collected by Father Du Halde." Europeans learned about China primarily through the scholarship of Jesuit missionaries. Early British Sinologists, such as Thomas Percy and William Jones, depended "on this older Jesuit tradition of Confucian sinology," including notable works such as Jean-Baptiste Du Halde's *Description Geographique, Historique, Chronologique, Politique, et Physique de L'Empire de la Chine* (1735).[7]

There was, however, some reason to doubt the veracity of Jesuit reports. Jesuits had been proselytizing in China since the sixteenth century. Their strategy was to convert the emperor of China and members of the ruling elite, who would then Christianize the rest of China.[8] Jesuit depictions of China reflected, in part, their peculiar interests, experiences, and conversion strategies. James Cobb was justifiably skeptical: "Whatever credit may be due to Father Du Halde on secular subjects, he does not fail to call in the assistance of miracles whenever the interest of the Church is in danger."[9]

By the late eighteenth century, diplomats and participants of various European embassies (Dutch, Portuguese, and Russian) were also publishing their own accounts of China. The writings of Johann Adam Schall von Bell, Everard Isbrand Ides, John Bell, Carlo Ambrogio Mezzabarba, and others, all participants in various diplomatic missions to China, guided Prime Minister Pitt and Henry Dundas as they planned Britain's first embassy.[10] But James Cobb warned against taking these secular accounts at face value: "Can we imagine that among all the petty princes who have called themselves sovereigns of the world, and claimed alliance with the sun moon and stars, any of them ever believed a word of the matter? Do we not address our own monarch as king of a country where he has not a foot of dominion, and as defender of a faith, which disqualifies its professors from holding any place of trust under the state? Such titles are baubles which swell the pomp of courtly civility without adding to its importance." Cobb reasoned that "we must not therefore form our ideas of the Chinese court from the bombast of an ambassadorial letter." Despite the difficulties of prior embassies and the arrogance of official Chinese rhetoric, Cobb strongly advised sending a British embassy to China.[11]

Eighteenth-century Britons who thirsted for knowledge about China had to content themselves with the writings of Jesuit missionaries and

European diplomats. Not so for Dundas. As de facto head of the Board of Control, he enjoyed access to another source of information: the East India Company. Dundas studied the Company's China Factory Records and compiled detailed quantitative information about the China trade.[12] The Board of Control's records are filled with extracts of letters, inquiries, and reports on the China trade.[13] In 1791, Henry Browne, Thomas Fitzhugh, David Lance, Henry Lane, William Fitzhugh, William Henry Pigou, all retired Company supercargos, were asked by the Court of Directors—most likely at the insistence of Dundas—to answer a long list of questions, for example, "What material alterations has the mode of conducting the trade in China undergone within your recollection?" and "Do you apprehend that the Company derive any advantage in consequence of the magnitude of their Trade over the Swedes, Danes and Dutch companies or over individuals such as the French Portuguese or Americans?" If their answers were insufficient, Dundas could also speak in person with retired Canton factory supercargos to obtain their expert opinions on China and the Canton trade. Both George Smiths recommended Dundas do just that. Smith of Canton proposed getting "genuine information" from them.[14] Smith of Madras recommended that Dundas contact several former supercargos then resident in London, including Thomas Lockwood of Mortimer Street, Cavendish Square; Thomas Fitzhugh of Portland Place; and James Flint of Kent. All had resided in China for decades and could offer Dundas their expert knowledge of China.[15] Dundas also received information from two family members in the employ of the East India Company: his nephew East Indiaman Captain Philip Dundas, known in Bombay as "the Spy," and his cousin James Drummond, who worked as a supercargo in Canton.[16]

Still, Dundas's appetite for knowledge about China was not sated. Private traders, most of them Scots, provided him with additional information and a different perspective on the East Indies. Dundas was drawn to Scottish private traders because, like him, they disdained monopoly and sought to establish an empire of free trade. This shared imperial vision was the foundation for one of Dundas's closest friendships.

David Scott, the fifth son in a family of thirteen children from Forfarshire (modern Angus) in Scotland, moved to India in the early 1760s and worked there for over twenty years as a private trader. In Bombay he earned a fortune as the "acknowledged leader among the private merchants, and head of a respected agency house with an unrivalled knowledge of eastern trading conditions, especially in western India." In 1786, Scott returned to Britain and began serving as a director of the East India Company (1788) as well as a member of Parliament for Forfarshire (1790). Knowledgeable and driven, unostentatious and warmhearted, Scott, not surprisingly, felt drawn to Dundas. He shared many of Dundas's better traits, but more importantly, he shared Dundas's imperial vision. According to C. H. Philips, the editor of Scott's correspondence, "they were on intimate terms and on Indian problems saw eye to eye." They both tried to fight the shipping interest of the East India Company and whittle away at the Company's monopoly on commerce with Asia. They worked together, often at Dundas's home, where Scott was frequently invited "to meet Pitt and confer on India business," and as the English war with France took more and more of Dundas's attention, Scott took more and more responsibility in London for India. Scott's private overland express news service from India to London provided information to share with Dundas, as did Scott's personal network of Indian informants.[17] Alexander Adamson, a former business partner of Scott's and a private cotton trader in Bombay, also corresponded extensively with Dundas about Indian affairs.[18]

Dundas's affinity to anti-monopolistic Scottish private traders and their friends should come as no surprise. While some historians have argued that Dundas "was far from convinced that an end to the Company's monopoly would be beneficial to the national interest," recent scholarship suggests, to the contrary, that Dundas's attitude toward the Company's monopoly was unequivocal.[19] Dundas (and Prime Minister Pitt) desired an end to the Company's monopoly on Asian trade sooner rather than later. According to Dundas's biographer Michael Fry, Dundas intended to subvert the Company's monopoly. Only "political circumstance had thus far obliged him to tolerate a more powerful Company than ideally he would have liked."[20] Yet through piecemeal and partial solutions, Dundas set the process in motion by which the Company would eventually "crumble in its own time."[21] He would be happy when it did.[22]

Dundas's imperial vision was undoubtedly shaped by the work of another influential Scot, Adam Smith. Not only had Dundas read *The Wealth of Nations* (published in 1776), but its author was an honored guest at Dundas's home. In 1787, Dundas assured Adam Smith, "You shall have a comfortable room and as the business is much relaxed we shall have time to discuss all your books with you every evening." Prime Minister Pitt even insisted that all the guests at Dundas's home stand till Smith was seated, "because they were all his pupils."[23] That is quite a powerful image: Britain's most powerful statesmen playing the role of eager and deferent pupils to Adam Smith. One historian, Alan Frost, has argued that in 1784, with Pitt in power, leading members of his administration "began approaching commercial questions in the consciousness of an ideology of free trade." In fact, "liberating British trade along the lines urged by Adam Smith had become something of an obsession with Dundas."[24] While Dundas was a savvy and pragmatic politician—he knew he must tread with caution when dealing with the Company—he had a clear vision for the British empire, and that vision did not include a place for monopolistic companies, at least not in the long run.

Like Adam Smith, George Smith of Canton was both a Scot and a free-trade advocate, and he, too, contributed to Dundas's thinking about Britain's imperial future, particularly the China trade. Like his more famous namesake, he was hosted several times at Dundas's home at Cannizaro House in Wimbledon.[25] Drawing from his own extensive "local experience" in China, Smith of Canton eagerly took on the role of Dundas's advisor.[26] He cautioned Dundas that "the only persons that can give genuine information are the supercargos . . . and some of the intelligent captains of Indiamen."[27] The day before Dundas's meeting with East India Company leaders, Smith of Canton prescribed healthy skepticism, there being "but one or two of the Directors that are at all informed regarding the Company's situation in China."[28]

Several years before George Smith of Canton began advising Dundas, George Smith of Madras arrived on the political scene in London. Smith of Madras probably came to Dundas's attention through Edmund Burke, a prominent Whig MP who enjoyed a long career in Parliament between 1765 and 1794. Like Dundas, Burke devoted more time and effort to India than to any of his other public commitments.[29] By 1785, "Burke almost certainly knew more about India than did any other man in public life who had not actually been there."[30] Burke's interest in India preceded Dundas's. During the late 1760s and early 1770s, he warned against state interference in the East India Company.[31] As a member of the Rockinghamite Whig political party, Burke fought to limit monarchial power; this included guarding the East India Company's sovereignty in India. In 1773, Burke went so far as to defend Lord Robert Clive, the notorious "nabob" who was then under attack for peculation and mismanagement in India. Yet not long after, Burke led a decade-long Melvillian quest to impeach Warren Hastings, governor-general of Bengal, for similar offenses.

It was corruption in Madras, however, not Bengal, that transformed Burke's views about India and the Company. In 1777, Burke learned that several members of the Company's Madras Council had suspended the non-complicit Council members and then commissioned the Company's military officers to ambush Lord Pigot, the governor of Madras, in his chaise while he was on his way to the Company's Garden House. For months, Pigot lived under house arrest at a Colonel Matthew Horne's home. He died mysteriously in May 1777. Events in Madras hit close to home for Burke because he and Governor Pigot had shared an allegiance to the same political faction, the Rockingham Whigs. When Pigot's brother, Admiral Hugh Pigot, organized a campaign to reinstate him as governor of Madras, Burke had played an active role.[32]

Edmund Burke's distant relative and oldest and closest friend in England, William Burke, also became deeply involved in the Madras scandal. William Burke was dispatched to Madras by London-based Pigot supporters as a messenger to the ousted governor, but he was too late. By the time William Burke arrived in Madras, Lord Pigot was dead. Burke quickly returned to London to represent the interests of the raja of Tanjore, whose nemesis, the nawab of Arcot, was deeply indebted to the East India Company as well as to numerous members of the Madras commercial community (George Smith of Madras had been one of his creditors).[33] Before the coup in 1776, Governor Pigot had tried to return land that was taken from the raja of Tanjore by the nawab of Arcot. But this policy was extremely unpopular among many members of the Madras community. During the 1760s and 1770s, just as the Hong merchants had done in Canton, the nawab borrowed great sums of money at high interest from British residents in Madras. The nawab's creditors would stop at little to ensure that he held on to the raja of Tanjore's land, which was considered to be the most fertile in the region. After all, future tax revenues from Tanjore land, estimated at two million pagodas, had already been mortgaged by the nawab to Paul Benfield and other private British creditors in Madras.[34]

Corruption in Madras so disturbed Edmund Burke that he "seems to have become almost a third Tanjore agent." Through pamphleteering and speeches in Parliament, he and William Burke sought to protect the raja of Tanjore's interests. In 1779, Burke tried another tactic. He acquired a £1,000 share in East India Company stock, securing himself a vote in the Company's Court of Proprietors—the highest body of the Company that could overrule the decisions of the Court of Directors.[35] He now had "a say in the deliberations of the Court of Proprietors in the matter of Paul Benfield."[36]

In December 1780, the East India Company investigated the suspect behavior and dubious character of Paul Benfield, a Company employee, banker, and major creditor of the nawab of Arcot. The Court of Proprietors deliberated over reinstating Benfield to his Company post in Madras. In preparation for the deliberations, Edmund Burke summoned George Smith of Madras to testify against Benfield. Burke may have learned about Smith of Madras through William Burke and his new associate, Claud Russell. During William Burke's short stay in Madras, he had become acquainted with Claud Russell, who happened to be one of Governor Pigot's sons-in-law and a former business partner of George Smith of Madras. William Burke had been selected by Russell to serve as the raja of Tanjore's agent, and several years later, when Russell made a bid for the Madras governorship, he received Edmund Burke's support.[37] Claud Russell may have been the link between the Burkes and George Smith of Madras.

Before returning to Britain in 1780, Smith of Madras had become deeply entangled in the Madras coup; he possessed sensitive information about Benfield and about corruption in Madras more generally. Four years before the Company began to investigate Benfield, Smith served as foreman of the jury for the coroner's inquest on Governor Pigot's mysterious death. It was at Smith's home that the jury met and decided that the conspirators had murdered Governor Pigot, but the Bengal Supreme Court quickly nullified these findings, citing insufficient evidence for an indictment of murder or manslaughter. We will never know whether Pigot, an avid gardener, died from overexposure to the sun from tending to his plants, whether "eating remarkably hearty of a turtle" (apparently a dangerously rich dish) during a Sunday meal led to his demise, or whether something more nefarious, perhaps poisoning by an agent of the nawab, was to blame. Company surgeon Gilbert Pasley deposed that "he died of a slow visceral fever, partial suppurations in the substance of his liver, and putrid bile" due to exposure.[38]

The year of the coup, Smith alerted Company authorities in Bengal and London to the "troubles" in Madras.[39] On October 10, 1776, he warned the Court of Directors:

> Duty and attachment to the Company, under whose protection I have lived for many years, being the incentive to this address it will I hope meet with your favorable reception attention and excuse. I am greatly concerned that a revolution (if not rebellion) has taken place in your settlements on this coast, by the seizure of Lord Pigot's person and government by a military force on the 24th of August last . . . For the manner in which Lord Pigot was seized, I beg leave to refer your honors to his Lordships' petition of Habeas Corpus herein inclosed. The first act of the new administration was to suspend Mess. Russell, Dalrymple, Stone and Lathom from your service . . . To subvert established Laws and a fixed government by the title of convenience or necessity being replete with many dangers and inconveniencies to the community and apprehensive of its proving so to the interest of the Company, is the reason why I have presumed to take the liberty of

> informing you with a circumstance which may so very materially affect them. You will be told that this resolution meets with the general concurrence of your settlements, the assertion is not true . . . That a man, cannot serve God and Mammon, is a very ancient maxim, whether a man can serve the Company and Mahomet, merits your deliberations, unhappily of late many of your servants have not entertained a doubt of the propriety of such a conduct.[40]

The "Mahomet" to which Smith of Madras referred was the nawab of Arcot. Smith criticized Company servants such as Benfield who undeniably put the nawab's and their own interests ahead of those of the Company and the Madras community.[41]

Burke must have been delighted to have a knowledgeable and respected ally in Smith of Madras. He described Smith as "an intelligent person concerned in trade" in the East Indies.[42] According to a newspaper account of the meeting of the Court of Proprietors, Burke moved "that Mr. George Smith, late Mayor of Madras, be requested to attend the court," and "he pledged himself, as a man of honour, that Mr. Smith was a man perfectly acquainted with the subject, and could give material information upon that and other essential parts of their enquiry; and that without his evidence, the case could not be so perfectly established in such a satisfactory manner as he could wish."[43] But Benfield's friends in the Company's Court of Proprietors objected to hearing Smith's testimony and barred him from speaking by a vote of 109 to 90.[44]

Although Smith of Madras did not utter a word during the Court of Proprietors' investigation, he eventually found an even more powerful audience: Parliament. In 1782, the Commons Select Committee on India, led by Edmund Burke, interviewed Smith for their *Ninth Report* on the affairs of India, printed in 1783.[45] Smith testified about the state of trade in Madras as well as the debts of the nawab of Arcot.[46] Smith's participation in the Parliamentary inquiry undoubtedly brought him to Henry Dundas's attention, and the evidence strongly suggests that Smith of Madras and Dundas communicated in London during the early 1780s.[47] Before Smith set sail for India again in 1783, a link between Smith of Madras and Dundas had been forged.

Between 1781 and 1791, Smith of Madras wrote hundreds of pages of letters to Dundas from England, Calcutta, Bombay, and Canton.[48] Many of his letters concerned India. Smith of Madras played a critical role in convincing Dundas of Bombay's importance to the British empire. It was, in part, due to Smith's efforts that the British settlement in Bombay was not abandoned by the British government.[49]

Smith of Madras wrote extensively to Dundas not just about India but also about China: "The national importance of that trade to Great Britain cannot have escaped your penetrating eye, nor that of the Right Honble the Board of Control, who no doubt will be very careful in preserving to Britain the present advantages arising from a branch of commerce, now very extensive and lucrative, but which in my opinion may be still more augmented to the benefit of the nation and Company." Like Smith of Canton, Smith of Madras expressed concern about Britain's trade deficit with China. He believed that the East India Company would have to send ships full of bullion to China regularly "to keep the trade to China even on its present footing," because the Company's Indian presidencies could not afford to send specie independently and because Chinese merchants could not conduct business on credit for extended periods. "One thing is absolutely necessary," explained Smith, "and that is, to owe the Chinese as little money as possible, and for as short a time as is possible." It was not because Chinese merchants were untrustworthy—on the contrary, the East India Company frequently owed money to the Hong merchants—but rather because "few if any of the brokers who we call merchants, and with whom we deal have any capitals of their own, but purchase the goods which we want from the country farmers, or merchants, who bring their teas to market." Because the Hong merchants lacked capital, they bought tea from farmers and brokers on credit, "agreeing to pay for them in full within a year." These upcountry tea farmers trusted the "liberty, integrity and honor of the English East India Company," and so they would wait up to, but no longer than, a year to be repaid by the Hong merchants. The viability of the tea trade, in Smith's view, depended on a steady flow of silver into Canton.[50]

Private traders in India, Smith of Madras argued, had long played a key role in pumping silver into Canton and financing the Company's tea trade. They shipped "cotton, opium, tin and sandal wood" to China and filled the Company's Canton treasury with silver. Private trade, therefore, "merits every encouragement from the Co[mpany]." A more favorable exchange rate on Company bills of exchange, in Smith's view, would ensure that private British wealth found its way to the British East India Company's Canton treasury rather than to those of other European East India companies, where it often went.[51]

Smith of Madras suggested several ways of expanding Britain's commercial reach between India and China through a chain of maritime bases in Southeast Asia.[52] In this, he shared much with his Scottish contemporary, Alexander Dalrymple, who had settled in Madras in 1753, at roughly the same time as Smith, and worked for over a decade as a Company employee. Like Smith of Madras, Dalrymple developed a friendship with Lord Pigot, the governor of Madras, and supported the governor against his enemies. Governor Pigot, in turn, supported Dalrymple's explorations and diplomatic missions in Southeast Asia.[53] Like Smith, Dalrymple encouraged the British government to establish naval and commercial bases in Southeast Asia to facilitate Britain's trade with China; he also corresponded frequently with Henry Dundas.[54] Given their similar circumstances, interests, and political connections, it is hard to imagine that Smith of Madras and Dalrymple never met. If they did, they surely had much to discuss.

Dalrymple took particular interest in the area between Borneo and Manila, and he personally led a mission in the 1760s to establish a British settlement on the island of Balambangan, off the northernmost tip of Borneo just south of Palawan, in the Philippines. Smith of Madras, in contrast, focused his attention on the western coast of the Malay Peninsula—more specifically, on Penang Island. In 1786, the island was claimed by another British private trader, Francis Light, on behalf of the East India Company, but Smith proudly took some credit for the new settlement. Not only had he been present (or so he claimed) when Light took possession of Penang, but, he boasted, the idea for a settlement in the area had originated with him: "I own I am partial to the island, for I consider it in a great degree as a child of my own, for Sir John Macpherson will do me the justice to acknowledge that I urged him to form a settlement at or near Queda, and also at Trangany, and recommended Mr. Light as the fittest man I know to make the settlement."[55] In this new British settlement only ten to twelve days' run from Madras, Smith saw many possibilities. Penang had an excellent harbor with ample space for the entire Royal Navy. In addition to its strategic naval value, Penang could support Britain's trade to China. The island produced tin, "which may prove a supply for China." Smith sent a sample of Penang's tin to Dundas via Captain Wall of the *Valentine*.[56] Penang's utility to "our oriental and China Trade" justified Britain's political and military support of the new colony.[57]

Not far from the Malay Peninsula, yet another kingdom caught Smith of Madras's attention, Pegu (now Bago), in modern Myanmar. The conquest of the Kingdom of Pegu, Smith believed, was "an object of great importance, as it would prove a key to the Empire of China which lies behind Pegu, and with which, a most advantageous branch of trade for the staples of England might be opened." Smith admitted that "territorial acquisitions" were "no favorite object" of his, but if it were a question of increasing Sino-British trade and opening the Chinese market to British manufactures, he would support Britain's territorial expansion in Asia.[58]

New colonies, however, had to be governed properly. Smith of Madras voiced particular concern for Britain's new possessions in India. His extensive experience in both China and India enabled him to do some comparative analysis, observing parallels between the Qing and British empires. In doing so, Smith of Madras was drawing on a long European literary tradition going back to Marco Polo. China had been studied, imagined, and constructed in various ways by numerous European writers over many centuries. During the eighteenth century, China, like the "Orient," increasingly came to serve as a conceptual device, as both a model and a foil against which British institutions and society could be compared, critiqued, and constructed.[59] China was good to think with. British writers and philosophers, though critical at times, tended to approach China with genuine curiosity and respect.

British and European perceptions of China, however, began to shift toward the end of the eighteenth century. Once considered rich, civilized, cultivated, and well governed, China was increasingly perceived as rigid, stagnant, oppressive, and barbaric. By the early 1790s, Britain's first ambassador to China, Lord Macartney, could arrogantly liken the empire of China to an "old crazy first rate man of war, which a fortunate succession of able and vigilant officers have contrived to keep afloat for these 150 years past and to overawe their neighbors merely by her luck and appearance; but whenever an insufficient man happens to have the command upon deck, adieu to the discipline and safety of the ship. She may perhaps not sink out right, she may drift some time as a wreck and will then be dashed to pieces on the shore, but she can never be rebuilt on the old bottom."[60] After the First Opium War, Karl Marx's condescending description of China as a "mummy carefully preserved in a hermetically sealed coffin" waiting to be broken out of its "barbarous and hermetic isolation from the civilized world" would have resonated with many of the readers of the *New York Daily Tribune*.[61]

Unlike Ambassador Macartney, Smith of Madras's attitude reflected the earlier thinking of European Sinophiles. Smith advised Dundas that Britain should learn from China's imperial example. He drew lessons from the mid-seventeenth-century Manchu conquest of China. While arguing that Britain should allow the native population in Bengal to retain Hindu and Muslim laws and institutions rather than imposing British institutions upon them, Smith of Madras pointed to the example set by the Qing-dynasty Manchus, to whom Smith referred as "Tartars." He offered information to Dundas about

> the Tartars who overran China in the last century, and who soon after the conquest endeavoured to enforce their laws and manners in the conquered. They began by commanding the Chinese to shave their heads, reserving only a lock of hair, in imitation of the Tartars, but this they would not obtain obedience to and whole cities were decapitated and disfranchised

> in consequence, but the Tartar barbarian soon perceived, that the country which he had conquered, would be lost to him, if he continued to press the execution of his orders, and wisely desisted, nay he did more, he adopted the laws of the conquered, and that vast Empire is at this day, governed by the Tartarman race, who has kept peaceful possession of the throne for about one hundred and forty years, and the Chinese in conformity with the manners of their rulers, do at this time, and of their own accord, wear that lock of hair which their ancestors lost their heads sooner than submit to what they thought an indignity and a badge of slavery.[62]

Smith of Madras's description of the Ming-Qing dynastic transition was partly correct. Dorgon, prince-regent of the Manchus, had in fact canceled his first decree that all Chinese men must wear their hair as the Manchus did, by shaving their foreheads and braiding their hair in the back into a queue. However, under pressure from his advisors, Dorgon reissued the unpopular decree in 1645. When many ethnically Chinese men—that is, Han Chinese—chose to keep their hair and lose their heads, Dorgon stood firm.[63] In Philip Kuhn's view, this decree was a constant source of political anxiety for Qing rulers: "it became a touch-stone by which the throne tested its servants." Yet the Manchus also had the "ability to implement flexible culturally specific policies aimed at the major non-Han peoples inhabiting the Inner Asian peripheries in the empire."[64] Qing rulers also respected and maintained Chinese governmental and intellectual institutions, including the centuries-old examination system.[65] Smith of Madras may have exaggerated the tolerance and leniency of Manchu governors toward the conquered population, but he was perceptive in appreciating the Manchus' ability to govern a large, culturally diverse territorial empire. Perhaps Henry Dundas was inspired to take notes.

In Qing China, Smith of Madras saw a model of imperial governance that should be emulated in British India. After Warren Hastings resigned his post as governor-general of Bengal in 1785 (having served for twelve years), Smith warned Dundas of the potential danger of allowing a governor to remain in power for too long: "I consider his voluntary resignation of this government little less than an abdication of a kingdom, nay an Empire, for were he not faithful, and loyal, he might have attempted, and successfully, a dismemberment of the country, from the British Empire." In case the next governor-general refused to relinquish the reins of power, Smith strongly advocated shorter terms, again pointing to the Chinese government as an example. In China "the Emperor always remov[es] his viceroys every three years generally from one province, to another, or recalling them to an honorary station at Court, in order to prevent the formation of undue connections in the provinces."[66] Smith's description of the Chinese bureaucracy was accurate. Not only were Qing-dynasty officials frequently rotated through the empire, but they were also prohibited from serving in their natal provinces. In reaction to Britain's recent imperial failures in America, Smith of Madras sought successful imperial models for Britain. Perhaps most striking is that he did not scour the Roman classics for examples. Instead, Smith looked to China.

Just before departing for India for the second time in 1783, Smith of Madras sent Dundas what was arguably his most important proposal, entitled "Establishment of the East India Company Trade to China, on a firm, and advantageous Basis, and to the procurement Virtually of an Exclusive right to that most lucrative Branch of Commerce, humbly submitted to the Consideration of the Right Honble the Lord Advocate."[67] Smith of Madras recommended that the British government send an embassy to China. This would be Britain's first official diplomatic contact with China.

But Smith of Madras was not the first to propose a British embassy to China. Rather, British creditors of the Hong merchants in Canton beat him to it by six years. It was actually Smith of Canton, not Smith of Madras, who first lobbied for an embassy to China. Doubting the possibility of "an honest and faithful representation to the Court of Pekin" from Canton, British creditors devised the idea of an embassy. They had become deeply disturbed by the "precarious state" of the China trade and were convinced of the "necessity and expediency of putting both the public and private concerns of China, upon a better and more permanent footing."[68] According to Smith of Canton, British creditors met in China in December 1777 and discussed the possibility of "immediate application to the Imperial government of China for relief." Smith of Canton explained: "It was thought that appearance of the crown of great Britain in behalf of their subjects would be sufficient, that a kings frigate might perhaps be spared from the Indian station to carry any person entrusted with such a commission, that by the port of Tianjing within fifty miles of Peking, an easy and ready access might be obtained to the Imperial Court, where a plain tale thus countenanced might answer the most sanguine expectations."[69] Smith of Canton and his colleagues dispatched a report and a representative to London "to assist in such information as might be derived from local knowledge."[70] Over a decade later in 1792, John Rogers, an East Indiaman captain, confirmed that "a representation to Peking" was "what the creditors ever had in view."[71]

A meeting for those with "money concerns in China" was advertised in the *London Chronicle* and held in October 1778 at the London Tavern, a popular haunt for merchants. The meeting's participants selected a committee of creditors, including Matthew Purling, John Hunter, George Paterson, John Clements, and Thomas Raikes. Purling, Hunter, Paterson, and Clements had all invested money in China and, with the exception of Hunter, had worked for the East India Company. Purling, who had formerly served as a Company council member at St. Helena, in the southern Atlantic Ocean, also represented the financial interests of Matthew Bazett, a fellow St. Helena Council member, and Daniel Corneille, lieutenant governor of St. Helena.[72] Thomas Raikes worked as a partner in the London counting house of Rumbold, Charlton, and Raikes. He also legally represented four British creditors in their efforts to recover money from Chinese merchants.

The committee of creditors first turned to the directors of the East India Company for help. According to Smith of Canton, the Canton brokers were "sensible of the impropriety of any application but through the Honble Company," so they "humbly submitted the mode and means of relief to the superior wisdom of the Honble Court." The Court of Directors, however, was slow to come to the aid of the creditors and strongly objected to sending a British embassy to China.[73] Frustrated by the Company's resistance, the creditors overcame their earlier sense of "impropriety" and

Ambassador Macartney's entrance into China, where he is greeted by a mandarin. Between the mandarin and the woman on the left, who represents commerce, stand three imperial soldiers. In the background is a cityscape with canals. George Staunton, *An Historical Account of the Embassy to the Emperor of China . . .* (London: Published by John Stockdale, 1797), frontispiece.

decided to turn to the British government directly for help. Two sources in Canton confirm that the British government was "applied to with regard to an embassy to be sent to Pekin on this subject, but [the] ministry would do nothing but through the East India Company."[74] The idea of a British embassy to China was born out of the Canton financial crisis.

At first the creditors' proposal did not get much traction in London. With time, though, the British government began to show interest in creating diplomatic ties with China. In 1782, Prime Minister Shelburne (William

Petty) contemplated sending an embassy to China. He was prodded by Royal Navy Captain Blankett: "The peace that ends the American War may be a proper time to make a trial at trade with Japan. It may be engrafted on the plan your lordship has in contemplation for extending the commerce of China."[75] The politically tumultuous period in which Shelburne served as prime minister afforded him little time to enact his plan, and in 1783, after nine months in power, he was dismissed. Now it was Prime Minister Pitt and Henry Dundas's turn to reach out to China.

Dundas received proposals from both Smith of Madras and Smith of Canton. Smith of Madras painted a bleak picture of the Canton trade. He warned Dundas, "It is now twenty one years since I left Canton, since which the obstructions to our trade have increased twenty one fold, the impositions of the superior, and inferior mandarins are become intolerable, as are the extortions on the merchants with whom we deal." The prices of Chinese commodities (even provisions) were increasing, foreign and Chinese merchants were being constantly fleeced by corrupt officials, and the China trade was "greatly clogged." An embassy was the only solution. In no uncertain terms he urged Dundas to act: "it appears to me Sir, that nothing less than any embassy can remove the evils now so justly complained of, that an embassy would remove them I am clearly convinced of."[76]

Smith of Madras had no shortage of recommendations for Dundas: the ambassador to China should introduce the manufactures of Britain, such as woolen cloth and firearms, into China; he should secure permission for the British to trade at Amoy and Ningbo as well as Canton; and he should obtain a guarantee from the Chinese government to back all contractual agreements between British and Chinese merchants. Smith of Madras also strongly advised that the ambassador negotiate a "treaty of friendship" between Britain and China according to which Britain would enjoy preferential status. If the Qianlong emperor were made aware of Britain's strong military and maritime presence in South Asia, perhaps he would be amenable to such a treaty. Should the emperor of China "be attacked by any European Power on his Coasts . . . we could bring a sufficient force to repel the assailants in two months after receipt of his advices in India." Smith of Madras also recommended that Britain and China enter into a

"League offensive and defensive" to protect China from the growing power of Russia. The ambassador should explain to the emperor that "the English are the only power able to defeat such intention in Russia." In return for British support, the emperor might cede a safe and convenient port on one of the Chinese islands.[77]

Like Smith of Madras, Smith of Canton advised Dundas on the embassy. He raised the issue of an interpreter, boasting about a Russian contact who knew a competent interpreter in Russia. The interpreter was willing to work for an annual salary of "twelve hundred rubles [and] to find his own board and lodging," and Smith would be happy "to go to Russia myself [to] finish the negotiation with the linguist [and] bring him with me to this country." Smith of Canton only asked in return that the government defray his few expenses, which "will not be thought unreasonable considering that I should thereby separate myself for so long a period from my wife and children."[78] Smith of Canton claimed that his advice came without any expectation of reward.[79] But he knew full well that a British embassy to China was his best chance "to procure from the Chinese government full payment of the just debts due by its hongs to their British creditors."[80] Smith of Canton pressed hard for the embassy.

Henry Dundas also obtained advice from several Company ship captains, most of whom traded ambitiously for private gain.[81] The private trade of Company ship captains in the East Indies was "innovative and dynamic" and "extensive and sophisticated."[82] Captain William Mackintosh, an East Indiaman captain who was selected to command the *Hindostan* as part of the Macartney embassy to China, corresponded with Dundas and transmitted several translated letters from China. The anonymous European author of these letters strongly advocated political intervention: "It gives me no small uneasiness when I reflect on the harsh and unjust treatment which the Europeans meet with at Canton, and I am certain that if the Emperor was acquainted with one hundredth part of the frauds and villainy of those mandarins, he would hang them everyone. The four millions (of Dollars) owing by the Chinese, would certainly be immediately discharged, and if no other way could be found, out of the public treasury, so just and strict is this emperor, more particularly where foreigners are concerned." According to the anonymous writer, only an embassy to China could address "the oppressions and abuses suffered by the Europeans who either reside in, or annually come to Canton to trade, there is no other mode of redress than to find some method of laying them before the Emperor who being a man of integrity, and desirous that justice should be done to every one, particularly to strangers, would immediately apply the proper remedy, and severely punish the guilty persons."[83] Another East Indiaman captain, John Rogers, agreed: "Many gentlemen were convinced an embassy to Peking was the sure means of obtaining redress in a cause where multitudes are concerned."[84] As a creditor of the Chinese Hong merchants, Captain Rogers had a personal interest in the embassy.

The East India Company's leaders in London took a different view. The chairmen of the Company believed that a British embassy to China was likely to damage their trade. According to one of their Canton supercargos, Thomas Fitzhugh, previous embassies to China from Portugal, Russia, and the Netherlands had all failed. A British embassy would be no different. In 1787, Fitzhugh warned the Company's chairmen: "The Chinese government is proud and insolent. It looks with contempt on all foreign nations. Its ignorance of their force gives it confidence in its own strength, which by experience is known to be superior to the border hordes of Tartars with whom it is commonly engaged in war; nor do I think it looks on embassies in any other light than acknowledgments of inferiority."[85]

The East India Company's leadership offered no outright opposition to the proposed British embassy to China, but it did use subtle means to stall it. The Company's chairmen repeatedly bickered with both Ambassadors Charles Cathcart and George Macartney about their salaries and the cost of the embassy; after all, the Company was footing the bill.[86] They also discouraged Ambassador Macartney by emphasizing the dangers of sending an embassy to China and the likelihood of failure. According to the chairmen, "The only chance of success in the embassy will arise from a perfect previous knowledge of the laws, customs and manners of the Chinese."[87] With time Dundas came to realize "that the Court of Directors are rather hostile to the expedition, and give out that it may be highly prejudicial to their interests." The Company's leaders were extremely risk-averse.

They feared that an embassy might create "jealousies among the Mandarins and other Chinese at Canton" and that the Company would be expelled from China.[88] It seemed better to the Company's leadership to maintain an extremely lucrative commerce under imperfect conditions than to exacerbate the situation or, worse yet, forfeit the trade completely. Business was booming. Why take the risk?

The Company's leadership also objected to two important aims of the embassy, namely, the appointment of a permanent British consul in China and the establishment of an independent commercial settlement in the name of the king of Great Britain. Both aims potentially threatened the East India Company's monopoly by creating an alternative source of British authority in China and opening Canton commerce to a wider pool of participants. A British consul, as recommended by George Smith of Madras, would establish a representative of the British state in China. Smith of Madras advised Dundas that this consul should receive the complaints of the Company's supercargos and all British subjects in China; it should also enjoy "at all proper times free access to the Viceroy, or Zuntoo of Canton to present any grievances imposed by the inferior mandarins which are to be immediately redressed by the viceroy."[89]

George Smith of Canton and David Scott also recommended that Britain acquire a permanent and independent commercial establishment in China. In 1786, Smith of Canton suggested "a permanent establishment in China," perhaps Danes Island, at Whampoa fourteen miles from Canton, or Portuguese Macao. A British establishment in China would bring many advantages, Smith of Canton argued: British supercargos would have more time to make their contracts, they would not have to shuttle back and forth every season between Canton and Macao, and they could enjoy a depot for the "mines, goods and manufactures of this country in order for their extension as much as possible, for instance tin, lumber, copper and other articles not hitherto exported from this country."[90]

David Scott had set his sights on Macao. In a letter to the directors of the East India Company (it was later published as a pamphlet), Scott argued that "the Portuguese gain nothing by Macao; if it could be purchased by our Company, it would be a most consequential acquisition."[91]

The third George Smith of our tale, George Smith of Bombay, albeit unwittingly, also helped to convince Henry Dundas of the urgent need for an independent British territory in China. While he does not seem to have ever corresponded with Dundas, unsettling reports about the *Lady Hughes* Affair reached London in 1785 and led the British government to reconsider "how to deal with the Qing at the international diplomatic level."[92] The *Lady Hughes* Affair went a long way toward persuading Dundas that "our Supercargos are denied open access to the tribunals of the country, and to the equal execution of its laws, and are kept altogether in a most arbitrary state of depression, ill suited to the importance of the concerns which are entrusted to their care, and scarcely compatible with the regulations of civilized society." He felt certain that the best way to avoid another "Canton War" was to "obtain a grant of a small tract of ground or detached island but in a more convenient situation than Canton where our present warehouses are at a great distance from our ships, and where we are not able to restrain the irregularities which are occasionally committed by the seamen of the Company's ships, and those of private traders."[93] Dundas instructed Ambassador Macartney that the new establishment in China would be taken in the name of Great Britain. There the British would enjoy the "power of regulating the police, and exercising jurisdiction over our own dependents, for which competent powers would be given so as effectually to prevent or punish the disorders of our people." Should the Chinese government object to British jurisdiction over Chinese subjects, that was acceptable to Dundas "provided British subjects can be exempted from the Chinese jurisdiction for crimes, and that the British chief or those under him be not held responsible if any culprit should escape the pursuit of justice, after search has been made by British and Chinese officers acting in conjunction."[94] It had become clear to Dundas that if the China trade were to thrive, Britain would require a safe place where the Company could control and govern its own employees, as well as private traders. British subjects would also require independence and exemption from what they increasingly perceived as the barbarism of Chinese laws.

J. Smith Burges and Francis Baring, the Company's chairmen, were extremely unsympathetic to these aims of the embassy. Unlike private traders, they painted a rosy picture of the situation in Canton. While it had been suggested that "disputes subsist at Canton between the servants of the company and the Chinese officers and magistrates," Francis Baring argued to the contrary: "So far from having disputes the Company conceive their servants to be on a better footing than formerly with the magistrates, officers, and other natives of China; which is evident from the improvement of the trade in every respect."[95] Baring and Burges insisted that if the emperor of China ceded territory to the British ambassador, it should "be made to the East India Company for their sole care and benefit during the continuance of their exclusive trade."[96] They feared that having a British territory in China that welcomed "ships of all nations" would undermine the Company's monopoly.[97] Baring felt so strongly about the issue that he refused to dispatch the embassy until Dundas consulted the Company's Court of Directors upon the subject.[98]

This delay enraged Dundas: "While you are trifling in that manner (for I can give it no better name) I know with certain knowledge that foreign nations are not losing time in frustrating the effects of the embassy."[99] Dundas, Pitt, and William Wyndham Grenville, foreign secretary and cousin of Prime Minister Pitt, knew they needed to tread carefully with respect to the Company's monopoly rights because the Company's charter was about to come up for renewal in 1793. They agreed it would be "imprudent to give them [the Company's leadership] a handle for saying that any measure suggested or promoted by government had proved prejudicial to them."[100] But on this matter, Dundas would not budge. He instructed Macartney: "Should a new establishment be conceded you will take it in the name of the King of Great Britain," not the East India Company.[101]

Private traders bartered information for privileges. In Henry Dundas they found a great ally, for he accepted information from a variety of sources: "I make it a rule to receive both verbal and written communications from every person who offers me information on Indian affairs. I get some very good, and likewise some very great [?] stuff in consequence of it."[102] In 1786, Dundas expressed his appreciation for George Smith of Madras's advice through his confidential clerk at the Board of Control, William Cabell. Cabell wrote to Smith of Madras to acknowledge "the receipt of your several letters, and to thank you for the useful information they contain." According to Cabell, Mr. Dundas had begged Smith to continue his communication of "every material information" and reassured him that his letters would receive an "early and attentive perusal."[103] Later, in May 1790, Smith could not contain his delight when he received a personal letter from Dundas.[104]

With the help of Dundas, private traders not only put an embassy to China on Britain's political agenda but helped to define the embassy's goals and strategies. Many of their recommendations, most notably for a permanent independent British settlement, a permanent British consul, and a treaty of friendship, found clear expression in the government's official instructions to Ambassadors Cathcart and Macartney, sometimes verbatim. Dundas also followed several of Smith of Madras's suggestions of gifts for the Qianlong emperor, instructing Ambassador Macartney to present a telescope, planetarium, globe, British porcelain, fine cloths, and guns to him. Ironically, some of these gifts would find their way back into British hands when British soldiers looted the Summer Palace during the Second Opium War (1856–60).[105]

Like Dundas, many of these private-trader informants—George Smith of Canton, George Smith of Madras, David Scott, and Captain Mackintosh—were of Scottish origin. Like Dundas, they sought free commerce and greater opportunity for private traders. They urged Dundas to use the power of the British state to intervene forcefully in India, Southeast Asia, and China, making "Leaden Hall Street the Emporium of the Asiatic trade to the western world."[106] Leaden Hall Street was the London location of the Company. Private traders led Dundas to believe that a British embassy to China "would be attended with the most salutary effects to the commerce of England in general."[107] Smith of Canton reassured Dundas of the embassy's probable success: "From the well known equitable maxims of the Chinese government, the most salutary effects might be expected from a favourable representation of the Court of Great Britain in their behalf."[108]

Dundas was less sanguine than his private-trader informants. According to the prevailing view, "the Chinese in general are studious to avoid any intimate connexion or intercourse with Europeans . . . a similar principle operates upon the Imperial Government of Pekin." Yet the reports of various travelers had also given Dundas the "strongest reason to believe that the Emperor himself is accessible, that the reception of foreigners at Pekin is courteous." Dundas "was especially solicitous about the development of the China trade" and extremely tempted by the promises of private traders.[109] Opening new markets in China to British goods, establishing a permanent British consul, and building an independent commercial settlement in China would, he believed, help to forge Britain's global commercial empire.[110] With guarded optimism and an admiration for Chinese civilization, Dundas ultimately decided that "a free communication with a people perhaps the most singular upon the globe, among whom civilization has existed, and the arts have been cultivated through a long series of ages, with fewer interruptions than elsewhere, is well worthy also, of this nation.'[111]

Epilogue

The Legacies of the Three George Smiths

George Smith of Canton

Throughout the 1780s and early 1790s, George Smith of Canton served as Henry Dundas's unofficial China advisor. The advice and information he provided came "without the expectation or thinking myself thereby entitled to any favor whatever, deeming it a duty incumbent upon every honest man to contribute to the welfare of his country as much as in his power."[1] He did, however, ask for something in return, and it was no small favor. Smith of Canton requested that the ambassador to China present British creditors' claims before the Qianlong emperor. The private financial interests of fifty or so creditors nearly made it onto the agenda of Britain's first embassy to China.

Although the handful of remaining Hong merchants in Canton (the rest had gone bankrupt during the financial crisis in 1779) had been ordered by the Chinese government to assume the debts of their insolvent colleagues and use a collective fund to repay British creditors in ten annual installments, the Chinese repayment plan included only one-tenth of the amount claimed by George Smith of Canton and others.[2] This left British creditors scrambling to recover the rest of their money. Smith of Canton hoped the British government could attain from the Chinese government full payment of Hong merchants' debts to British creditors.[3] He tried to convince Dundas that "the debts due by the Chinese to British subjects will be extremely influential in forwarding the obtaining [of] a permanent and solid regulation of the trade to China" and would also "strongly aid the ambassador in obtaining from the Court of Peking redress of the Company's grievances, and putting their trade on a respectable footing."[4] Bringing British creditors' complaints to the emperor's attention would promote the objectives of the embassy, or so Smith of Canton reasoned. He even went so far as to offer to "accompany the embassy to Peking and render it every service in my power."[5] Mr. Smith hoped to go to China again, this time as a participant in Britain's first embassy to China.

Dundas was ambivalent about intervening. He felt it was "improper to load the intended mission with any official instructions relative to the debt," far less to take any of the creditors to China as assistants in the mission.[6] At the same time, Dundas must have sympathized with Smith of Canton to some degree because he left open the possibility of state intervention on the British creditors' behalf. He explained to Smith of Canton: "If any of you will at any time wait upon Colonel Cathcart, he will, with my approbation, be glad to receive every information from you, and to be of any service to you that lays in his power, not inconsistent with the important object of his mission."[7] Dundas also did Smith the favor of passing to Ambassador Cathcart Smith's "hints in writing" with which he had earlier "favored Mr. Dundas relative to the Chinese Government."[8] During the planning of the Macartney Mission to China five years later (Ambassador Cathcart died on the voyage to China in 1788), Dundas again expressed his ambivalence about the creditors' plight. On the one hand, he had been pressured by Francis Baring and J. Smith Burges, the Company's chairmen, "to forbear mentioning the Chinese debts in the instructions to be given to the Ambassador."[9] The Chinese debts issue, as a result, never found its way into the official instructions to Macartney. On the other hand, Dundas could not ignore the creditors' pleas entirely. In a private letter, he instructed Macartney to find out what he could:

> With a due attention to the important interest alleged to be brought into risk by your Lordship's interference; and considering that the East India Company are at the expense of the embassy, I think it totally incompatible with my duty to give your Lordship the instructions which I have been requested to give to you. At the same time as the property of British subjects to so large an amount is stated to be at stake, I cannot receive their representations with indifference. It is therefore my wish that your Lordship should inform yourself with as

> much accuracy as your situation and local circumstances will enable you to do, of the real state of these transactions, of the disposition of the Emperor of China respecting them, and how far in your judgment any interposition can be used for the recovery of those debts, without injuring any of the interests of the East India Company in the exercise of their commerce and connection with China, and I shall be glad to be informed by you what is the result of your observations respecting those particulars.[10]

There was "a disposition on the part of government" to aid the creditors, not an overwhelming enthusiasm, but Dundas could not ignore Smith's pleas.[11] While he would not go so far as to instruct Ambassadors Cathcart and Macartney to represent the debts to the emperor of China, Dundas still recommended unofficially that both ambassadors look into the matter and see what they could do. Dundas opted to leave it to the discretion of the two ambassadors. The fate of George Smith of Canton and the other British creditors lay in the hands of Charles Cathcart and, five years later, George Macartney.

Had Ambassador Cathcart survived the journey to China, he probably would have brought the Canton debts to the attention of the Qianlong emperor. While in London, Cathcart was extremely receptive to the creditors. He met with Smith of Canton and corresponded with him many times, going so far as to notify him exactly when he planned to leave for China.[12] Cathcart made a proposal to the creditors: "With [Prime Minister] Pitt's permission," he suggested that the British creditors delegate to George Smith of Canton, John Hunter, George Vansittart, and Ewan Law—two private traders and two Company employees—"full powers to treat with government, and to send secret instructions to their agents in China relative to a plan which they Messrs. Smith etc. have concerted with a view to the recovery of the debts."[13] Ambassador Cathcart used his "endeavors to bring their case into some form."[14]

Smith of Canton appreciated Ambassador Cathcart's efforts, writing, "The aid of government was most joyfully and thankfully accepted."[15] He

62. George Vansittart to Robert Palk, Aug. 14, 1772, BL Mss Eur F331/19.
63. Weiller and Mirowski, "Rates of Interest in 18th Century England"; Price, *Capital and Credit,* pp. 58–59.
64. George Vansittart to Robert Palk, Patna, Aug. 14, 1772, BL Mss Eur F331/19; Weiller and Mirowski, "Rates of Interest in 18th Century England," pp. 1–28.
65. Trivellato, "Credit, Honor, and the Early Modern French Legend of the Jewish Invention of Bills of Exchange," pp. 289–94.
66. Marshall, *East Indian Fortunes,* p. 222.
67. Morse, *The Chronicles of the Company Trading to Canton,* vols. 2, 5, passim.
68. Van Dyke and Mok, *Images of the Canton Factories,* p. xv.
69. Nov. 18, 1774, BL IOR/R/10/7.
70. BL IOR/H/411, pp. 55–79.
71. Nightingale, *Trade and Empire in Western India,* p. 24.
72. George Smith, "Narrative of the proceedings for the recovery of debts owing by the Chinese merchants to British subjects" and "General statement of debts made up to the end of the season 1787/88," July 12, 1787, BL IOR/G/12/18, pp. 91–112.
73. Captain Rogers, "Some remarks on the heavy debt now owing by the Chinese to European subjects," BL IOR/G/12/91, vol. 2.
74. Pritchard, *The Crucial Years of Early Anglo-Chinese Relations,* pp. 395, 400.
75. Quincy, *The Journals of Major Samuel Shaw,* p. 169.
76. CUL, Copies of the East India Company Records, and Other Documents Relating to China and the China Trade Prepared for Lord Macartney's Information, vol. 1, "Queries put by the court of directors to persons now in England who have served the Company in China with the answers thereto 1791–2."
77. Marshall, *East Indian Fortunes,* p. 223.
78. Nov. 30, 1779, BL IOR/G/12/67.
79. Nightingale, *Trade and Empire in Western India,* p. 23.
80. Bowen, "British Exports of Raw Cotton from India to China," p. 123.
81. Nightingale, *Trade and Empire in Western India,* pp. 16, 72.
82. Letter from Court, Jan. 10, 1787, in *Fort William–India House Correspondence,* vol. 10, pp. 205–9.
83. China Council to Court of Directors, Dec. 21, 1767, BL IOR/R/10/6.
84. James Kerr to the Court of Directors, Nov. 9, 1773, BL Mss Eur K45.
85. Thomas Fitzhugh to the Court of Directors, July 7, 1782, BL IOR E/1/71, pp. 7–10.

expressed his gratitude to the ambassador prior to his departure for China: "I cannot think of letting you depart without first in the sincerity of my heart most cordially acknowledging and rendering you my ever grateful thanks for your politeness and attention, during the whole of my exertions, from the time they were put immediately under your direction."[16] Unfortunately for Smith of Canton, Cathcart never reached China. His untimely death at the age of twenty-eight on board the *Vestal* in the Straits of Sunda meant that matters would be left to the next ambassador to China, Lord Macartney.

Born to an Irish landowner and educated at Trinity College, Dublin, George Macartney moved in elite social circles. He was tutored by a friend of Edmund Burke's, befriended Rousseau and Voltaire, and later married Lady Jane Stuart, the daughter of former prime minister John Stuart, third earl of Bute, and Mary Wortley Montagu.[17] Having begun his career as a diplomat to Russia, chief secretary to Ireland, and later governor of Grenada, Tobago, and the Grenadines, Macartney's first experience with the East Indies came in 1781, when he was selected by the East India Company to serve as governor of Madras, considered by many at the time as the most corrupt settlement in India. Macartney was anything but corrupt. According to Holden Furber, during his tenure as governor from 1781 to 1787, he "gained a reputation for personal integrity which had seldom been approached in the whole history of the Madras Presidency."[18] His reputation as an honest civil servant earned him the respect and trust of Henry Dundas.

The peculiar circumstances of Macartney's service in Madras during the 1780s made him unlikely to sympathize with George Smith of Canton. In Madras, Macartney had already dealt with a group of creditors, namely those of the nawab of Arcot, Muhammad Ali Khan Wallajah. The financial scandal in Madras was so encompassing by 1780 that the Company decided to send out a replacement governor, and so it was left to George Macartney to take on the infamous local corruption. Not surprisingly, his tenure was marked by acrimonious quarrels, including one that escalated into a duel with a Company army general. When Governor Macartney learned that the Board of Control for Indian affairs in London had succumbed to pressure from Warren Hastings, governor of Bengal, and the Madras creditors' lobbyists, and had overturned his decision regarding the nawab's revenues, Macartney resigned his post and returned to England in disgust.[19] Macartney may not have enjoyed his tenure as governor of Madras, but at least he fared better than his predecessor, Governor Pigot.

Several years later, when the British government approached Macartney about leading Britain's first embassy to China, he expressed skepticism. Macartney refused to be a stooge to those looking to use the embassy for private gain. "Will there not be fifty knaves and blockheads, who on the first hint of what is in agitation, will, by the means of connections and other circumstances, intrude themselves into the business, destroy all the credit that able and honest men might acquire in it, and defeat all the benefits intended to the public?" he asked his secretary George Leonard Staunton. Certainly not he, "nor any wise man," would embark on the ambassadorial mission "unless there was a fair prospect of making an honorable and prosperous voyage."[20]

He eventually overcame his reservations. During the nine-month voyage on board the *Lion,* Macartney took up creative writing to pass the time. In an appendix to his journal, entitled the "First Supplement to the Head. Trade and Commerce," he told the story of Paul Plunder, George Grasp, Patrick O'Robbery, and Ander MacMurder, who

> set their heads together and project a money voyage to another country where altho' lending money to the natives even at legal interest be against Laws, and consequently must be doubly criminal, if at usury; nevertheless such is the force of habit and the allurements of lucre, they run the risk and prosecute the adventure. They take bonds from the Chinese bearing 18 percent for some little time, receive regular payments and hug themselves for their sagacity in discovering these new Indies of enrichment. However what everyone, not absolutely blinded by cupidity, might expect soon happened; The borrowers were ruined by this exorbitant rate of interest, and became absolutely incapable to fulfill their engagements.

The lenders then cry out in all the fury of disappointed voracity and loudly reprobate as a fraud the insolvency, of which they themselves were the authors. As indefatigable, as insatiable, they pursue their object, without remission, and without any consideration whatsoever before them but the recovery of their losses. They had the audacity to commit the honour of their sovereign in the infamy of their proceedings and engage his admiral to send an English man of war to enforce their scandalous demands at Canton. Notwithstanding the illegality of their claim, the regency of Canton listen to it, with attention and order a considerable part of it to be paid out of the emperor's treasury reserving to themselves the settlement of the business of the debtors. The Chinese government however acted on this occasion with their usual artifice and policy. As they could recover nothing from debtors, who they found had been already stripped, they were resolved not to be entirely the dupes of the claimants, and that the emperor should not pay out of his own pocket what he had received no value for. As the right of making such regulation in their own ports as they judge fit cant well be disputed altho' it may be complained of, they, in order to reimburse themselves laid an additional tax upon the foreign trade to Canton, intending it to fall, as indeed it does, chiefly upon the English, who then considered as the occasion of the trouble of expence they had been put to, so that by this adventure of a few usurers from India not only the English East India Company, but all the other European Companies at Canton, are saddled with a new burden on their commerce, which it may be very difficult, if even impossible, to get free from. But this is not all, these money lenders instead of being satisfied with having got, what they had no right to expect, are vociferous for more and actually importune the minister to make himself the shylock of their rapacity, and to exact for them all the penalties and forfeitures of the bonds.[21]

Macartney had no sympathy for either "George Grasp" or George Smith. He criticized these "usurers from India" for their "cupidity," their disregard for Chinese law, and their audacious sense of entitlement to the British government's support. They were making Prime Minister Pitt and Henry Dundas the "shylock of their rapacity" and saddling the East India Company "with a new burden on their commerce."[22]

Macartney did not stop there. He also penned a satirical piece that told the story of several Chinese merchants who petitioned the king of England to recover 40,000 taels from two British traders, Peter Paneras and Samuel Smithfield. The tables were now turned. The Chinese petitioners reasoned that since the British government had so generously helped Plunder, Grasp, O'Robbery, and MacMurder, the same could be done for them. What motivated Macartney to write these tales? Perhaps we can take him at his word that he wrote "merely for his own amusement and to pass away some tedious time of a very long sea voyage." Whatever his motivation, Ambassador Macartney would not be a "stooge" to the British creditors.[23] Had Ambassador Cathcart survived the voyage to China in 1788, the British creditors' complaints would have been presented to the Qianlong emperor by Britain's first ambassador to China. The vagaries of history had it otherwise.

George Smith of Canton finally had to give up any hope of recovering his fortune in China. A new bankruptcy bill being discussed in Parliament in 1794, however, might have at least released him from the grip of his creditors. The bill, officially titled "An act for the relief of certain insolvent debtors," originated in the House of Lords and was read in the House of Commons on May 12, 1794. Smith hoped that an amendment might be added to the bill in the House of Commons (where two of his creditors, George Vansittart and Ewan Law, served as MPs) absolving Smith of his debts.

Smith of Canton turned to his powerful "dear friend" David Scott for help.[24] Scott was initially reluctant to get involved, but Smith appealed to his compassion: "Let me entreat you my friend to deliver my letter to Mr. Dundas, consider how anxious I must be to get relieved from my oppressed situation."[25] Moved by his friend's pleas, he ultimately suggested to Dundas that the British government should help Smith, citing "the long series of distresses which the unfortunate George Smith has gone through owing to the Chinese government and our having no law to give him relief (as it would have done had he met his misfortune in this country)."[26] Scott described Smith of Canton as a "very honest man, he has a very large family and if at liberty indefatigable industry."[27] Moreover, he indicated that Smith's creditors in the House of Commons would move for Smith's amendment if Dundas would support it.[28] All seemed to be riding on Dundas.

Smith's petition was read in the House of Commons. It presented the general state of trade in Canton in addition to the particulars of his case. Smith offered to testify in person at the bar of the House if it were deemed necessary. He claimed to have been waiting for years "to state my whole case at the bar," to present "a plain tale . . . easily told, and a more oppressive one I will venture to say never came before the house. I thank my god I am afraid of no man or set of men that exists."[29] The House decided to refer Smith's petition to a committee; the petition was also referred to "Mr. Law, Mr. Francis etc.," who were to meet the following morning at nine in the Speaker's Chamber and who "had the power to send for persons, papers and records."[30]

A couple of days later, the committee's report was read in the House of Commons. Two former Company supercargos, themselves also creditors of the Chinese merchants, were questioned, and confirmed the veracity of Smith's petition.[31] Several members of the House verified that Smith had promptly delivered a statement of his accounts to his creditors when he returned to England in 1782. Joseph Ward, solicitor to the Commission of Bankruptcy, testified that all but thirteen of Smith's numerous creditors had consented to relinquish their claims on him. Several members of the House later corrected Ward's statement; only eight refused to release Smith from his financial obligations to them. The House then ordered that the "report do lie on the table."[32]

The committee's report seems to have died on the table. Smith's petition and the committee's report on that petition do not appear to have been officially discussed in Parliament again.[33] Smith's clause was not included in any of the amendments added by the House of Commons to the Lords bill, nor did Smith's clause appear in the final draft of the Insolvent Debtors Bill, which was passed by both houses and received royal assent.[34]

Several years later, in 1798, Smith of Canton again asked his "most sincere friend" David Scott to present his case to Dundas. Unfortunately for Smith, "the opinion was that however hard your case certainly was, yet our Laws were by the great majority deemed rather too lenient already . . . there could be no chance of carrying the alteration at present as proposed by you." Scott was "very sorry for this, but there is no help for it."[35]

Smith of Canton died on February 1, 1808, in Stoke-next-Guilford, Surrey, and was buried in the yard adjoining St. John's Stoke Church, where the Smith family's memorial plaque still hangs today.[36]

But before we conclude too hastily that George Smith of Canton died in penury, the evidence suggests, to the contrary, that he and his family managed to lead a comfortable life after returning to England. That the Smith family survived this ordeal is largely thanks to Smith of Canton's wife, Charlotte. She and her family in Surrey provided Smith a financial cushion and refuge from his business failures in Canton.

Charlotte Smith née Peche had brought her own property to the marriage. She possessed £6,000 in addition to "diamonds, pearls and jewels" that she had inherited from her late husband, James Smith, Esq., of Bombay, who had been employed by the East India Company before his death.[37] When George and Charlotte were married, they placed her inheritance in a trust under the management of David Scott, George Moubray, John Fergusson, and James Sibbald, all prominent Scottish traders in India who were also friends and relatives of the Smith family. According to David Scott, the principal of £6,000 was remitted to England in 1786 through the Company's bills of exchange. Realizing that the interest "would only yield £223 per annum, for the maintenance of the family," Sibbald transferred the principal back to India and placed it in the East India Company's treasury in Bombay. During the early 1800s, Alexander Adamson, a former business partner of David Scott's and prominent cotton trader in Bombay, was helping Charlotte Smith earn high "Indian" returns, 9 percent per year, on her marriage settlement.[38]

According to the law of coverture in early modern Britain, "a husband and wife were one person—the husband—and therefore their property was his." Because Charlotte was a femme "covert" (legally "covered" by her husband), the property she brought to her marriage to Smith of Canton should have come under his immediate control.[39] By creating a trust in Charlotte's name, the Smiths instead placed legal responsibility for Charlotte's wealth in the hands of the Smiths' friends and colleagues. The trust secured her "a good and sufficient jointure against all the risques that may happen by loss in trade."[40] It was not atypical for widows who remarried to protect their property. Charlotte may have insisted on this type of marriage settlement to secure her own finances and establish a degree of legal and economic autonomy from her husband despite Britain's patriarchal laws.

It is also possible that the Smiths used Charlotte's trust to protect their new family's assets from the hazards and uncertainties of George Smith's business. By 1778, Smith of Canton already had more than an inkling of the pending financial crisis in Canton. With the establishment of Charlotte's trust, even if Smith of Canton went bankrupt, his creditors could not touch her £6,000. This financial strategy became increasingly common among middle-class shopkeepers during the nineteenth century, with over one-third of them placing in trust the property of their wives and daughters in an effort to protect family assets against potential creditors. Commercial lobbyists responded by pressing for legislation that would make married women "partly liable for familial debt." This pressure encouraged Parliament to pass the Married Women's Property Act in 1870, a historic piece of legislation that gave married women much greater control over their earnings and property.[41]

Charlotte also brought real estate to the marriage. When the East India Company finally expelled the Smith family from China in 1782, George, Charlotte, and their young daughters, Charlotte Eleanora and Harriet Ann, settled in her family's natal village of Stoke-next-Guildford, Surrey. From 1791 to 1807, George Smith paid one pound sixteen shillings per year in land tax as the proprietor and occupier of a piece of property in Surrey. In 1808, the year of Smith's death, Charlotte Smith appears in the land tax records instead, paying the same amount on a piece of property. This may have been the same property that Charlotte's father, John Peche, indirectly transferred to her in 1793 through a trust managed by David Scott, George Moubray, Henry Browne, and Lestock Wilson.[42] These trustees were clearly close friends and relations of the Smith family, since the Smiths named several of their children after the first three men. Once again, property was put into a trust in Charlotte's name to protect it from the debts and liabilities of her husband's business. Charlotte's father stipulated that the property not be subject to George Smith's "intermeddling or disposal nor shall the same or any part thereof be any ways subject to the debts power controul or engagements."[43]

In 1808, just four months after George Smith's death, Charlotte sold the property for £900 and moved to Devonshire Street, Portland Place, in Middlesex County, London.[44] The wealth of Charlotte Smith, along with the strategic use of trusts and the loyalty of well-connected friends and relatives, allowed the Smith family to emerge intact from George Smith's financial disaster in China and subsequent bankruptcy. The Smiths were "neither destitute of friends or of money," and so the Smith family survived.[45]

Still, George and Charlotte worried about their finances and the future prospects of their children. None of Charlotte's letters survive, but we can glean some of her thoughts and concerns from David Scott's correspondence with her. While Charlotte, the wife of a major Canton financier, insisted she was "a stranger to the subject of finances," she had no trouble taking charge of her family's finances when her husband was ill and writing directly to Scott about the management of her money. She angrily referred to the £6,000 under Scott's management as "the wreck" of her marriage settlement and complained that it was "incumbered with long unsettled accounts." Scott tried to convince Charlotte to put her situation in perspective: "You may regret that you are not richer, but I should think you would receive satisfaction were you to take a view of many genteel families not having near so much, and deeming themselves happy, to be so well off." Regarding the future of the Smith children, Scott expressed more compassion: "As to the children unprovided for, I feel with you, the anxiety they must," but he blamed their father, George, for not taking Scott's advice and accepting a Bengal cadetship when Smith's son had reached the appropriate age. Perhaps the Smiths had set their sights on a civil rather than military position in the Company.[46]

The Smith children ultimately thrived. With their mother's death in 1833, they inherited £900 to be divided equally among themselves. Charlotte bequeathed her home in Portland Place, as well as her plate, linen, china, pictures, books, clothing, and furniture, to her two eldest daughters, whom she hoped would live together there. She left an annuity of £100 to another daughter, Caroline Moubray, and gave her youngest son, David Scott Smith, the sum of £500. She directed in her will that her daughters "shall have and enjoy their respective shares of my said residuary estate to and for their separate use respectively and free from the interference control debts or engagement of any husband or husband whom they or either of them have married or shall happen to marry; and I do hereby authorize and empower my said daughters or any or either of them not withstanding their coverture to give or dispose of their said respective shares by deed or will as they or any or either of them shall think proper."[47] As the widow of a bankrupted trader, Charlotte must have felt particularly anxious to keep her daughters' inheritance out of the hands of potential future husbands.

The two eldest daughters, Harriet Ann and Charlotte Eleanora, who had both been born in Macao, never married. Financially speaking, they apparently had no need to. Harriet Ann and Charlotte Eleanora both left wills (an achievement in itself), demonstrating that they lived comfortable lives independent of men.[48] As "fund-holders," those who could live off of the interest and profits from their stocks, annuities, and investments, Charlotte Eleanora and Harriet Ann supported themselves and their brother's children. At some point, Harriet Ann moved from her Portland Place home in Middlesex, which she had inherited from her mother, to the fashionable nineteenth-century spa-town, Cheltenham, in Gloucester. According to the 1851 census, she employed two female servants in her home, Chandos Cottage.[49]

In 1856, Charlotte Eleanora bequeathed £100 to be paid annually to her brother David Scott, £1,000 to be divided between David's two sons, all her plate and plated goods to go to her nieces, and twenty-nine shares in an assurance society to go to other kin.[50] What is perhaps most informative, she instructed her trustees about the management of her investments, authorizing them "to continue the present investments of my property or to alter vary and change the same from time to time as they may think proper. And I declare that such investments are not to be unnecessarily confined to the funds of Great Britain but may include those of foreign governments and stock of the East India Company."[51]

Caroline Moubray Smith and Louisa Scott Smith, unlike their two older sisters, chose to marry. Their choices in marriage partners suggest that the Smith family enjoyed relatively high social status in England. Caroline Moubray's husband, Colonel Edward Boscawen Frederick of Berkeley Square, Middlesex, served as lieutenant colonel in the British Army.[52] And Louisa Scott's husband, William Seton Charters, was the officiating surgeon for the East India Company's presidency in Calcutta. Their marriage lasted until Louisa's death in 1833 at the age of thirty-nine after "severe sufferings endured on board the *Lord Amherst*" in a hurricane. She left three young daughters behind.[53]

Two of George and Charlotte's four sons achieved significant success. George Fordyce and George Moubray obtained positions as officers in the East India Company's military in Madras, but they both died in India relatively young.[54] Henry Browne was the only Smith son who survived his military service in India. He was "fitted out" by his mother, Charlotte, "at a considerable expense" when he took his position in India.[55] He rose to the rank of colonel in the East India Company's army before retiring in 1839 and moving to Bristol, where he died in 1866, leaving an estate worth just under £8,000.[56] He was already so successful by 1833 that his mother believed he was "sufficiently provided for" such that there was no need to make "any further provision for him" in her will.[57]

Henry Browne and his wife, Jane Maria, raised six children during their time in Madras. Their only son, Mowbray Henry Ochterlony, later became a captain in Her Majesty's East Indian Army.[58] Their eldest daughter, Jane, never married and, like her aunts Charlotte Eleanora and Harriet Ann, was described as a "fundholder" in the 1861 British census. The two youngest daughters, Emily Matilda Jane and Anna Mary, both married East India Company Army officers. Emily Matilda Jane's husband,

Henry Charles Zachary Claridge, was a colonel in the Madras Staff Corps "who served for many years in the 7th Madras Grenadiers." The couple had seven children, all born in Tamil Nadu, India.[59] An elaborate grave, a "house like" stone tomb with a Celtic cross, still stands in the Ryde New Cemetery on the Isle of Wight, just off the southern coast of England, commemorating both Colonel Claridge and his wife, Emily Matilda Jane Claridge née Smith, who died in 1899 and 1918, respectively.[60] Anna Mary and her husband, Captain Charles Tulloch, raised two children in India as well.

David Scott Smith, Esq., George and Charlotte Smith's youngest son, did not follow in the path of his older brothers. Instead, he remained in England, where he worked as superintending clerk in the Admiralty, the department of the government in charge of the Royal Navy. He and his wife, Amelia Louisa Hare, lived in Marylebone and Kensington, Middlesex, where they raised four children (Edward Fordyce, Amy Harriet, Charlotte Cecil, and James Stuart) with the help of a governess and five other female servants.[61] When David Scott Smith, Esq., died, he left an estate worth slightly less than £6,000.

George Smith of Madras

Like George Smith of Canton, George Smith of Madras worried about his family's future. After leaving Madras and setting sail for England in 1779, George and his wife, Margaretta Aurora, and their children, Aurora Catherine, Catherine Frances, George, Jemima Claudia, and Henrietta Christiana, made their new home in Upper Harley Street in the parish of St. Marylebone in Middlesex. This surpassed Smith's earlier prediction that he would probably only earn enough to retire to his native Scotland.

Smith of Madras's bankruptcy in 1782, however, changed everything.[62] He was able to make payments to his creditors in 1783, 1784, 1786, 1789, and 1790 and placed on auction at the Bank Coffee-House his "remarkably large oriental ruby," advertised to be "of the first colour and perfection and weighing one hundred and four grains and three quarters." He decided, though, that the only escape from bankruptcy was to return to the East Indies. His creditors allowed him to retain a "certain sum out of such his late estate" so that he could settle in India and try to regain his fortune.[63]

In 1783, Smith and his wife, Margaretta Aurora, said their goodbyes to each other. He set sail on the *Bessborough* for Calcutta, hoping that he might "make some comfortable provision for a family of hopeful children."[64] Smith set up his own "agency and scrivener's office," which was removed to No. 125 Neemtullah in the Cossitolla Bazaar in Calcutta.[65] In a newspaper advertisement, he announced to "his friends and the public in general" that his agency continued to "transact, as usual, all money and commercial matters, as well as all kinds of conveyancing and notarial business on the most reasonable terms. N.B. Company's paper [i.e., Company bonds], &c. bought and sold on commission."[66] Smith of Madras also advertised that bills of exchange on Madras, Bombay, and England could be had on application at his office in the bazaar, where he faithfully negotiated "all money matters, remittances and commercial transactions."[67] The Calcutta newspaper ads suggest that Smith of Madras was a jack of many trades, providing various commercial services to the community as notary and scrivener, real-estate agent, commission merchant, wholesale and retail merchant, stock trader, and broker.[68]

Although Smith of Madras based his business in Calcutta, he was frequently at sea, on business trips to various parts of India, Southeast Asia, and China. He traded extensively at various locations up and down both sides of the Indian coastline from Bengal in the northeast to Bombay in the northwest, in addition to the island of Ceylon (Sri Lanka). He also ventured to Sumatra, Penang (then called Prince of Wales Island), and China. He was at sea so often that he requested letters to him to be sent to his attorneys, Andrew Ross of Madras or John Fergusson of Calcutta, "either of whom will forward it to me wheresoever I may be."[69] Smith of Madras traded extensively with Indian merchants and artisans and claimed to possess "knowledge of the industry, and ability of the native merchants" in addition to "mercantile authority derived from the information of very considerable native merchants."[70]

For all his effort, Smith of Madras never managed to restore his fortune. He had no choice but to set sail, season after season, to ply his trade throughout the Indian Ocean and the South China Sea. He was probably nearing sixty years of age toward the end of the 1780s. Exhausted by his perpetual migratory situation and "anxious to provide for a large and hopeful family of children," he wished to have a "fixed abode" to collect his children under his "parental eye."[71] He repeatedly attempted to evoke Henry Dundas's sympathy by describing his "intention to leave Calcutta in search of bread for myself and family, which I must do, but at my time of life a residence on shore is to be preferred to voyaging and ploughing the ocean," and expressing his hope that Dundas's "generous and powerful influence will succeed for my establishment here in such manner as will prove creditable and advantageous to me."[72] In a November 1785 letter he proposed Awadh as a territory where he might hang his hat and make a living engaging in local trade, "this being a field unconnected with the privileges deemed within the provinces, by the covenanted servants of the Company."[73] Dundas seems not to have replied to this request, so Smith was forced to keep braving the oceans. Once again, in 1787, Smith complained to Dundas: "I am far advanced in life, unfortunate therein without employment, and a certain subsistence, or provision for a large and hopeful family."[74]

Smith of Madras also agonized over securing employment for his only son, George Junior. He continually pleaded with Dundas to appoint George Jr. as a writer for the East India Company in Bengal. In 1785, Smith described his son as a "fine promising" nine-year-old who studied at school with the Reverend Mr. Mannery Kensington Gore. George Jr. had also been educated in writing and merchant's accounts under the supervision of the headmaster of the prestigious Harrow School.[75] While Smith understood that seeking a writership for such a young child might seem ridiculous, he reminded Dundas in the postscript to his letter that should Dundas need precedents, "the Directors [of the East India Company] will I have no doubts be so candid as to furnish them in cases in point, with respect to the promotion of their own sons, and nephews at a similar age into the service."[76] In 1791, just several months before his death, Smith of Madras again beseeched Dundas for help, reminding him of "my dear boy . . . a word from you Sir, will provide for the Boy for life, the obligation thereby conferred on the Father never can be effaced from his memory."[77]

In 1793, two years after his father's death, George Jr. obtained a Company writership in Bombay.[78] He had sailed to Bengal in 1791 on a Company ship, the *Cornwallis,* and only learned of his Company appointment in 1795, after returning to England on the *Manship.* George Jr. hastily sailed back to India to take up his position in Bombay.[79] His career in India was short-lived, though. In 1807, the *Gentleman's Magazine* reported the death of "George Smith, esq. collector of Guntroa Circar, son of the late Geo. Smith, esq. of Bengal."[80] He left all his worldly belongings to his younger sister, Jemima Claudia, who had married a British Army captain in the 12th Regiment of Foot named Walter Ruding at the Cape of Good Hope in 1797.[81]

In 1797, the same year Jemima Claudia got married, George and Margaretta Aurora's youngest daughter, Henrietta Christiana, the child who had been born at the Cape of Good Hope on the Smith family's journey with William Hickey from Madras to Britain in 1779–80, married an East India Company man, Thomas Frederick Bevan, Esquire, in Berahmpore, Bengal.[82] Thomas Frederick worked his way up the Company ranks to senior merchant before his death in 1808.[83] The couple's only child, Henrietta Anne Bevan, was born in Berahmpore (Baharampur), Bengal, in 1803.[84]

George and Margaretta Aurora Smith's eldest daughter, Aurora Catherine, also lived in Berhampore, where she married twice. Her marriage in 1792 to Robin Maxwell, a captain in the Company's army, lasted just over a year. In 1793, she married another Company Army officer, Lieutenant Colonel John Clerkson, with whom she had several children. Eleven years after her second husband's death, in Cawnpore (Kanpur) in 1801, she petitioned for, and was granted, a pension from the East India Company to support herself and her children. The family's relationship with the Company continued through Aurora Catherine and John Clerkson's son, Henry Chambers Clerkson. With the support of his grandmother, Margaretta Aurora Smith, seventeen-year-old Henry Chambers Clerkson applied for and was granted a cadetship in the East India Company's Bengal infantry in 1812.[85]

The Smith family's connection to India continued in curious ways that George Smith of Madras could not have imagined. A little over a year after his death in Bengal in 1791, Smith's wife, Margaretta Aurora, remarried. This time she chose William Petrie, a high-ranking East India Company employee who had worked off and on in Madras between 1765 and 1807. Margaretta Aurora's family, the Munros, had deep roots in Madras, so it is likely the two were acquaintances, perhaps friends, in Madras before the Smith family left for England in 1779. Given the length and danger of the voyage between England and India, William Petrie commuted between Madras and London surprisingly frequently.[86] He even escorted George Jr., George Smith of Madras's fifteen-year-old son, to Bengal on the *Cornwallis* in 1791.[87] It seems likely that William Petrie played some role in arranging a Company appointment for George Jr., who obtained the writership in Bombay not long after his mother's marriage to Petrie.

The new couple also produced their own son, William Petrie Jr., who later went to work for the East India Company in Bengal. While living in London during the 1790s, William Petrie, the father, served as a member of Parliament for East Retford from 1796 to 1802, but the large debts he accrued, the result of imprudent investments, drove him to return to Madras in 1799 to regain his fortune. Sixteen years after Margaretta Aurora and George Smith of Madras said their good-byes, she bade farewell to yet another insolvent India-bound husband.[88]

William Petrie, during his final stint in the East Indies, served not only as the acting governor of Madras but also as the governor of Penang until his death in 1816. Coincidentally, just two decades earlier, the island's praises had been sung by none other than George Smith of Madras. In 1790, Smith had strongly urged Henry Dundas to continue supporting the young British settlement and even claimed partial responsibility for the colonization of Penang in 1786. Could Smith of Madras ever have imagined that his wife, Margaretta Aurora, would marry the future governor of the British colony he claimed "as a child of my own"? In his darkest moments in Bengal during the last few years of his life, Smith of Madras might have found

William Petrie's grave in Northam Road Cemetery, George Town, Penang. Photograph by the author.

it difficult to picture his family's future success: the five leasehold houses in London, the library of books, the house full of servants, the diamond and coral jewelry, the investments and £2,000 annuity—all the wealth his wife enjoyed after his death.[89]

George Smith of Bombay

Out of the three Smiths, it was George Smith of Bombay who achieved the greatest commercial success. Only he managed to hold on to his fortune until his death. In 1789, Smith of Bombay set sail on the East Indiaman the *Winterton* to return at long last to his native Scotland. He never made it home.

The *Winterton* had already rounded the Cape of Good Hope and was heading toward St. Helena in the Atlantic Ocean when Smith of Bombay found his "strength daily diminishing." Dr. Wilson, the ship's surgeon, did what he could, but on January 22, 1790, Smith of Bombay passed away. He was fifty-two. His death was recorded in the ship's log: "At ½ past 10 PM departed this life Mr. George Smith a passenger, at ½ past 11 PM committed his body to the deep."[90] The mood on board the *Winterton* the next morning was undoubtedly somber when Smith's will was read out loud, "as he desired before his death," and his effects were "disposed of . . . as he directed." For "trouble and care of attention to me," Dr. Wilson received 100 German Crowns, a silver chocolate pot "as a memorandum of me," and various trinkets and curiosities, including Smith of Bombay's seal, printed books, a small French watch, a pair of pistols, and one gun. Smith's servant, David Lockwood, received money in addition to his wages, all of Smith's table linen, furniture, clothes, bed linen, bedding, a pair of pistols, one gun, a camphor-wood chest, and a basket of seeds. To Lieutenant George Manuel, Smith bequeathed "a silver cup with a cover as a token of my esteem." George Dundas, the ship's captain, received Smith's remaining liquors and provisions.[91]

Smith of Bombay died a bachelor, and he appears to have had only one living child, the daughter named Felicia whom he fathered with Esperanza Gaspar D'Almina in India. Although Smith of Bombay did not bring D'Almina and Felicia with him on his return voyage to Scotland, he ensured that his daughter was well provided for. This was standard practice for Scots who fathered children with Indian women. Andrew Mackillop, who sampled the wills of Scots who died in Madras and Bombay between 1780 and 1790, found not one Scotsman who "made any provision for Indian women to be sent to Europe with their children," although several bequeathed money to their offspring and lovers.[92] Smith of Bombay left his daughter £1,500 to be given to her when she married or turned eighteen, whichever came first. Until then, the money would be entrusted to Alexander Adamson and James Forbes, prominent private traders in Bombay, who would act as Felicia's legal guardians. Smith of Bombay directed them to invest the money in securities of 3 percent consolidated stock. When Felicia turned five years old, she would receive annual interest from this fund not exceeding £50 per year. This money was intended to support

Felicia and cover her education costs. Besides child support, Smith did not leave anything in his will to Felicia's mother.[93]

While Smith of Bombay made provision for his daughter in India, he "left the bulk of his estate to be divided among his five sisters or their descendents." Only three of the Smith sisters established their claim to his estate, so the rest was donated, as Smith of Bombay had directed in his will, to his hometown of Fordyce. He instructed his executors that £1,000 should be deposited in the hands of the magistrates of Banff to endow an infirmary or hospital. Another £25 per year should be paid to the parson or minister of the town and parish of Fordyce to augment his yearly stipend.

Perhaps most important, Smith of Bombay used his East Indies fortune to endow a school, later known as Fordyce Academy. He arranged for £40 per year to go to a schoolmaster skilled in English and modern commercial languages (French and Dutch) in accounts and mathematics who would reside in Fordyce "for the purpose of teaching and educating during the term of five years as many boys of the name Smith (giving a preference to those who can prove a relationship to me) as the interest of the remaining part and residue of the unclaimed shares and reversions of

Old postcard of Fordyce Academy.

my estate can maintain and admit of at the yearly allowance of twenty five (25) pounds sterling to each boy." Smith of Bombay further directed "that the children of my sisters and their issue to the fourth generation of what name soever may be admitted to and partake of this bounty (which shall be called and known by the name of George Smith's bounty) if they claim it and prove their right."[94] According to a historian of the Fordyce Academy, the Banff magistrates received over £10,297 in government bonds, which provided a yearly revenue of roughly £308 to run the school. "George Smith's bounty," which was administered by the magistrates of Banff from 1801 to 1890, made it possible for generations of Scottish boys to follow in Smith of Bombay's footsteps.[95]

The travels of the three Mr. Smiths and their families have shown the inner workings of a global financial system connecting Britain, India, and China that depended on private British capital and helped to extend Britain's imperial reach in Asia. Their actions and motives have given a new perspective on the planning of Britain's first embassy to China. The importance of Scots in the British empire, not only in America, India, and Australia but also in China, is underlined by their adventures, just as the journeys, letters, investments, marriages, and minutiae of their lives have made visible the connections among a variety of seemingly disparate cultural, social, political, and economic phenomena across the eighteenth-century world—specifically, tea drinking, migration, global finance, social mobility, cross-cultural trade, diplomacy, and imperial expansion.

Over half a century ago, historians expressed pessimism about the possibility of uncovering the origins and business practices of a "small but peculiarly compact merchant community of free traders, whose economic basis was the Country Trade with India."[96] By moving beyond state- and company-centric histories and paying attention to the "drivers of empire," who were often obscure individuals and families "operating at or beyond different frontiers who acted in their own interest," we see with fresh eyes how empires spread, how globalization happens.[97] Sustained examination of the three George Smiths and their economic relationships with Asian elites in India and China reveals the risky ways global commerce was financed. It also shows how the British empire was made at the micro-economic level through countless financial exchanges in the port cities of maritime Asia. The economic and political effects of these financial relationships were felt far and wide. The adventures and mishaps of the three George Smiths and private traders like them changed the course of world history. If it is true that "the archives are bursting with as-yet-untold stories of people living on the eastern edges of empire," then more of these stories need to be told.[98]

Eighteenth-Century Currency Equivalents

A British pound	is equivalent to	20	shillings
		3	taels
		10	rupees
		4	Spanish dollars
		2.50	pagodas
A Spanish dollar	is equivalent to	5	shillings
		0.07	taels
		2.50	rupees
		0.63	pagodas
An Indian rupee	is equivalent to	2	shillings
		0.33	taels
		0.40	Spanish dollars
		0.25	pagodas
An Indian pagoda	is equivalent to	8	shillings
		1.20	taels
		4.00	rupees
		1.50	Spanish dollars
A Chinese tael	is equivalent to	6	shillings and 8 pence
		1.39	Spanish dollars
		3.06	rupees
		0.83	pagodas

(Adapted from Pritchard, *The Crucial Years of Early Anglo-Chinese Relations*, p. 103)

Notes

Abbreviations of Archives

BL	British Library
BLYU	Beinecke Library, Yale University Library
CUL	Cornell University Library
DRO	Durham Record Office
JRL	John Rylands Library
NAH	National Archives, The Hague
NAS	National Archives of Scotland
NLA	National Library of Australia
NLS	National Library of Scotland
NMA	Nordiska Museet Arkivet
NMM	National Maritime Museum
NRO	Northumberland Record Office
PRO	National Archives (Kew), Public Record Office
RAC	National Archives (Rigsarkivet)
SHC	Surrey History Centre
TBA	The Baring Archive

Introduction

1. Mistakes regarding the identities of the three George Smiths can be found in the following works: Greenberg, *British Trade and the Opening of China,* p. 20; NLS, Handlist to Melville Papers, Mss., 1053–61, "Letters of George Smith Member of the Bengal Council, 1785–91" (George Smith of Madras was never a member of the Bengal Council); Morse, *Chronicles of the East India Company Trading to China,* vol. 2, pp. 4–5; vol. 5, pp. 102–3 (Morse confuses George Smith of Madras with George Smith of Canton); McGilvary, *East India Patronage and the British State,* pp. 175–76 (McGilvary confuses Smith of Madras with Smith of Bombay); Furber, *Henry Dundas, First Viscount Melville,* p. 49 (refers to "George Smith, a Bengal revenue official"); Dermigny, *La Chine et l'Occident,* vol. II, pp. 905–6; Van Dyke, *The Canton Trade,* p. 124 (Van Dyke repeats Morse's error); Warren, *The Sulu Zone,* pp. 41, 45–46 (Warren confuses George Smith of Madras with a Captain

George Smith who was active in trade several years after Smith of Madras's death in 1791).

2. Van Dyke, "The Anglo-Dutch Fleet of Defense."
3. Wills, "Trade and Diplomacy with Maritime Europe," pp. 192–93; Chang and Farrington, et al., *The English Factory in Taiwan,* p. 11.
4. Van Dyke, *The Canton Trade,* pp. 167–69.
5. BL Mss Eur C387/1–4 Scattergood Papers, passim.
6. Linqua and Anqua to John Scattergood, Feb. 1, 1715/16, BL Mss Eur C387/2 Scattergood Papers; Van Dyke, *Merchants of Canton and Macao,* vol. 1, pp. 20, 75.
7. Furber, *John Company at Work,* pp. 161–62.
8. Prakash, *European Commercial Enterprise in Pre-Colonial India,* p. 287.
9. Yang, Wu, and Deng, *Ming Qing Shiqi Aomen Wenti Dangan Wenxian Huibian,* Memorial from Governor Sun Shi Yi, 1784/12/30, Doc. 287, pp. 459–61.
10. Andrade, "A Chinese Farmer, Two African Boys, and a Warlord"; Ogborn, *Global Lives,* p. 9; Finn, "Anglo-Indian Lives in the Later Eighteenth and Early Nineteenth Centuries"; Wrightson, *Ralph Tailor's Summer,* p. xii; Ward, *Networks of Empire,* p. 31. See also Trivellato, "Is There a Future for Italian Microhistory in the Age of Global History?"
11. Cain and Hopkins, "Gentlemanly Capitalism and British Expansion Overseas I"; Cain and Hopkins, *British Imperialism,* pp. 68–76; Zahedieh, *The Capital and the Colonies,* pp. 28, 55–57; Mentz, *The English Gentleman Merchant at Work,* ch. 3; Webster, *Gentlemen Capitalists,* p. 21; Bowen, *The Business of Empire,* ch. 4; Bowen, "Investment and Empire in the Later Eighteenth Century."
12. There is an extremely large literature on this topic, but some of the key works include: G. Parker, *The Military Revolution;* Cipolla, *Guns, Sails, and Empires;* Pearson, "Merchants and States"; Jones, *The European Miracle;* Landes, *The Wealth and Poverty of Nations;* Mokyr, *Lever of Riches;* Hoffman, *Why Did Europe Conquer the World?*
13. Frank, *Re-Orient;* Pomeranz, *The Great Divergence;* Rosenthal and Wong, *Before and Beyond Divergence;* Parthasarathi, *Why Europe Grew Rich and Asia Did Not;* Clulow, *The Company and the Shogun,* p. 10.
14. Andrade, "Koxinga's Conquest of Taiwan in World History"; Clulow, *The Company and the Shogun,* p. 10.
15. J. Parker, "Scottish Enterprise in India"; Tomlinson, "The Empire of Enterprise"; Tomlinson, "From Campsie to Kedgerie"; Rothschild, *The Inner Life of Empires;* Cain, *The Cornchest for Scotland;* Bryant, "Scots in India in

the Eighteenth Century"; George McGilvary, *East India Patronage and the Indian State.*

16. Devine, *Scotland's Empire,* p. xxvii.
17. Frederic Davy to a Friend, May 30, 1776, BLYU, Osborn c594.
18. McCarthy, *A Global Clan;* Murdoch and Grosjean, *Scottish Communities Abroad in the Early Modern Period;* Murdoch, *Network North.*
19. Devine and McCarthy, "Introduction," p. 2.
20. Grace, *Opium and Empire;* Blake, *Jardine Matheson;* Watt, *Robert Fortune;* Rose, *For All the Tea in China;* Cheong, *Mandarins and Merchants.*
21. Prakash, *European Commercial Enterprise,* p. 287; Greenberg, *British Trade and the Opening of China,* p. 20.
22. Devine and McCarthy, "Introduction," p. 5.
23. Ward, *Networks of Empire;* Games, *Web of Empire;* Ballantyne, *Orientalism and Race.*
24. PRO, PROB 11/2243/311; PRO, PROB 11/1615/393.
25. Hall and Rose, "Introduction," p. 31. There has been much debate about the extent and nature of the empire's impact on British society. Some notable works include: Wilson, *Island Race;* B. Porter, *The Absent-Minded Imperialists;* Mackenzie, *Propaganda and Empire;* Burton, *Burdens of History.*
26. Cormack, *An Historic Outline of the George Smith Bounty.*
27. Harlow, *The Founding of the Second British Empire,* vol. 2, p. 486; Pritchard, *The Crucial Years of Early Anglo-Chinese Relations,* pp. 231–32.

Chapter One. Tea and Finance

1. See Berg, *Luxury and Pleasure in Eighteenth-Century Britain;* Berg et al., *Goods from the East.*
2. There is a growing literature on chinoiserie in early modern Britain. See Honour, *Chinoiserie;* Impey, *Chinoiserie;* Beevers, *Chinese Whispers;* Jenkins, *A Taste for China;* Sloboda, *Chinoiserie.*
3. For recent studies of the ways in which China was constructed and depicted in seventeenth- and eighteenth-century British Sinology, literature, and theater see: D. Porter, *The Chinese Taste in Eighteenth-Century England;* Kitson, *Forging Romantic China;* Markley, *The Far East and the English Imagination;* Yang, *Performing China.*
4. See Sharma, *Empire's Garden;* Gardella, *Harvesting Mountains,* p. 8.
5. Benn, *Tea in China,* p. 6; Sharma, *Empire's Garden,* pp. 30–31.
6. Sharma, *Empire's Garden,* pp. 35–37.

7. See Jordan Goodman's forthcoming book on Joseph Banks.
8. Sir Joseph Banks's letter to the deputy chairman of the East India Company, Dec. 27, 1788, BL Mss Eur D993.
9. Latham, *The Shorter Pepys,* p. 81.
10. Benn, *Tea in China,* p. 6.
11. Gardella, *Harvesting Mountains,* pp. 22–23; Benn, *Tea in China,* pp. 3–4.
12. Gardella, *Harvesting Mountains,* p. 25.
13. Benn, *Tea in China,* pp. 5–9.
14. Gardella, *Harvesting Mountains,* p. 30.
15. Benn, *Tea in China,* p. 17.
16. Xu Guoqi as quoted in Gardella, *Harvesting Mountains,* p. 21.
17. Van Dyke, *Merchants of Canton and Macao,* vol. 1, pp. 14–16.
18. Ibid.
19. Burnett, *Liquid Pleasures,* p. 50; Mair and Hoh, *The True History of Tea,* p. 169.
20. Rappaport, *A Thirst for Empire,* p. 34.
21. Dermigny, *La Chine et l'Occident,* vol. I, p. 382.
22. Chaudhurie, *The Trading World of Asia and the English East India Company,* p. 538.
23. Cole, "Trends in Eighteenth-Century Smuggling," pp. 395–410.
24. Shammas, "Changes in English and Anglo-American Consumption from 1550 to 1800," pp. 183–84.
25. Cunningham, ed., *The Letters of Horace Walpole,* vol. 1, p. 224.
26. *The Gentleman's Magazine,* 1731, vol. 1, p. 37; *Read's Weekly Journal; or, British Gazetteer,* Dec. 17, 1737, issue 693; *Weekly Miscellany,* Feb. 23, 1740, issue 374; *Read's Weekly Journal; or, British Gazetteer,* Mar. 10, 1750, issue 1332; *Gazetteer and London Daily Advertiser,* Nov. 8, 1760, issue 9853; Macfarlane and Macfarlane, *Green Gold,* p. 69; Nierstrasz, "The Popularization of Tea," p. 266.
27. Mair and Hoh, *The True History of Tea,* p. 175.
28. Burnett, *Liquid Pleasures,* pp. 52–53.
29. Shammas, "Changes in English and Anglo-American Consumption from 1550 to 1800," p. 184.
30. Hanser, "Teatime in the North Country."
31. Mackillop, "A North Europe World of Tea," pp. 297–98.
32. Carr and Walsh, "The Standard of Living in the Colonial Chesapeake," pp. 135–59.
33. Breen, "An Empire of Goods," pp. 467–99.
34. S. Smith, "Accounting for Taste," pp. 183–214.

35. W. Smith, *Consumption and the Making of Respectability,* pp. 123–24; Mintz, *Sweetness and Power,* pp. 108–22; Sheridan, *Sugar and Slavery,* pp. 18–29.
36. Macfarlane and Macfarlane, *Green Gold,* pp. 82–86.
37. DRO, Londonderry Papers, D/LO/F/751.
38. Weatherill, *Consumer Behaviour,* p. 159.
39. Lawson, "Women and the Empire of Tea," p. 9; Weatherill, *Consumer Behaviour,* p. 189.
40. *Newcastle Gazette,* Aug. 5, 1752; Rappaport, *A Thirst for Empire,* p. 39.
41. Elizabeth Carter to Elizabeth Robinson Montagu, Jan. 31, 1759, *Letters from Mrs. Elizabeth Carter to Mrs. Montagu*, vol. 1, p. 24.
42. NRO, Grey MSS, NRO 753, Box 1 G–I, Jan. 14, 1745, Ralph William Grey of Backworth.
43. Instructions to Cathcart, Nov. 30, 1787, BL IOR G/12/90, pp. 108–28.
44. Mui and Mui, "Smuggling and the British Tea Trade," pp. 44–73.
45. Mui and Mui, "'Trends in Eighteenth-Century Smuggling' Reconsidered."
46. Mui and Mui, "Smuggling and the British Tea Trade."
47. Mui and Mui, "William Pitt and the Enforcement of the Commutation Act."
48. Rappaport, *A Thirst for Empire,* p. 46.
49. Pritchard, *The Crucial Years of Early Anglo-Chinese Relations,* p. 146.
50. Henry Dundas, "Mr. Dundas's Letter to Mr. Baring on the East-India Trade," in East India Company, *Three Reports of the Select Committee,* 1793, pp. 130–40.
51. Letter from Court, Jan. 23, 1759, in H. N. Sinha, *Fort William–India House Correspondence,* vol. II, pp. 124–25.
52. Lord Cornwallis to Mr. Dundas, Nov. 4, 1788, NLS MS 3385.
53. Sinha, *Fort William–India House Correspondence,* vol. II, Jan. 23, 1759, pp. 124–25; vol. III, Dec. 31, 1760, p. 61; Dec. 23, 1761, p. 121.
54. Marshall, *The Making and Unmaking of Empires,* pp. 136–37; Arasaratnam, *Maritime Commerce and English Power,* pp. 2–3.
55. Arasaratnam, *Maritime Commerce and English Power,* p. 1.
56. Marshall, *Bengal,* p. 102.
57. Marshall, *East Indian Fortunes,* ch. 9.
58. Tripathi, *Trade and Finance in the Bengal Presidency,* ch. 1; Furber, *John Company at Work,* pp. 237–40.
59. Marshall, *East Indian Fortunes,* pp. 41–42.
60. Gurney, "The Debts of the Nawab of Arcot," pp. 38–39.
61. Marshall, *East Indian Fortunes*, pp. 70–72; Gurney, "The Debts of the Nawab of Arcot," pp. 37-53.

86. Henry Watson to Bengal Council, Mar. 29, 1781, BL IOR P/2/46, p. 182.
87. George Smith to Warren Hastings, Nov. 30, 1785, BL Add MS 29169, f. 138.
88. Thomas Fitzhugh to the Court of Directors, July 7, 1782, BL IOR E/1/71, pp. 7–10.
89. "Summary of Proceedings in the Third Session of Parliament," *The Gentleman's Magazine,* vol. 56, Part 2, pp. 967–68.
90. CUL, Copies of the East India Company Records, and Other Documents Relating to China and the China Trade Prepared for Lord Macartney's Information, vol. 1, "Queries put by the court of directors to persons now in England who have served the Company in China with the answers thereto 1791–2."
91. Ibid.
92. Morse, *The Chronicle of the Company Trading to Canton,* vol. 2, pp. 140–41.
93. Greenberg, *British Trade and the Opening of China,* pp. 112–13.
94. Bowen, *The Business of Empire,* p. 224; Van Dyke, *The Canton Trade,* p. 159.

Chapter Two. George Smith of Madras

1. Devine, *Scotland's Empire,* p. 252.
2. For a study on the British public's reception of nabobs during the eighteenth century see: Nechtman, *Nabobs.*
3. Marshall, "The Bengal Commercial Society of 1775."
4. Marshall, *East Indian Fortunes,* p. 48.
5. Frederic [Davy] to Brother Charles, Feb. 8, 1776, Letters January 1773, 1773-1777, BLYU, Osborn c594.
6. George Smith to Robert Palk, Oct. 4, 1770, BL Add MS 34686, p. 136; Marshall, *East Indian Fortunes,* pp. 216–17.
7. Frederic [Davy] to a Friend, May 30, 1776, Letters January 1773, 1773-1777, BLYU, Osborn c594.
8. Mackillop, "Accessing Empire."
9. Catterall, "Scots along the Mass," p. 171.
10. Meijers, *News from the Republick of Letters,* p. 2.
11. Macinnes and Hamilton, *Jacobitism, Enlightenment and Empire,* p. 1.
12. Grace, *Opium and Empire,* p. 3.
13. Plank, *Rebellion and Savagery,* pp. 8-9.
14. Grace, *Opium and Empire,* p. 5.
15. Ibid., p. 6. Plank, *Rebellion and Savagery,* pp. 1–26.

16. Marshall, *East Indian Fortunes,* pp. 20–21.
17. Parmentier, *Tea Time in Flanders;* Mueller, "Scottish and Irish Entrepreneurs in Eighteenth-Century Sweden."
18. Marshall, *East Indian Fortunes,* pp. 21–22.
19. Furber, "Madras in 1787," p. 256.
20. Marshall, *East Indian Fortunes,* pp. 22–23.
21. Morse, *The Chronicles of the East India Company Trading to China,* vol. 5.
22. *Nassau,* Monday, Dec. 20, 1779, BL IOR L/MAR/B/544G-H.
23. Spencer, *Memoirs of William Hickey,* vol. 2, p. 131.
24. Marshall, *East Indian Fortunes,* pp. 218–19.
25. "The most humble petition of the British European merchants to the Supreme Emperor of China," CUL, MSS DS117, George Macartney Papers, Asia Collections, vol. 10, doc. 430.
26. Capt. Mackintosh to Mr. Dundas, Dec. 20, 1791, G/12/91 Part 1.
27. G. Vansittart to Robert Palk, Calcutta, Apr. 2, 1773, Mss Eur F331/19, pp. 72–73.
28. Marshall, *East Indian Fortunes,* pp. 28, 240–41.
29. Frederic Davy to Charles Davy, Feb. 3–8, 1776, BLYU, Osborn c594.
30. Tripathi, *Trade and Finance in the Bengal Presidency,* pp. 9–10; Marshall, *East India Fortunes*, pp. 246–49.
31. Marshall, *East Indian Fortunes,* pp. 248–49; Marshall, "The Bengal Commercial Society of 1775"; Tomlinson, "The Only Merchant in Calcutta."
32. Prakash, *European Commercial Enterprise in Pre-Colonial India,* p. 287.
33. Frederick Davy to Charles Davy, Nov. 19, 1775, BLYU, Osborn c594.
34. McGilvary, *East India Patronage and the Indian State,* pp. 78–83.
35. Devine, *Scotland's Empire,* p. 269.
36. Love, *Vestiges of Old Madras,* vol. 3, pp. 550–51; McGilvary, *East India Patronage and the British State*, pp. 81–82.
37. Ibid., vol. 2, pp. 430, 456–57; vol. 3, p. 550; Dalrymple, *White Mughals,* p. 63.
38. Will of Andrew Munro, BL IOR/P/328/60, p. 147; Love, *Vestiges of Old Madras*, vol. 2, pp. 458–59; vol. 3, p. 553.
39. Will of Andrew Munro.
40. Ibid.
41. Smith to Dundas, Apr. 27, 1785, Nov. 30, 1785, Feb. 14, 1785, BL IOR/H/434.
42. BL IOR/J/1/15, pp. 241–45.
43. Devine, *Scotland's Empire,* pp. 262–63.
44. Smith to Bengal Council, Dec. 15, 1783, BL IOR/P/2/65, p. 151.

45. Smith to Thomas Saunders, Dec. 24, 1759, BL Add MS 34686.
46. Van Dyke, *Merchants of Canton and Macao,* vol. 1, pp. 29, 137–47.
47. Smith to Thomas Saunders, Dec. 24, 1759, BL Add MS 34686.
48. Van Dyke, *Merchants of Canton and Macao,* vol. 1, p. 144.
49. RAC Ask 1141–55, Negotieprotocolor for Kinafarere, Dec. 20, 1759, Dec. 22, 1761, Dec. 11, 1762, Dec. 24, 1763, Dec. 7, 1764. Thanks to Paul Van Dyke for generously sharing Swedish and Danish sources with me.
50. NMA, Inkomna skrivelser G-H (volym 4), Michael Grubb to His Brother, Sept. 11, 1763, Sept. 13, 1763, Sept. 19, 1763, Oct. 9, 1763, Oct. 14, 1763, May 5, 1764; NMA, Räkenskaper, Huvudbok, 1765–1766, enskilda affärer, register; Van Dyke, *The Canton Trade,* p. 123; Van Dyke, *Merchants of Canton and Macao,* vol. 1, p. 119; Van Dyke, *Merchants of Canton and Macao,* vol. 2., pp. 43–57.
51. Mann Horner and William Rous to the Council, Aug. 18, 1764, BL IOR/R/10/5; G. Mandevile and William Harrison to Mr. Fitzhugh and Council, Aug. 8, 1764, BL IOR/R/10/5.
52. Consultations, Aug. 18, 1764, BL IOR/R/10/5.
53. Dermigny, *La Chine et l'Occident,* vol. II, pp. 905–6. Here, Dermigny confuses George Smith of Canton with George Smith of Madras.
54. Consultations, Aug. 18, 1764, BL IOR/R/10/5.
55. Consultations, Aug. 23, 1764, and Consultations, Aug. 28, 1764. BL IOR/R/10/5.
56. For a history of Macao see: Souza, *Survival of Empire.*
57. Puga, *The British Presence in Macau,* p. 87.
58. Consultations, Sept. 5, 1764, Sept. 11, 1764, Sept. 30, 1764, BL IOR/R/10/5; George Smith to the Council, Sept. 4, 1764, BL IOR/R/10/5, p. 72; George Smith to the Council, Sept. 9, 1764, BL/IOR/R/10/5; Consultations, Sept. 30, 1764, BL IOR/R/10/5.
59. George Smith to the Council, Sept. 17–30, 1764, BL IOR/R/10/6, pp. 73–79.
60. Council to George Smith, Sept. 18, 1764, BL IOR/R/10/6, p. 74.
61. Smith to Alexander Wynch, Mar. 6, 1773, No. 205, *Report on the Palk Manuscripts,* London, 1922, pp. 216–17.
62. Marshall, *The Making and Unmaking of Empires,* p. 142; Love, *Vestiges of Old Madras,* vol. 3, pp. 61–63.
63. Marshall, *The Making and Unmaking of Empires,* pp. 230–37.
64. Smith to Palk, Oct. 4, 1770, BL Add MS 34686, p. 136.
65. Love, *Vestiges of Old Madras,* vol. 3, pp. 12–14, 554; Smith to Alexander Wynch, Mar. 6, 1773, No. 205, *Report on the Palk Manuscripts,* London, 1922, pp. 216–17.

66. Smith to Palk, Oct. 4, 1770, BL Add MS 34686.
67. Mentz, *The English Gentleman Merchant at Work,* p. 216.
68. Dalrymple, *White Mughals,* pp. 48–51.
69. Smith to Palk, May 7, 1768, No. 48, *Report on the Palk Manuscripts,* London, 1922, pp. 73–74.
70. BL IOR/N/2/1, f. 321.
71. Mentz, *The English Gentleman Merchant at Work,* p. 250.
72. Smith to Palk, Oct. 4, 1770, BL Add MS 34686, p. 136.
73. BL IOR/N/2/1, p. 372; BL IOR/J/1/15, p. 243; BL IOR/N/2/1, p. 389; BL IOR/N/2/1, p. 348.
74. Quincy, *The Journals of Major Samuel Shaw,* pp. 281–82.
75. Mentz, *The English Gentleman Merchant at Work,* p. 254.
76. Love, *Vestiges of Old Madras,* vol. 3, pp. 61–63.
77. Ibid., p. 60.
78. Mentz, *The English Gentleman Merchant at Work,* p. 254.
79. Quincy, *The Journals of Major Samuel Shaw,* p. 282.
80. Spencer, *Memoirs of William Hickey,* vol. 2, pp. 217–18.
81. Charles Smith to Culling Smith, Jan. 24, 1767, Charles Smith Papers, BL Mss Eur E340/2.
82. Love, *Vestiges of Old Madras,* vol. 3, p. 118; Spencer, *Memoirs of William Hickey,* vol. 2, p. 194.
83. Mentz, *The English Gentleman Merchant at Work,* p. 243.
84. Smith to Palk, Oct. 4, 1770, BL Add MS 34686.
85. Ibid.
86. Bassett, *The British in South-East Asia,* p. 72.
87. Furber, *John Company at Work,* p. 234.
88. George Smith to Robert Palk, May 7, 1768, No. 48, *Report on the Palk Manuscripts,* London, 1922, pp. 73–74.
89. Bassett, *The British in South-East Asia,* p. 73.
90. Drummond, "Monckton, Hon. Edward (1744–1832), of Somerford Hall, Staffs."
91. Bassett, "British 'Country' Trade and Local Trade Networks in the Thai and Malay States," pp. 625–43.
92. Bassett, *The British in South-East Asia,* p. 73.
93. Aug. 30, 1772, BL IOR/R/10/9.
94. Governor and Council of Fort St. George to China Council, July 24, 1771, BL IOR/R/10/7, p. 35.
95. John Crichton to Canton Council, Oct. 12, 1769, BL IOR/R/10/7; Mr. Crichton and Dalrymple to Canton Council, Dec. 30, 1771, BL IOR/R/10/7. *Lon-*

don Chronicle, Saturday, Dec. 21, 1782, issue 4067; *Morning Herald and Daily Advertiser* (London), Saturday, Feb. 1, 1783, issue 706; *General Evening Post* (London), Tuesday, May 23, 1786, issue 8200; *General Evening Post* (London), Saturday, June 14, 1788, issue 8516; *London Gazette,* Saturday, Jan. 22, 1791, issue 13276.

96. Canton Council to the Court of Directors, Nov. 20, 1769, BL IOR/R/10/7.
97. John Crichton to the Canton Council, Oct. 12, 1769, BL IOR/R/10/7, p. 43.
98. Canton Council to the Court of Directors, Nov. 20, 1769, BL IOR/R/10/7, pp. 49–51.
99. Consultation, Aug. 24–Oct. 1, 1775, BL IOR/R/10/8.
100. Mr. Crichton and Dalrymple to Canton Council, Dec. 30, 1771, BL IOR/R/10/7; Marshall, *East Indian Fortunes,* p. 227.
101. George Smith of Madras to Robert Palk, Oct. 4, 1770, Add Mss 34686, p. 136.
102. Governor and Council of Fort St. George to the China Council, July 10 and July 23, 1773, BL IOR/R/10/7; Governor and Council of Fort St. George to the China Council, Aug. 1, 1774, BL IOR/R/10/7; George Smith to the Bengal Council, Dec. 15, 1783, BL IOR/P/2/65, p. 151; Crichton and Dalrymple to the China Council, Dec. 30, 1771, BL IOR/R/10/7, p. 90.
103. Smith to Palk, Oct. 4, 1770, BL Add MS 34686, p. 136.
104. Hellman, "Navigating the Foreign Quarters," pp. 147–48.
105. NMA, Utgåebde brev Brevkopieböker (volym 1B), Michael Grubb to George Smith, Nov. 29, 1765; NMA, Inkomna skrivelser G-H (volym 4), Letter from Michael Grubb to his Brother and Friend, Sept. 13, 1753.
106. Marshall, *The Making and Unmaking of Empires,* pp. 136–46; Arasaratnam, *Maritime Commerce and English Power,* pp. 3, 7; Marshall, *Writings and Speeches of Edmund Burke,* vol, 5, pp. 553–56.
107. Charles Smith to Culling Smith, Jan. 24, 1767, Charles Smith Papers, BL Mss Eur E340/2; NMA, Inkomna skrivelser G-H (volym 4), Letter from Jacob Hahr a Country Gentleman, May 13, 1767.
108. Charles Smith to Culling Smith, Jan. 24, 1767, Charles Smith Papers, BL Mss Eur E340/2.
109. George Smith to Robert Palk, May 7, 1768, No. 33, *Report on the Palk Manuscripts,* London, 1922, pp. 73–74.
110. Crichton and Dalrymple to the China Council, Dec. 30, 1771, BL IOR/R/10/7, p. 90; Cheong, "The Decline of Manila as the Spanish Entrepôt in the Far East."
111. Cheong, "Changing the Rules of the Game." This was during Smith of Madras's second stint in India. Between 1783 and 1791 he lived in Bengal.

112. George Smith to Robert Palk, Oct. 30, 1767, No. 33, *Report on the Palk Manuscripts,* London, 1922, pp. 53–54.
113. Bassett, "British 'Country' Trade and Local Trade Networks in the Thai and Malay States."
114. Bassett, *The British in South-East Asia,* pp. 74–85.
115. George Smith to Robert Palk, Oct. 30, 1767, No. 33, *Report on the Palk Manuscripts,* London, 1922, pp. 53–55.
116. J. Parker, "Scottish Enterprise in India."
117. Smith to Palk, Oct. 30, 1767, No. 33, *Report on the Palk Manuscripts,* London, 1922, pp. 53–55.
118. *Nassau,* BL IOR L/MAR/B/544G-H.
119. Marshall, "William Hickey."
120. Spencer, *Memoirs of William Hickey,* vol. 2, pp. 204–5.
121. Ibid., pp. 205–7.
122. *Nassau,* BL IOR L/MAR/B/544G-H; Spencer, *Memoirs of William Hickey,* vol. 2, pp. 213–15.
123. Spencer, *Memoirs of William Hickey,* vol. 2, pp. 217–18.
124. Ibid., pp. 221–22.
125. George Smith to Robert Palk, Feb. 1, 1773, No. 198, *Report on the Palk Manuscripts,* London, 1922, pp. 213–14.
126. Smith to Dundas, Apr. 15, 1786, BL IOR/H/434.
127. *London Gazette,* Feb. 16–19, 1782, issue 12271.

Chapter Three. George Smith of Canton

1. BL IOR/H/411, pp. 55–79.
2. SHC Guildford HT Baptisms and Burials 1558–1783, SHC GUHT1/1–2; SHC Guildford St. Mary Baptisms and Burials 1698–1753 GUM/1/3; SHC Guildford St. Mary Baptisms and Burials 1755–1812 GUM/1/4.
3. PRO, PROB 11/1513/130; PRO, Duties Paid on Apprentices' Indentures, IR1/22, Aug. 18, 1759.
4. BL IOR/L/MAR/B/482G; BL IOR/N/1/5, 1797–1801, f. 64; BL IOR/D/156, 1802, ff. 229–30; BL IOR/D/157, 1803, f. 248; BL IOR/E/1/55, Apr, 11, 1771, ff. 368–369v; Hodson, *List of the Officers of the Bengal Army;* Farrington, EIC Register, India Office List, Indian Army List, Savannah 2012.
5. Will of Joseph Smith, BL IOR/P/416/98, p. 3a; Bombay Proceedings, June 28, 1779, BL IOR/P/417/37, pp. 676–80.
6. Bombay Proceedings, June 28, 1779, BL IOR/P/417/37, pp. 676–80; BL IOR/N/3/3, p. 362.

7. Burke, *The General Armory of England, Scotland, Ireland, and Wales,* p. 785.
8. J. Smith, *The Heraldry of Smith in Scotland;* Burke, *A Genealogical and Heraldic History of the Landed Gentry,* vol. 1, pp. 1487–88.
9. Spencer, *Memoirs of William Hickey,* vol. 1, p. 218.
10. Quincy, *The Journals of Major Samuel Shaw,* pp. 163, 241–42.
11. Nightingale, *Trade and Empire in Western India,* p. 24.
12. Letter Book of David Scott, BL IOR/H/731, pp. 125, 191–92, 135–36, 200, 206–7; Bombay Proceedings, June 28, 1779, BL IOR/P/417/37, pp. 676–80; SHC BR/T/1266/7.
13. Love, *Vestiges of Old Madras,* vol. 3, pp. 137, 229, 370, 402, 424, 537, 554–56, 568.
14. PRO, PROB/11/1700/378, Will of George Moubray.
15. Anglican Parish Register, Woking, Surrey: England, SHC, 1764–1803.
16. Spencer, *Memoirs of William Hickey,* vol. 1, pp. 197–98.
17. Van Dyke, *The Canton Trade,* pp. 103–4.
18. Van Dyke, "Floating Brothels and the Canton Flower Boats"; Spencer, *Memoirs of William Hickey,* vol. 1, pp. 198–200.
19. Spencer, *Memoirs of William Hickey,* vol. 1, pp. 198–99.
20. Bulley, *Free Mariner,* p. 73.
21. Spencer, *Memoirs of William Hickey,* vol. 1, pp. 201–2; Bulley, *Free Mariner,* p. 73.
22. John McQueen, 1757–59, BL Mss Eur D675.
23. Bulley, *Free Mariner,* p. 73.
24. Bulley, *Free Mariner,* pp. 78–79, 175; Spencer, *Memoirs of William Hickey,* vol. 1, pp. 201, 209; John McQueen, 1757–59, BL Mss Eur D675.
25. See Richard, "Uncovering the Garden of the Richest Man on Earth in Nineteenth-Century Canton."
26. Bulley, *Free Mariner,* p. 175.
27. Van Dyke, *Merchants of Canton and Macao,* vol. 2, pp. 61–66.
28. Spencer, *Memoirs of William Hickey,* vol. 1, pp. 223–24.
29. Van Dyke, "The Shopping Streets of Canton in the Foreign Quarter at Canton."
30. M. Mok, "Trading with Traders"; Van Dyke and Mok, *Images of the Canton Factories,* p. xxi; Conner, *The Hongs of Canton,* p. 2.
31. Nov. and Dec. 1772, BL IOR/R/10/9; Jan. 22, 1773, BL IOR/R/10/9; Nov. 18, 1774, BL IOR/R/10/7; Nov. 9, 1776, BL IOR/G/12/59; Feb. 1777, BL IOR/G/12/61; Nov. 1777, BL IOR/G/12/62; Jan. 22, 1779, BL IOR/G/12/64.

32. Aug.–Oct. 1775, BL IOR/R/10/8; Oct. 16, 1779, BL IOR/G/12/68; Jan. 15, 1779, BL IOR/G/12/64; Jan. 15, 1779, BL IOR/R/10/8.
33. Nov. 17, 1775, BL IOR/R/10/8; Aug. 23, 1775, BL IOR/R/10/8.
34. Sept. 27–Oct. 1775, BL IOR/G/12/58; Aug. 1, 1774, BL IOR/R/10/7.
35. Aug. 23, 1775, BL IOR/R/10/8.
36. Dec. 31, 1775, BL IOR/R/10/8; Aug. 23, 1775, BL IOR/R/10/8; Sept. 1, 1775, BL IOR/G/12/58; Nov. 17, 1775, BL IOR/R/10/8; Dec. 31, 1775, BL IOR/R/10/8; Jan. 1, 1776, BL IOR/R/10/8.
37. Aug. 25, 1775, BL IOR/R/10/8; Jan. 1, 1776, BL IOR/R/10/8; Dec. 4, 1775, BL IOR/R/10/8; BL IOR/H/411, pp. 55–79.
38. BL IOR/H/411, pp. 55–79; Aug. 24, 1775, BL IOR/G/12/58.
39. Jan. 29, 1779, NAH, Canton 88. Thanks to Paul Van Dyke for sharing and translating this reference; Bombay Proceedings, June 21–28, 1779, BL IOR/P/417/37, pp. 645–54, 676–80.
40. Bombay Proceedings, June 28, 1779, BL IOR/P/417/37, pp. 683–84; Bombay Proceedings, May 17, 1779, BL IOR/P/417/37, p. 522.
41. Bulley, *Bombay Country Ships,* pp. 182, 187, 200–202.
42. George Smith to the Company Supercargos, Jan. 19, 1779, BL IOR/R/10/8.
43. BL IOR/H/411, pp. 55–79.
44. Feb. 3, 1781, BL IOR/G/12/20ff. 300–301.
45. Feb. 17, 1781, BL IOR/G/12/20, ff. 304–5; Feb. 26, 1781, BL IOR/G/12/20, f. 306.
46. Feb. 26, 1781, BL IOR/G/12/20, f. 306.
47. Apr. 7, 1781, BL IOR/G/12/20, f. 307.
48. Nov. 10, 1781, BL IOR/G/12/20, ff. 308–9.
49. Ibid.
50. Nov. 26, 1781, BL IOR/G/12/73; Jan. 2, 1782, BL IOR/G/12/73.
51. Feb. 10, 1781, BL IOR/G/12/20, ff. 302–3.
52. SHC Guildford HT Baptisms and Burials 1558–1783, SHC GUHT1/1–2; SHC Guildford St. Mary Baptisms and Burials 1698–1753, SHC GUM/1/3; SHC Guildford St. Mary Baptisms and Burials 1755–1812 GUM/1/4.
53. Dec. 31, 1781, BL IOR/G/12/73; Jan. 22, 1782, BL IOR/G/12/75; BL IOR L/MAR/B/319B.
54. Sept. 24, 1782, BL IOR L/MAR/B/319B.
55. Oct. 1782, BL IOR L/MAR/B/319B.
56. *Journals of the House of Commons*, May 12, 1794, vol. 49, pp. 585–86.
57. Hoppit, *Risk and Failure in English Business,* p. 41.
58. Smith to Cathcart, Nov. 16, 1787, BL IOR/G/12/90, p. 39; *Journals of the House of Commons*, May 12, 1794, vol. 49, pp. 585–86.

59. *Journals of the House of Commons*, May 12, 1794, vol. 49, pp. 585–86.
60. Ibid.
61. Ibid.; Hoppit, *Risk and Failure in English Business,* pp. 35–36.
62. John Crichton's letter to the Hoppo, July 8, 1779, BL IOR G/12/68.
63. Hoppit, *Risk and Failure in English Business,* p. 36.
64. Ibid.
65. John Crichton's letter to the Hoppo, July 8, 1779, BL IOR G/12/68.
66. Smith to Dundas, May 7, 1794, NLS MS 1069, ff. 100–101.
67. Ibid.
68. *London Chronicle,* Saturday, Dec. 23, 1782, issue 4067.
69. Ibid.; *Public Advertiser* (London), Wednesday, Feb. 5, 1783, issue 15191; *London Chronicle,* Saturday, Feb. 8, 1783, issue 4088; *London Chronicle,* Saturday, Mar. 15, 1783, issue 4110; *Morning Chronicle and London Advertiser,* Saturday, Mar. 22, 1783, issue 4320.
70. *London Gazette,* Saturday, May 10, 1783, issue 12439.
71. *London Gazette,* Tuesday, July 6, 1784, issue 12558; *Morning Chronicle and London Advertiser,* Monday, May 16, 1785, issue 4993; *General Evening Post* (London), Tuesday, May 23, 1786, issue 8200; *London Gazette,* Tuesday, July 4, 1786, issue 12766; *London Gazette,* Saturday, Apr. 14, 1787, issue 12847; *General Evening Post* (London), Saturday, June 14, 1788, issue 8516; *World* (London), Monday, Nov. 23, 1789, issue 899; *London Gazette,* Tuesday, Oct. 26, 1790, issue 13249; *London Gazette,* Saturday, June 18, 1791, issue 13318.

Chapter Four. Financial Crisis

1. Wong, "Global Positioning," p. 105; Van Dyke, *Merchants of Canton and Macao,* vol. 1, p. 19.
2. Wong and Rosenthal, *Before and Beyond Divergence,* p. 161.
3. George Smith of Canton to Company Supercargos, Nov. 17, 1775, BL IOR/R/10/8.
4. Grant, *The Chinese Cornerstone of Modern Banking,* pp. 33, 99.
5. Van Dyke, *Merchants of Canton and Macao,* vol. 1, pp. 17–19, 221–22; Memorial of Viceroy of Guangdong and Guangxi, Jueluo Bayansan, and Guangdong Superintendent of Customs, Tu Ming-a, to the Qianlong Emperor, *Qinggong Yue Gang Ao Shangmao Dang'an Quanji,* vol. 5, Doc. 501, pp. 2688–2700, Qianlong 45th year, 10th month, 26th day; Li Zhi-ying and Tu Ming-a's Memorial to the Qianlong emperor, 45/04/12, National Palace Museum, Taipei, Taiwan, Junjichu Dang Zhejian, 26992.

6. Chen, *The Insolvency of the Chinese Hong Merchants,* p. 184; Captain Rogers, "Some remarks on the heavy debt now owing by the Chinese to European subjects," BL IOR/G/12/91, vol. 2; Jing, "Legislation Related to the Civil Economy in the Qing Dynasty"; "The Fooyuern and Hoppo's answer to Sir Edward Vernon's letter concerning the debts," in Consultation, Nov. 10, 1779, BL IOR/G/12/68; Consultation, Apr. 7, 1780, BL IOR/G/12/68.
7. Van Dyke, *Merchants of Canton and Macao,* vol. 1, p. 17.
8. Consultation, Oct. 7, 1779, BL IOR/G/12/66.
9. Captain Rogers, "Some remarks on the heavy debt now owing by the Chinese to European subjects," BL IOR/G/12/91, vol. 2.
10. Grant, *The Chinese Cornerstone of Modern Banking,* pp. 93–101.
11. Van Dyke, *Merchants of Canton and Macao,* vol. 1, pp. 17–18, 220; Chen, *The Insolvency of the Chinese Hong Merchants,* p. 218.
12. Consultation, Oct. 7, 1779, BL IOR G/12/66.
13. Van Dyke, *The Canton Trade,* pp. 20–21. Van Dyke adds that complaints might be brought to the attention of the Hoppo while he measured ships at Whampoa. A European might also deliver a document in person to the sentry at the Yaoulan city gate, although this method was inconvenient and time-consuming.
14. "Debt due from Chinese merchants to Englishmen," Warren Hastings Papers, BL Add MS 29210, f. 343; "Letter from Capt. Mackintosh to Mr. Dundas dated 20th December 1791 enclosing a plan for obtaining a redress of the grievances and oppressions of Europeans at Canton," BL IOR G/12/91, vol. 1.
15. CUL, Copies of the East India Company Records, and Other Documents Relating to China and the China Trade Prepared for Lord Macartney's Information, vol. 10, Consultation, Aug. 7 and Sept. 5, 1755.
16. Van Dyke, *Merchants of Canton and Macao,* vol. 1, p. 130.
17. "Debt due from Chinese merchants to Englishmen," Warren Hastings Papers, BL Add MS 29210, f. 343.
18. Consultation, Oct. 16, 1779, BL IOR/G/12/68.
19. Memorial of Li Zhi-ying and Tu Ming-a to the Qianlong Emperor, 45/04/12, National Palace Museum, Taipei, Taiwan, Junjichu Dang Zhejian, 26992.
20. Van Dyke, *Merchants of Canton and Macao,* vol. 1, p. 17.
21. Consultation, Oct. 16, 1779, BL/IOR/G/12/68.
22. Extract letter from the Select Committee at Canton to the EIC: outstanding debts, with an abstract of sums owed by the Hong merchants, Jan. 15, 1780, BL IOR/G/12/19, ff. 30–38; F. Baring and J. Smith Burges to Henry Dundas, July 25, 1792, BL IOR/G/12/91, vol. 2.

23. "Debt due from Chinese merchants to Englishmen," Warren Hastings Papers, BL Add MS 29210, f. 343; Letter from Matthew Raper to John Raper, Feb. 20, 1778, CUL, MSS DS117, George Macartney Papers, Asia Collections, vol. 2, Doc. 6.
24. Cheong, *Hong Merchants of Canton,* pp. 246–47.
25. Memorial of Li Zhi-ying and Tu Ming-a to the Qianlong Emperor, 45/04/12, National Palace Museum, Taipei, Taiwan, Junjichu Dang Zhejian, 26992.
26. John Crichton's letter to the Hoppo, July 8, 1779, BL IOR/G/12/68.
27. George Vansittart and Ewan Law to the Court of Directors, Nov. 1, 1785, BL IOR/E/1/73, ff. 400–405.
28. Letter Books of George Vansittart, BL Mss Eur F331/19–21.
29. Killican to Graham, Dec. 5, 1784, NAS, GD 2061/24.
30. This was the same Killican of the Bengal Agency House for whom the young Ralph Davy had gone to work in 1775.
31. NAS GD 2061, passim. Both Dacres and Crommelin were born in Bombay and came from Huguenot families. It appears that they were brothers-in-law. See: Richard Pugh, "Charles Crommelin (1717–1788): A Governor of Bombay," Crommelin Family Foundation, http://www.crommelin.org/history/Biographies/1763CharlesRussel/02-CharlesGovOfBombay.htm.
32. Killican to Graham, Oct. 30, 1780, NAS GD 2061/20; Feb. 13, 1779, NAS GD 2061/16a; Apr. 23, 1778, NAS GD 2061/14a; Sept. 17, 1777, NAS GD 2061/11.
33. Grant, *The Chinese Cornerstone of Modern Banking,* p. 112; Van Dyke, *Merchants of Canton and Macao,* vol. 1, pp. 128–30.
34. "Debt due from Chinese merchants to Englishmen," Warren Hastings Papers, BL Add MS 29210, f. 343.
35. George Smith of Canton to Company Supercargos, Nov. 17, 1775, BL IOR/R/10/8.
36. Matthew Raper to John Raper, Feb. 20, 1778, CUL, MSS DS117, George Macartney Papers, Asia Collections, vol. 2, doc. 6.
37. John Crichton's letter to the Hoppo, July 8, 1779, BL IOR/G/12/68.
38. John McIntyre to his wife [Kattie], Canton, Feb. 25, 1779, BL Mss Eur F558.
39. Smith of Bombay also loaned money to Chinese merchants at 18 percent annual interest, although his bonds to Geowqua and Pinqua are dated December 1, 1787, so they may have been made after the financial crisis in Canton. PRO, Prob 11/1198/107.
40. George Smith to Thomas Saunders, Dec. 24, 1759, and Jan. 26, 175? BL Add MS 34686, pp. 1–2.

41. George Smith to Robert Palk, Oct. 2, 1770, BL Add MS 34686, p. 136.
42. Consultation, Oct. 16, 1779, BL IOR/G/12/68.
43. George Smith, "Narrative of the proceedings for the recovery of debts owing by the Chinese merchants to British subjects" and "General statement of debts made up to the end of the season 1787/88," July 12, 1787, BL IOR/G/12/18, ff. 91–112; Consultation, Mar. 18, 1780, BL IOR G/12/68.
44. Smith, Crichton, and Hutton to the Fooyuern and Quanpoo, Apr. 11, 1780, BL IOR G/12/68.
45. Leslie to the Company Supercargos, Nov. 10, 1777, BL IOR/G/12/60; Dec. 14, 1773, BL IOR/R/10/7; Nov. 10, 1777, BL IOR/G/12/60; Company Supercargos to Leslie, Oct. 5, 1778, BL IOR/R/10/8.
46. Morse, *The Chronicles of the East India Company Trading to China,* vol. 5, pp. 161–62.
47. PRO, PROB 11/973/225.
48. Letter 104, Petition of Thomas Hutton to the Court, BL IOR/E/1/71, ff. 232–233v.
49. Pugh, "Charles Crommelin"; Extract of the general letter from Bengal, Oct. 23, 1783, BL IOR H/219; BL IOR H/24, p. 116.
50. BL IOR J/1/2, f. 358; John Crichton's letter to the Hoppo, July 8, 1779, BL IOR/G/12/68; PRO, Will of Robert Gordon, PROB 11/073.
51. Abraham Leslie, Thomas Hutton, John Crichton, Charles Gordon, and George Smith, "The most humble petition of the British European merchants to the Supreme Emperor of China," CUL, MSS DS117, George Macartney Papers, Asia Collections, vol. 10, doc. 430.
52. Li Zhi-ying and Tu Ming-a's Memorial to Emperor Qianlong, 45/04/12, National Palace Museum, Taipei, Taiwan, Junjichu Dang Zhejian, 26992.
53. Consultation, Feb. 16, 1780, BL IOR/G/12/68; George Smith, "Narrative of the proceedings for the recovery of debts," July 12, 1787, BL IOR/G/12/18, ff. 91–112; John Crichton's letter to the Hoppo, July 8, 1779, BL IOR/G/12/68; "Translation of the chop from the Military General and Fooyuern Governor of the Province of Canton," in Consultation, Feb. 10, 1780, BL IOR/G/12/68.
54. Pritchard, *The Crucial Years of Early Anglo-Chinese Relations,* pp. 130–31.
55. Abraham Leslie, Thomas Hutton, John Crichton, Charles Gordon, and George Smith, "The most humble petition of the British European merchants to the Supreme Emperor of China," CUL, MSS DS117, George Macartney Papers, Asia Collections, vol. 10, doc. 430.
56. Copy of a Letter from Mr. Crichton to the Governor and Council of Fort St. George, July 26, 1779, BL IOR/G/12/68.

57. Copy of a Letter to Rear Admiral Sir Edward Vernon, BL IOR/G/12/68; Quincy, *The Journals of Major Samuel Shaw,* p. 307.
58. Copy of a Letter to Rear Admiral Sir Edward Vernon, BL IOR/G/12/68.
59. Sir Edward Vernon to the Fouyuern, Nov. 4, 1779, BL IOR/G/12/68; Sir Edward Vernon to the Council at Fort St. George, BL IOR G/12/68.
60. Sir Edward Vernon to the Fouyuern, Nov. 4, 1779, BL IOR/G/12/68; Sir Edward Vernon to the Council at Fort St. George, BL IOR G/12/68; Copy of a letter to the President and Council of Fort St. George from the Creditors of the Chinese merchants, June 15, 1780, BL IOR/G/12/68; The Memorial of Andrew Ross, BL IOR/H/168, pp. 535–38; Hughes to the President and Council of Fort St. George, BL IOR/H/168, p. 547; Hughes to the Viceroy, June 14, 1780, BL IOR/H/168, p. 555; Extract of Vice-Admiral Sir Edward Hughes's Letter to the Secretary of State, Jan. 15, 1783, NMM, SAN/F/40.
61. BL IOR/G/12/18, pp. 91–112; Captain Rogers to Henry Dundas, "China Debts to Europeans," BL IOR/G/12/91, vol. 2; *Journals of the House of Commons,* May 12, 1794, vol. 49, pp. 585–86.
62. Protest of the Select Committee to Captain Panton, Oct. 19, 1779, BL IOR G/12/69; Consultation, Feb. 10–16, 1780, BL IOR/G/12/68; Consultations Apr. 1–2, 1780, BL IOR/G/12/68.
63. Company Supercargos to Madras Council, Nov. 8, 1779, BL IOR G/12/68; Company Supercargos to Captain Panton, Oct. 7, 1779, BL IOR/G/12/68; Quincy, *The Journals of Major Samuel Shaw,* p. 314.
64. Consultation, Mar. 11, 1780, BL IOR/G/12/68.
65. Li Zhi-ying and Tu Ming-a's Memorial to Emperor Qianlong, 45/04/12, National Palace Museum, Taipei, Taiwan, Junjichu Dang Zhejian, 26992.
66. Consultation, Oct. 24, 1779, BL IOR/G/12/68; Cheong, *Hong Merchants of Canton,* p. 258.
67. Li Zhi-ying and Tu Ming-a's Memorial to Emperor Qianlong, 45/04/12, National Palace Museum, Taipei, Taiwan, Junjichu Dang Zhejian, 26992; Translation of Military General and Fooyuern's Chop to Company Supercargos dated Nov. 5, 1779, in Consultation, Feb. 16, 1780, BL IOR G/12/68.
68. Fooyuern and Quanpoo's Chop to Company Supercargos, Mar. 3, 1780, BL IOR/G/12/68.
69. Consultation, Mar. 4, 1780, BL IOR/G/12/68.
70. Smith, Crichton, and Hutton to the Fooyuern and Quanpoo, Apr. 11, 1780, BL IOR/G/12/68.
71. BL IOR/G/12/18, ff. 91–112.
72. David Lance and William Fitzhugh to Henry Lane, Jan. 15, 1781, BL IOR G/12/20, ff. 310–21.

73. Consultation, Apr. 17, 1780, BL IOR/G/12/68; David Lane and William Fitzhugh to Henry Lane, Jan. 15, 1781, BL IOR/G/12/20.
74. Translation of Chop from the Quanpoo given on 45th year of the Emperor Qianlong, the 6th Day of the 2nd Moon, Apr. 10, 1780, BL/IOR/G/12/68.
75. Consultation, May 8, 1780, BL IOR/G/12/68.
76. BL IOR/G/12/18, ff. 91–112; Consultation, May 8–13, 1780, BL IOR G/12/68.
77. Consultation, Oct. 9, 1779, BL IOR/G/12/66; Leslie to the Company Supercargos, Dec. 18, 1780, BL IOR/G/12/69; Leslie to the Company Supercargos, Oct. 26, 1779, BL IOR/G/12/66; Van Dyke, *The Canton Trade*, p. 98.
78. Consultation, Sept. 22–24, 1780, BL IOR/G/12/68; Consultation, May 19, 1781, BL IOR/G/12/72; Extract letter from the Select Committee to the EIC: debt negotiations and general affairs, Dec. 16, 1780, BL IOR/G/12/19, ff. 57–75; Van Dyke, *The Canton Trade,* p. 98; Leslie to the Company Supercargos, Dec. 18, 1780, BL IOR/G/12/69.
79. Extract of the Instructions proposed to be sent to the Company's Supra Cargoes in China, BL IOR/G/12/19, ff. 137–61.
80. NMM, Sandwich Papers, Letter from Sir Edward Hughes, Jan. 13, 1783, SAN/T/2.
81. Memorial of Li Zhi-ying and Tu Ming'a to the Qianlong emperor, dated 45/04/12, National Palace Museum, Taipei, Taiwan, Junjichu Dang Zhejian, 26992.
82. Hanser, "From Cross-Cultural Credit to Colonial Debt."

Chapter Five. George Smith of Bombay and the *Lady Hughes* Affair

1. Cormack, *An Historic Outline of the George Smith Bounty;* Cormack, *More about Founder of Fordyce Academy.*
2. Grosjean and Murdoch, "The Scottish Community in Seventeenth-Century Gothenburg," p. 191.
3. Mackillop, "Accessing Empire."
4. Cormack, *An Historic Outline of the George Smith Bounty;* Cormack, *More about Founder of Fordyce Academy.*
5. Meijers, *News from the Republick of Letters,* p. 3; Murdoch, *Network North,* pp. 148–49.
6. Catterall, "Scots along the Maas," pp. 172–73.
7. Mackillop, "Accessing Empire."
8. Nierstrazs, "The Popularization of Tea," p. 272; Hodacs and Mueller, "Chests, Tubs and Lots of Tea," p. 278.

9. Cormack, *An Historic Outline of the George Smith Bounty;* Cormack, *More About Founder of Fordyce Academy.*
10. Index of Court Minutes, BL IOR/B/80–84.
11. Percival Spear as quoted in Nightingale, *Trade and Empire in Western India,* p. 12.
12. Nightingale, *Trade and Empire in Western India,* p. 12.
13. Marshall, *The Making and Unmaking of Empires,* p. 241.
14. Nightingale, *Trade and Empire in Western India,* p. 13.
15. Davies, "British Private Trade Networks in the Arabian Seas," p. 58.
16. Marshall, *The Making and Unmaking of Empires,* p. 320.
17. Nightingale, *Trade and Empire in Western India,* p. 13.
18. Ibid.
19. Smith to Dundas, Mar. 12, 1786, NLS MS 1060, ff. 210–21.
20. Smith of Bombay to the Bengal Council, Apr. 24, 1785, BL IOR/P/3/11, f. 254.
21. Ibid.; Bayly, *Indian Society,* p. 62.
22. Nightingale, *Trade and Empire in Western India,* p. 23.
23. Frederic Davy to Father, May 21, 1776, Letters January 1773, 1773-1777, BLYU, Osborn c594.
24. "Summary of proceedings in the third session of Parliament," *The Gentleman's Magazine,* July 1786, vol. 56, Part 2, p. 967.
25. Nightingale, *Trade and Empire in Western India,* pp. 53, 72.
26. Bulley, *Bombay Country Ships,* p. 177.
27. PRO, PROB/11/1198; Mackillop, "Accessing Empire."
28. Dalrymple, *White Mughals,* pp. 27–28.
29. Nightingale, *Trade and Empire in Western India,* p. 24.
30. PRO, PROB/11/1198/107.
31. Ibid.; Grant, *The Chinese Cornerstone of Modern Banking,* p. 215.
32. Several historians mention the *Lady Hughes* Affair in their works. See, for example: Chen, *Chinese Law in Imperial Eyes,* ch. 1; Spence, *The Search for Modern China,* pp. 126–27; Wakemen, *Strangers at the Gate,* p. 81; Pritchard, *The Crucial Years of Early Anglo-Chinese Relations,* pp. 226–27; Fay, *The Opium War,* pp. 37–39; Chang, *Commissioner Lin and the Opium War,* pp. 12, 139, 197.
33. Spencer, *Memoirs of William Hickey,* vol. 1, p. 197; Smith of Madras to the Bengal Council, Feb. 10, 1785, BL IOR/P/3/10; BL L/MAR/B257A; RAC ASK 954, 1078, 1079. Thanks to Paul Van Dyke for sharing these references with me.
34. Smith of Madras to the Bengal Council, Feb. 9, 1784, BL IOR/P/3/2.

35. Smith of Bombay to the Bengal Council, Apr. 24, 1785, BL IOR/P/3/11.
36. "A Particular Account of the Unfortunate Accident . . . ," BL IOR/G/12/18, pp. 25–42. A "chop boat" is a Chinese vessel involved in the Canton customs procedure.
37. *Ta-Ch'ing Li-ch'ao Shi lu,* CL 49:11:11 (Dec. 23, 1784), in Fu, *A Documentary Chronicle of Sino-Western Relations,* p. 297; *Xiangshan Ming Qing Dang'an Jilu,* pp. 196–98, Doc. 3.23.
38. *Qianlong Chao Shangyu Dang,* vol. 12, pp. 361–62.
39. *Qinggong Yue Gang Ao Shangmao Dang'an Quanji,* vol. 5, Doc. 532, 2825–29.
40. Chen, *Chinese Law in Imperial Eyes,* p. 45.
41. *Qianlong Shangyu Dang,* vol. 12, pp. 361–62.
42. Chen, *Chinese Law in Imperial Eyes,* p. 45.
43. "A Particular Account of the Unfortunate Accident . . . ," BL IOR/G/12/18, pp. 25–42.
44. Chen, *Chinese Law in Imperial Eyes,* pp. 48–49.
45. *Qianlong Shangyu Dang,* vol. 12, pp. 361–62.
46. Ibid.
47. *Xiangshan Ming Qing Dang'an Jilu,* pp. 196–98, Doc. 3.23.
48. "A Particular Account of the Unfortunate Accident . . . ," BL IOR/G/12/18, pp. 25–42.
49. *Xiangshan Ming Qing Dang'an Jilu,* pp. 196–98, Doc. 3.23.
50. *Qianlong Chao Shangyu Dang,* vol. 12, pp. 361–62.
51. Ibid.
52. "A Particular Account of the Unfortunate Accident . . . ," BL IOR/G/12/18, pp. 25–42.
53. Ibid.
54. Yang, Wu, and Deng, *Mingqing Shiqi Aomen Wenti Dangan Wenxian Huibian,* 1784/12/30, Doc. 287, pp. 459–61.
55. "A Particular Account of the Unfortunate Accident . . . ," BL IOR/G/12/18, pp. 25–42.
56. Ibid.
57. Van Dyke, *The Canton Trade,* p. 117.
58. "A Particular Account of the Unfortunate Accident . . . ," BL IOR/G/12/18, pp. 25–42.
59. Ibid.
60. Ibid.; Quincy, *The Journals of Major Samuel Shaw,* pp. 186–91.
61. "A Particular Account of the Unfortunate Accident . . . ," BL IOR/G/12/18, pp. 25–42.

62. Ibid.
63. Supercargos to Court of Directors, Feb. 5, 1785, BL IOR/G/12/18.
64. "A Particular Account of the Unfortunate Accident . . . ," BL IOR/G/12/18, pp. 25–42.
65. Yang, Wu, and Deng, *Mingqing Shiqi Aomen Wenti Dangan Wenxian Huibian,* 1784/12/30, Doc. 287, pp. 459–61.
66. "A Particular Account of the Unfortunate Accident . . . ," BL IOR/G/12/18, pp. 25–42.
67. *Xiangshan Ming Qing Dang'an Jilu,* pp. 196–98, Doc. 3.23; Yang, Wu, and Deng, *Mingqing Shiqi Aomen Wenti Dangan Wenxian Huibian,* 1784/12/30, Doc. 287, pp. 459–61.
68. "A Particular Account of the Unfortunate Accident . . . ," BL IOR/G/12/18, pp. 25–42.
69. Kuhn, *Soulstealers,* pp. 14–22, 170–75.
70. Consultation, Dec. 2, 1784, BL IOR/G/12/79.
71. *Qinggong Yue Gang Ao Shangmao Dang'an Quanji,* Doc. 532, 2825–29.
72. *Ta-Ch'ing Li-ch'ao Shi lu,* CL 49:11:11 (Dec. 23, 1784), in Fu, *A Documentary Chronicle of Sino-Western Relations,* p. 297; Chen, *Chinese Law in Imperial Eyes,* p. 34.
73. *Qinggong Yue Gang Ao Shangmao Dang'an Quanji,* Doc. 532, 2825–29.
74. "East India Intelligence," *The Gentleman's Magazine,* Aug. 1785, vol. 55, p. 655; Yang, Wu, and Deng, *Mingqing Shiqi Aomen Wenti Dangan Wenxian Huibian,* 1784/12/30, Doc. 287, pp. 459–61.
75. Supercargos to the Court of Directors, Feb. 5, 1785, BL IOR/G/12/18; "East India Intelligence," *Gentleman's Magazine*, Aug. 1785, vol. 55, p. 655.
76. *Qinggong Yue Gang Ao Shangmao Dang'an Quanji,* Doc. 532, 2825–29.
77. Morse, *Chronicles,* vol. 5, pp. 15–19. Thanks to Paul Van Dyke for providing information about the Dutch cases.
78. See Chen, *Chinese Law in Imperial Eyes,* ch. 1.
79. Supercargos to the Court of Directors, Feb. 5, 1785, BL IOR/G/12/18; *India Gazette, or Calcutta Public Advertiser*, vol. 5: Apr. 25, 1785, issue 232; vol. 5: Jan. 31, 1785, issue 220.
80. Quincy, *The Journals of Major Samuel Shaw,* p. 186.
81. "Riot at China," *The Times,* Friday, July 8, 1785, p. 3, issue 166.
82. *India Gazette, or, Calcutta Public Advertiser,* Monday, Jan. 17, 1785, vol. 5, issue 218.
83. "Riot at China," *The Times,* Friday, July 8, 1785, p. 3, issue 166; "East India Intelligence," *Gentleman's Magazine*, Aug. 1785, vol. 55, p. 655.
84. *Public Advertiser* (London), July 22, 1785, issue 15962.
85. Capt. Mackintosh to Mr. Rose, Nov. 19, 1791, BL IOR G/12/91 vol. 1.

Chapter Six. Mission to China

1. Furber, *Henry Dundas, First Viscount Melville,* p. 11.
2. Ibid., p. 10.
3. Ibid., p. 11; Phillips, "Parliament and Southern India."
4. Furber, *Henry Dundas, First Viscount Melville,* p. 29.
5. Ibid., p. 30.
6. Dundas, *Heads of Mr. Dundas's Speech on the State of Affairs of the East India Company,* p. 3.
7. "Report on European relations with, and history of, China, relative to a projected embassy to that country drawn up by Mr. Cobb of the East India House," Add MS 13875, 1792; Kitson, *Forging Romantic China,* pp. 28–29.
8. For histories of early Christian missionaries in China see Spence, *Memory Palace of Matteo Ricci;* Brockey, *Journey to the East.*
9. "Report on European relations with, and history of, China, relative to a projected embassy to that country drawn up by Mr. Cobb of the East India House," Add MS 13875, 1792.
10. Ibid.
11. Ibid.
12. List of Mr. Dundas's Papers of Accounts, BL IOR/H/340.
13. Ibid.; Selection of Papers exhibiting a view of the East India Company's Commercial Concerns by R. Wissett, BL IOR/H/449.
14. CUL, Copies of the East India Company Records, and other Documents Relative to China and the China Trade Prepared for Lord Macartney's Information, Vol. 1, "Queries put by the Court of the Directors to persons now in England who have served the Company in China with answers thereto 1791–2"; Smith to Dundas, March 28, 1787, NLS MS 1069, ff. 15–16.
15. Smith, "Some propositions tending to the Establishment of the East India Companys Trade to China on a firm, and advantageous basis," Feb. 16, 1783, BL IOR/H/434.
16. JRL, Melville Papers, English MS 697, "Letters from India," passim; NLS, Melville Papers, MS 1069, passim; NAS, GD51/3/531; Nightingale, *Trade and Empire in Western India,* p. 26.
17. Philips, *The Correspondence of David Scott,* pp. ix–xxii.
18. Bulley, *Bombay Country Ships,* pp. 177–81; JRL, Melville Papers, English MS 697, "Letters from India," passim; NLS GD 51/3/81.
19. Webster, *Twilight of the East India Company,* p. 31; Philips, *The East India Company,* p. 71.
20. Fry, *The Dundas Despotism,* p. 195.
21. Ibid., pp. 218–19.

22. Frost, *The Global Reach of Empire,* p. 179.
23. Fry, *The Dundas Despotism,* pp. 173–75.
24. Frost, *The Global Reach of Empire,* p. 170.
25. Smith to Dundas, Mar. 28, 1787, NLS MS 1069, ff 15–16; Smith to Dundas, Sept. 19, 1790, NLS MS 1069, ff. 61–62.
26. Smith to Dundas, May 27, 1786, NLS MS 1069, f. 9.
27. Smith to Dundas, March 28, 1787, NLS MS 1069, ff. 15–16.
28. Ibid.
29. Whelan, *Edmund Burke and India,* p. 3.
30. Marshall, *Writings and Speeches of Edmund Burke,* vol. 5, p. 1.
31. Whelan, *Edmund Burke and India,* p. 43.
32. Marshall, *Writings and Speeches of Edmund Burke,* vol. 5, p. 5.
33. Ibid., pp. 5–6.
34. Phillips, "A Successor to the Moguls."
35. O'Brien, *The Great Melody,* pp. 307–8; Marshall, *Writings and Speeches of Edmund Burke*, vol. 5, pp. 5–6.
36. O'Brien, *The Great Melody,* p. 307.
37. Ibid., pp. 307–8; Marshall, *Writings and Speeches of Edmund Burke*, vol. 5, pp. 5–6.
38. Love, *Vestiges of Old Madras,* vol. 3, pp. 105–19.
39. Elijah Impey to Andrew Ross, Oct. 11, 1776, BL Add MS 16266, f. 24.
40. Smith to the Court of Directors, Oct. 10, 1776, BL IOR/H/129.
41. Gurney, "The Debts of the Nawab of Arcot,"Appendix 1. In 1767, Smith's mother-in-law and aunt, Francis Mary Munro, and his brother-in-law and first cousin, Robert Duncan Munro, claimed 5,700 and 1,600 pagodas from the Nawab, respectively.
42. Marshall, *The Writings and Speeches of Edmund Burke,* vol. 5, p. 230.
43. *Morning Post and Daily Advertiser* (London), Tuesday, Jan. 23, 1781, issue 2561.
44. Ibid.; *London Courant and Westminster Chronicle,* Monday, Jan. 22, 1781; *Lloyd's Evening Post* (London), Wednesday, Jan. 17–19, 1781, issue 3679.
45. Marshall, *The Writings and Speeches of Edmund Burke,* vol. 5, p. 9.
46. Ibid., vol. 5, pp. 553–56.
47. Smith to Dundas, Apr. 15, 1786, BL IOR/H/434.
48. The bulk of these letters can be found in the Home Miscellaneous Series, BL IOR/H/434, in the British Library and in Melville Papers MS 1060 of the National Library of Scotland.
49. Nightingale, *Trade and Empire in Western India,* pp. 36–55.
50. Sept. 10, 1787, NLS MS 1060, ff. 246–54.

51. Smith to Dundas, Nov. 26, 1786, NLS MS 1060, ff. 226–39.
52. Sept. 10, 1787, NLS MS 1060, ff. 246–54.
53. Harlow, *The Founding of the Second British Empire,* vol. 1, pp. 72–75, 81; Cook, "Alexander Dalrymple."
54. Alexander Dalrymple to Henry Dundas, July 17, 1784, Mar. 12, 1791, Nov. 16, 1791, Feb. 1, 1791, June 4, 1792, Sept. 28, 1792, Nov. 2, 1792, Feb. 3, 1794, Nov. 7, 1797, July 26, 1802, Sept. 4, 1802, NLA, MS 43/1, MS 43/7–12, 14–15, 18, 20–21.
55. Smith to Dundas, Jan. 10, 1790, NLS MS 1060, ff. 272–75.
56. Smith to Dundas, Nov. 26, 1786, NLS MS 1060, ff. 226–36.
57. Smith to Dundas, Jan. 10, 1790, NLS MS 1060, ff. 272–75.
58. Smith to William Cabell, Jan. 10, 1790, BL IOR/H/434.
59. Said, *Orientalism;* Oliver Goldsmith, *Citizen of the World.* For works on British and European constructions of China see: D. Porter, "A Peculiar but Uninteresting Nation"; Markley, *The Far East and the English Imagination;* Spence, *The Chan's Great Continent;* Batchelor, "Concealing the Bounds."
60. Ambassador Macartney, "A Journal of the Embassy to China in 1792 n 1793 n 1794," OSB fd 12/2, vol. 2, pp. 307–8.
61. Marx, "Revolution in Europe and in China."
62. Smith to Dundas, Apr. 23, 1781, BL IOR/H/434.
63. Spence, *The Search for Modern China,* p. 38.
64. Kuhn, *Soulstealers;* p. 58; Rawsky, *The Last Emperors,* p. 7.
65. Spence, *The Search for Modern China,* p. 40.
66. Smith to Dundas, Jan. 27, 1785, BL IOR/H/434.
67. Smith, "Some Propositions tending to the Establishment of the East India Companys Trade to China on a firm and advantageous basis," Feb. 16, 1783, BL IOR/H/434.
68. George Smith of Canton, Narrative of the Canton Debts, BL IOR/G/12/18, pp. 91–112.
69. Ibid.
70. Ibid.
71. Captain Rogers to Dundas, 1792, BL IOR G/12/91, vol. 2.
72. *London Chronicle,* Saturday, Sept. 3–5, 1778, issue 3394; BL IOR/G/12/90, pp. 53–64.
73. George Smith of Canton, Narrative of the Canton Debts, BL IOR/G/12/18, pp. 91–112.
74. Consultation, Oct. 7, 1779, BL IOR/G/12/68; Jan. 15, 1781, BL IOR/G/12/20, pp. 310–21.
75. Blankett to Lord Shelburne, Dec. 8, 1782, and Jan. 27, 1783, BL Bowood Manuscripts. Thanks to P. J. Marshall for sharing these references with me.

76. Smith to Dundas, Nov. 26, 1786, NLS MS 1060, ff. 226–35.
77. Smith, "Some Propositions tending to the Establishment of the East India Companys Trade to China on a firm and advantageous basis," Feb. 16, 1783; Smith to Dundas, Apr. 15, 1786, BL IOR/H/434.
78. Smith to Dundas, Sept. 19, 1790, NLS MS 1069, ff. 61–62.
79. Smith to Dundas, May 27, 1786, NLS MS 1069, f. 10.
80. *Journals of the House of Commons*, May 12, 1794, vol. 49, pp. 585–86.
81. Captain Mackintosh to Mr. Rose, Nov. 19, 1791, BL IOR G/12/91, vol. 1; Captain Mackintosh to Henry Dundas, Dec. 20, 1791, BL IOR G/12/91, vol. 1; Captain Rogers, "China Debts to Europeans," BL IOR G/12/91, vol. 2.
82. Bowen, "Privilege and Profit."
83. Captain Mackintosh to Mr. Rose, Nov. 19, 1791, BL IOR G/12/91, vol. 1; Captain Mackintosh to Henry Dundas, Dec. 20, 1791, BL IOR G/12/91, vol. 1.
84. Captain Rogers, "China Debts to Europeans," BL IOR, G/12/91, vol. 2
85. Copy of a letter from Thomas Fitzhugh to Nathaniel Smith, Aug. 28, 1787, BL IOR G/12/91, vol. 1.
86. BL IOR G/12/90–91, vols. 1–2, passim.
87. Macartney to Dundas, Jan. 23, 1792, BL IOR G/12/91, vol. 1.
88. Ross, *Correspondence of Charles, First Marquis Cornwallis,* vol. 2, pp. 1–2.
89. Smith to Dundas, Apr, 15, 1786, BL IOR/H/434.
90. Smith to Walsingham, July 18, 1786, NLS MS 1069, ff. 7–8.
91. Scott, *Remarks and Ideas on the Export Trade from Great Britain to India.*
92. Spence as quoted in Chen, *Chinese Law in Imperial Eyes,* p. 26.
93. Instructions to Lord Macartney, Sept. 8, 1792, CUL, MSS DS117, George Macartney Papers, Asia Collections, vol. 5, doc. 228.
94. Ibid.
95. Smith Burges and Baring to Dundas, Jan. 20, 1792, BL IOR G/12/91.
96. Memorandum, in the hand of Sir Francis Baring, TBA, c1792, NP1.C22 10a.
97. Cathcart to Dundas, Aug. 18, 1787, BL IOR/G/12/90.
98. Baring to Dundas, Sept. 4, 1792, TBA, NP1.C22.8.
99. Dundas to Baring, Sept. 4, 1792, TBA, NP1.C22.8.
100. Ross, *Correspondence of Charles, First Marquis Cornwallis,* vol. 2, pp. 1–2.
101. Instructions to Lord Macartney, Sept. 8, 1792, CUL.
102. Dundas to Sir Archibald Campbell, July 27, 1787 (copy), Mel. MSS Eskbank "Grange" letter-book, as cited in Furber, *Henry Dundas, First Viscount Melville,* p. 59.
103. William Cabell to Smith, July 21, 1786, NLS MS 1060,f. 224.
104. Smith to Dundas, Nov. 10, 1790, NLS MS 1060, ff. 288–93.

105. Smith to Dundas, Feb. 16, 1783, and Apr. 15, 1786, BL IOR H/434; Peyrefitte, *Immobile Empire,* pp. 73–75; Platt, *Autumn in the Heavenly Kingdom,* pp. 109–10.
106. Sept. 10, 1787, NLS MS 1060, ff. 246–54; Nightingale, *Trade and Empire in Western India,* p. 55.
107. George Smith of Madras to Dundas, Apr. 15, 1786, BL IOR/H/434.
108. George Smith of Canton, "Narrative of the Canton Debts," BL IOR/G/12/18, pp. 91–112.
109. Instructions to Lord Macartney, Sept. 8, 1792, CUL, MSS DS 117, George Macartney Papers, Asia Collections, vol. 5, doc. 288; Furber, *Henry Dundas, First Viscount Melville,* p. 68.
110. Frost, *Global Reach of Empire,* pp. 173–80.
111. Instructions to Lord Macartney, Sept. 8, 1792, CUL.

Epilogue

1. Smith to Dundas, May 27, 1786, NLS MS 1069, ff. 9–10.
2. Memorial of Viceroy of Guangdong and Guangxi, Jueluo Bayansan, and Guangdong Superintendent of Customs, Tu Ming-a, to the Qianlong Emperor, *Qinggong Yue Gang Ao Shangmao Dangan Quanji,* Doc. 501, pp. 2688–2700, Qianlong 45th year, 10th month, 26th day.
3. *Journals of the House of Commons,* May 12, 1794, vol. 49, pp. 585–86.
4. Smith to Dundas, March 28, 1787, NLS MS 1069, ff. 15–16.
5. Smith to Dundas, Sept. 19, 1790, NLS MS 1069, ff. 61–62.
6. Cathcart to Dundas, Aug. 18, 1787, BL IOR/G/12/90.
7. Ibid.
8. Cathcart to Smith, Nov. 19, 1787, BL IOR/G/12/90, p. 41.
9. Baring and Burges to Dundas, July 25, 1792, BL IOR/G/12/91, vol. 2.
10. Dundas to Macartney, Sept. 8, 1792, BL IOR/G/12/91, vol. 2.
11. Cathcart to Dundas, Aug. 31, 1787, BL IOR/G/12/90.
12. Cathcart to Smith, Nov. 19, 1787, BL IOR/G/12/90.
13. Cathcart to Dundas, Aug. 31, 1787, BL IOR/G/12/90.
14. Cathcart to Lord Sydney, Dec. 2, 1787, BL IOR/G/12/90.
15. Smith to Cathcart, Nov. 20, 1787, BL IOR/G/12/90.
16. Ibid.
17. Thorne, "Macartney, George, Earl Macartney (1737–1806)."
18. Furber, *Henry Dundas, First Viscount Melville,* p. 50.
19. Ibid., pp. 50–54.
20. Staunton as cited in Pritchard, *The Crucial Years of Early Anglo-Chinese Relations,* p. 274.

21. George Macartney, *Travel Journal,* BLYU, OSB fd12 ½.
22. Ibid.
23. Ibid.
24. Smith to Scott, May 10, 1794, NLS MS 1069, f. 104. The first David Scott was born in 1791 but died young. The second David Scott was born in 1796 and survived to adulthood.
25. Ibid.
26. Scott to Dundas, May 11, 1794, NLS, MS 1069, ff. 102–3.
27. Ibid.
28. Ibid.
29. Smith to Scott, May 10, 1794, NLS MS 1069, f. 104.
30. *Journals of the House of Commons*, May 12, 1794, vol. 49, pp. 585–86.
31. *Journals of the House of Commons*, May 15, 1794, vol. 49, pp. 595–96.
32. Ibid.
33. *General Index to the Journals of the House of Commons,* vol. 35, A.D. 1774–vol. 55, A.D. 1800.
34. Ibid.; An Act for the Relief of certain Insolvent Debtors, *House of Lords Sessional Papers, 1714–1805,* 1 January 1760–2 July 1801.
35. Letter Books of David Scott, Scott to Smith, May 8, 1798, BL IOR/H/729, p. 185.
36. Anglican Parish Registers, Woking, Surrey, SHC STK/1/5.
37. BL IOR/P/416/98, f. 3a.
38. Letter Books of David Scott, Scott to Charlotte Smith, no date, circa 1803?; Scott to Charlotte Smith, Jan. 31, 1804, BL IOR/H/731, pp. 135–36; Bulley, *Bombay Country Ships,* pp. 177–80.
39. Erickson, *Women and Property in Early Modern England,* pp. 19–24.
40. Bombay Proceedings of the Mayor Court, Bombay Proceedings, June 28, 1779, BL IOR/P/417/37, pp. 676–80.
41. Combs, "'Concealing Him from His Creditors.'"
42. SHC QS6/7/53–54.
43. SHC BR/T/1266/7, Dec. 27–28, 1793.
44. SHC BR/T/1266/11, June 1–2, 1808.
45. Letter Books of David Scott, Scott to Charlotte Smith, Jan. 31, 1804, BL IOR/H/731, pp. 191–92.
46. Ibid.; Letter Books of David Scott, Scott to Charlotte Smith, No date, circa 1803?, BL IOR/H/731, pp. 135–36.
47. PRO, PROB 11/1818/63.
48. For Harriet's will see: PRO, PROB 11/2135/102.
49. 1841 Census, HO1070 0675/01, fol. 18, p. 29: 8 Devonshire St., Marylebone, ST MARYLEBONE, MDX; 1851 Census, HO107 1468, fol. 842, hse 86:

18 Pembridge Villas, Kensington, KENSINGTON, MDX; 1851 Census, HO107 1593, fol. 375, hse 42: Byfleet, CHERTSEY, SRY; 1851 Census, HO107 1973, fol. 828, hse 5: Chandos Cottage, Thurslstone rd, Cheltenham, CHELTENHAM, GLS.

50. PRO, PROB 11/2243/311.
51. Ibid.
52. PRO, PROB 11/1976/202.
53. *The Asiatic Journal and Monthly Register for British and Foreign India, China and Austalasia,* new series, vol. 13 (Jan.–Apr. 1834): 205.
54. BL IOR/L/MIL/9/258/52v–53, 55v–56; BL IOR/L/MIL/9/116, p. 364; BL IOR/L/MIL/9/258/146v–47.
55. PRO, PROB 11/1818/63.
56. BL IOR/L/AG/23/10/1 no. 949; IOR/L/MIL/9/258/52v–53, 55v–56.
57. PRO, PROB 11/1818/63.
58. BL IOR/L/AG/23/10/1 no. 949.
59. BL IOR/L/MIL/9/208, f. 287.
60. Ryde New Cemetery Section H Plot 2104; Clark, *The East India Register and Army List for 1845,* p. 155; BL IOR L/AG/34/29/299.
61. 1861 Census, RG9 0770, fol. 70 hse 153: "Romans," Norwood, Uxbridge, MDX.
62. *London Gazette,* Feb. 16–19, 1782, issue 12271.
63. *London Gazette,* Apr. 15–18, 1786, issue 12743; *London Chronicle,* Saturday, Dec. 26, 1789, issue 5211; *Public Advertiser* (London), Wednesday, Jan. 27, 1790, issue 17324; *London Gazette,* Tuesday, Apr. 4, 1786, issue 12740; *Public Advertiser* (London), Thursday, June 24, 1784, issue 15625; *London Gazette,* Saturday, July 19, 1783, issue 12459.
64. Smith to Hastings, Nov. 30, 1785, BL Add MS 29169, f. 138.
65. *Calcutta Gazette; or, Oriental Advertiser,* vol. 05: 1786, issue 130.
66. Ibid.
67. *Calcutta Gazette; or, Oriental Advertiser,* vol. 06: 1786–1787, issue 149.
68. *Calcutta Chronicle; and General Advertiser,* vol. 02: 1787–1788, issue 89; *Calcutta Gazette; or, Oriental Advertiser,* vol. 06: 1786–1787, issue 153; *Calcutta Gazette; or, Oriental Advertiser,* vol. 10: 1788–1789, issue 237; *Calcutta Gazette; or, Oriental Advertiser,* vol. 06: 1786–1787, issue 150.
69. Smith to Dundas, Oct. 5, 1785, BL IOR/H/434.
70. Smith to Dundas, Dec. 6, 1785, BL IOR/H/434.
71. Smith to Dundas, Mar. 19, 1786, BL IOR/H/434; Smith to Dundas, Apr. 15, 1786, BL IOR/H/434.
72. Smith to Dundas, Oct. 5, 1785, BL IOR/H/434.

73. Smith to Dundas, Nov. 25, 1785, BL IOR/H/434.
74. Smith to Dundas, Sept. 10, 1787, NLS, Melville MS 1060, ff. 246–54.
75. BL IOR/H/434, Oct. 1, 1785, Smith to Dundas; BL IOR/J/1/15, pp. 241–45.
76. Smith to Dundas, Oct. 1, 1785, BL IOR/H/434.
77. Smith to Dundas, Jan. 20, 1791, BL IOR/H/434.
78. BL IOR/J/1/15, pp. 426–31; BL IOR/J/1/15, pp. 241–45.
79. BL IOR/J/1/15, pp. 241–45.
80. *The Gentleman's Magazine,* 1807, vol. 77, pt. 2, p. 1172.
81. PRO, PROB 11/1478/169. The marriage does not appear to have been a happy one. Walter Ruding sued Jemima Claudia in 1821 for using his last name. He also attempted to have the court declare their marriage null and void, since she was under the legal age at the time of their marriage and did not have permission from a guardian. *The Annual Register, or a View of the History, Politics and Literature of the Year 1821* (London, 1821).
82. BL IOR/N/1/5, f. 57.
83. *The Gentleman's Magazine,* 1809, vol. 79, pt. 1, p. 477.
84. BL IOR/N/1/7, f. 6.
85. Lord Clive Military Fund and Pension Registers and Payment books—widows in Madras, BL IOR/L/AG/23/2/14; BL IOR L/MIL/9/126/1-6; BL IOR/N/1/4, ff. 193, 201; IOR/N/1/6 f. 88.
86. A. Symonds, "Petrie, William (1747–1816), of 14 Hanover Street, Hanover Square, Mdx."
87. BL IOR/J/1/15, pp. 241–45; BL IOR/J/1/15, pp. 426–31.
88. Symonds, "Petrie, William (1747–1816), of 14 Hanover Street."
89. PRO, PROB 11/1615/393.
90. BL IOR/L/MAR/B/451C.
91. Ibid.; PRO, PROB/11/1198/107.
92. Mackillop, "Europeans, Britons, and Scots."
93. PRO, PROB/11/1198/107.
94. Ibid.
95. Cormack, *An Historic Outline of the George Smith Bounty;* Cormack, *More About Founder of Fordyce Academy.*
96. Greenberg, *British Trade and the Opening of China,* pp. 34–35.
97. Bowen, "Gentlemanly Capitalism and the Making of a Global British Empire."
98. Jasanoff, *Edge of Empire,* p. 8.

Bibliography

Principal Manuscript Sources Cited

Collections in Australia

CANBERRA: NATIONAL LIBRARY OF AUSTRALIA (NLA)

MS 43/1, MS 43/7–12, 14–15, 18, 20–21, Papers of Alexander Dalrymple, 1784–1806

Collections in Denmark

COPENHAGEN: NATIONAL ARCHIVES (RIGSARKIVET; RAC)

Ask 954, 1078-9, 1141-1155, 1116-1229 Negotieprotocolor for Kinfarere 1735–1833

Collections in Sweden

STOCKHOLM: NORDIC MUSEUM ARCHIVE (NORDISKA MUSEET ARKIVET; NMA)

F17:1–17 Ostindiska Kompagnier Documenter and Private Trade Documents 1744–1767 Skepps instrukioner, kassabokfoering, protokollsutdrag, och inventariefoerteckning Bokfoering med Compradoren 1762–1766. Jean Abraham Grill Papers, 1736–1792
Inkomna skrivelser G–H (volym 4)
Raekenskaper, Huvudbok, 1765–1766, enskilda affaerer, register
Utgåebde brev Brevkopieböker (volym 1B)

Collections in Taiwan

TAIPEI: NATIONAL PALACE MUSEUM ARCHIVES

Ming-Qing Archives, Junjichu Dang Zhejian 明清檔案: 軍機處檔摺件 [Grand Council Archives]

Collections in the Netherlands

NATIONAL ARCHIVES, THE HAGUE (NAH)

Canton 88, 1779.01.26

Collections in the United Kingdom

BRITISH CENSUSES

1841 Census, HO1070 0675/01 fol. 18, p. 29: 8 Devonshire St. Marylebone, St. Marylebone, Middlesex

1851 Census, HO107 1468 fol. 842 hse 86: 18 Pembridge Villas, Kensington, Kensington, Middlesex

1851 Census HO107 1593 fol. 375 hse 42: Byfleet, Chertsey, Surrey

1851 Census HO107 1973 fol. 828 hse 5: Chandos Cottage, Thurslstone Rd., Cheltenham, Cheltenham, Gloucestershire

1861 Census, RG9 0770 fol. 70 hse 153: "Romans," Norwood, Uxbridge, Middlesex

EDINBURGH: THE NATIONAL ARCHIVES OF SCOTLAND (NAS)

GD 2061

GD 2061/11, 16a, 14a, 20, 24

GD 51/3/81

EDINBURGH: THE NATIONAL LIBRARY OF SCOTLAND (NLS)

MS 1060 (Melville Papers: India)

MS 1069 (Melville Papers: China)

MS 3385 (Melville Papers: Correspondence with Lord Cornwallis)

GREENWICH: NATIONAL MARITIME MUSEUM (NMM), THE CAIRD LIBRARY

SAN/F/40

SAN/T/2

LONDON: THE BARING ARCHIVE (TBA)

NP1.C22 1792–97 (Documents Relating to the 1st Lord Macartney's Embassy to China)

LONDON: BRITISH LIBRARY (BL)

Add MS 13875 (Marquess Wellesley: Collection of letters and papers . . .)

Add MS 16266 (Letter Books of Sir Elijah Impey)

Add MS 29169, 29210 (Correspondence of Warren Hastings)

Add MS 34686 (Correspondence and Papers of Robert Palk)

Add MS 38310 (Liverpool Papers)

Add MS 45436 (Anderson Papers)
Bowood Manuscripts (Uncatalogued)

European Manuscripts

Mss Eur C387/1–4 (Scattergood Papers)
Mss Eur D675 (John Mcqueen)
Mss Eur D993 (Sir Joseph Banks Papers)
Mss Eur E340/2 (Charles Smith Papers)
Mss Eur F331/19–21 (Vansittart Collection)
Mss Eur F558 (Papers of the Macintyre and Anderson families c. 1770–1882)
Mss Eur K45 (Dr. Kerr's Observation upon Natural History)

India Office and Oriental Collections: Records

B/80–84 (Minutes of the East India Company's Directors and Proprietors)
D/156, 157 (Minutes and Memoranda of General Committees, 1700–1858)
E/1/55, 63, 71, 73, 168 (General Correspondence, 1602–1859)
G/12/18–20, 46–102 (East India Company Factory Records, c. 1595–1858)
H/24, 129, 168, 219, 228, 340, 411, 434, 449, 729, 731, 795 (Home Miscellaneous Series, c. 1600–1900)
IOR/B/80–84 (Minutes of the Court of Directors and Court of Proprietors 1599–1858)
J/1/15, J/1/2 (East India College, Haileybury, Records, and Records of Other Institutions, 1749–1925)
L/AG/23/10/1–2, L/AG/23/2/14, L/AG/23/10/5, L/AG/34/29/299 (Accountant-General's Records, c. 1601–1974)
L/MAR/B257A, L/MAR/B/544G-H, L/MAR/B/482G, L/MAR/B/319B, L/MAR/B/451 (Marine Records, c. 1600–1879)
L/MIL/9/116, 126, 208, 258 (Military Department Records, 1708–1959)
L/P&S/2/1 (Political and Secret Department Records, 1756–c. 1950)
N/1/4, N/1/5, N/1/6, N/1/7, N/2/1, N/3/3 (Returns of Baptisms, Marriages and Burials, 1698–1969)
P/2/51, P/2/65, P/3/2, P/3/11, P/3/10; P/3/27, P/3/34, P/328/60, P/416/98, P/417/37 (Proceedings and Consultations, 1702–1945)
R/10/5–9, 33, 67 (China: Canton Factory Records, 1623–1841)

LONDON: THE NATIONAL ARCHIVES (KEW), PUBLIC RECORD OFFICE (PRO)

PRO 30/11/9, 30/11/11 (Charles Cornwallis Papers)

PROB 11/973/225, 11/1615/393, 11/1198/107, 11/1478/169, 11/1513/130, 11/1700/378, 11/1976/202, 11/2135/102, 11/2243/393, 11/973/225, 11/1818/63, 11/2243/311 (Prerogative Court of Canterbury: Will Registers)

IR1/22 (Duties Paid on Apprentices' Indentures)

MANCHESTER: JOHN RYLANDS LIBRARY (JRL)

English MS 697 (Melville Papers)

NORTHUMBERLAND: NORTHUMBERLAND COUNTY RECORD OFFICE (NRO)

Grey MSS, NRO 753, Box 1 G–I, Jan. 14, 1745 (Ralph William Grey of Backworth)

WOKING: SURREY HISTORY CENTRE (SHC)

GUHT1/1–2 (Guildford HT Baptisms and Burials, 1558–1783)

GUM /1/3 (Guildford St. Mary Baptisms and Burials, 1698–1753)

GUM /1/4 (Guildford St. Mary Baptisms and Burials, 1755–1812)

SHC QS6/7/53–54

SHC STK/1/5 (Anglican Parish Registers, Woking, Surrey) BR/T/1266/7, BR/T/1266/11

Collections in the United States of America

ITHACA, NY: CORNELL UNIVERSITY LIBRARY (CUL)

Copies of the East India Company Records, and Other Documents Relating to China and the China Trade Prepared for Lord Macartney's Information, vols. 1, 10.

MSS DS117, George Macartney Papers, Asia Collections, Cornell University Library, vols. 2, 5, 10.

NEW HAVEN, CT: BEINECKE LIBRARY, YALE UNIVERSITY (BLYU)

OSB fd12 ½ (George Macartney's Travel Journal)

Osborn c594 (Letters January 1773, 1773-1777)

Principal Printed Primary Sources Cited

Periodicals

The Asiatic Journal and Monthly Register for British and Foreign India, China and Australasia, new series, vol. 13.
Calcutta Chronicle; and General Advertiser, vol. 02: 1787–1788, issue 56.
Calcutta Chronicle; and General Advertiser, vol. 02: 1787–1788, issue 89.
Calcutta Gazette; or, Oriental Advertiser, vol. 05: 1786, issue 130.
Calcutta Gazette; or, Oriental Advertiser, vol. 06: 1786–1787, issue 149.
Calcutta Gazette; or, Oriental Advertiser, vol. 06: 1786–1787, issue 150.
Calcutta Gazette; or, Oriental Advertiser, vol. 06: 1786–1787, issue 153.
Calcutta Gazette; or, Oriental Advertiser, vol. 10: 1788–1789, issue 237.
Calcutta Gazette; or, Oriental Advertiser, vol. 14: 1790–1791, issue 357.
Calcutta Gazette; or, Oriental Advertiser, vol. 16: 1791–1792, issue 392.
General Evening Post (London), Tuesday, May 23, 1786, issue 8200.
General Evening Post (London), Saturday, June 14, 1788, issue 8516.
The Gentleman's Magazine, January 1731, vol. 1, p. 37.
The Gentleman's Magazine, August 1785, vol. 55, p. 655.
The Gentleman's Magazine, July 1786, vol. 56, part 2, pp. 967–68.
The Gentleman's Magazine, December 1807, vol. 77, part 2, p. 1172.
The Gentleman's Magazine, 1809, vol. 79, p. 477.
India Gazette, or, Calcutta Public Advertiser, Monday, January 17, 1785, vol. 5, issue 218.
India Gazette, or Calcutta Public Advertiser, vol. 5, January 31, 1785, issue 220.
India Gazette, or Calcutta Public Advertiser, vol. 5, April 25, 1785, issue 232.
Lloyd's Evening Post (London), Wednesday, January 17, 1781, issue 3679.
London Chronicle (London, England), September 3–5, 1778, issue 3394.
London Chronicle, Saturday, December 21, 1782, issue 4067.
London Chronicle, Saturday, February 8, 1783, issue 4088.
London Chronicle, Saturday, March 15, 1783, issue 4110.
London Chronicle, Saturday, December 26, 1789, issue 5211.
London Courant and Westminster Chronicle, Monday, January 22, 1781.
London Gazette, February 16, 1782–February 19, 1782, issue 12271.
London Gazette, Saturday, May 10, 1783, issue 12439.
London Gazette, Tuesday, July 6, 1784, issue 12558.
London Gazette, Saturday, July 19, 1783, issue 12459.
London Gazette, Tuesday, March 14, 1786, issue 12734.
London Gazette, Tuesday, April 4, 1786, issue 12740.
London Gazette, April 15, 1786–April 18, 1786, issue 12743.

London Gazette, Tuesday, July 4, 1786, issue 12766.
London Gazette, Saturday, April 14, 1787, issue 12847.
London Gazette, Tuesday, October 26, 1790, issue 13249.
London Gazette, Saturday, January 22, 1791, issue 13276.
London Gazette, Saturday, June 18, 1791, issue 13318.
Morning Chronicle and London Advertiser, Saturday, March 22, 1783, issue 4320.
Morning Chronicle and London Advertiser, Monday, May 16, 1785, issue 4993.
Morning Herald and Daily Advertiser (London), Saturday, February 1, 1783, issue 706.
Morning Post and Daily Advertiser (London), Tuesday, January 23, 1781, issue 2561.
Public Advertiser (London), Wednesday, February 5, 1783, issue 15191.
Public Advertiser (London), Thursday, June 24, 1784, issue 15625.
Public Advertiser (London), Friday, July 22, 1785, issue 15962.
Public Advertiser (London), Wednesday, January 27, 1790, issue 17324.
The Times (London), Friday, July 8, 1785, p. 3, issue 166.
World (London), Monday, November 23, 1789, issue 899.

Pamphlets and Literature

Burke, Edmund, *Mr. Burke's Speech on the motion made for papers relative to the Directions for charging the nabob of Arcot's private debts to Europeans on the revenues of the Carnatic, February 28th, 1785* (London: J. Dodsley, 1785).
Dundas, Henry, *Heads of Mr. Dundas's Speech on the State of Affairs of the East India Company the 25th February 1793* (London, 1793).
East India Company, *Three Reports of the Select Committee, appointed by the Court of Directors to take into consideration the export trade from Great Britain to the East Indies, China, Japan, and Persia; laid before the Lords of the Committee of Privy Council. With the appendixes. Also, Mr. Secretary Dundas's letter to Mr. Baring; a concise statement of the East India Company's income; and the heads of their agreement for a new charter* (London: J. S. Jordan, 1793).
Goldsmith, Oliver, *Citizens of the World: or, letters from a Chinese philosopher, residing in London, to his friends in the East* (1760–61).
Scott, David, *Remarks and Ideas upon the Export Trade from Great Britain to India with a Plan and Proposals for the Increase thereof* (London, 1787).

Parliamentary Sources

General Index to the Journals of the House of Commons, vol. 35, A.D. 1774–vol. 55, A.D. 1800.

House of Lords Sessional Papers, 1714–1805, January 1, 1760–July 2, 1801.

Journals of the House of Commons, vol. 49, 1794.

Edited Collections of English Sources

Chang Hsiu-Jung and Anthony Farrington, et al., eds., *The English Factory in Taiwan, 1670–1685* (Taipei: National Taiwan University Press, 1995), 9–16.

Great Britain, Royal Commission on Historical Manuscripts, *Report on the Palk Manuscripts in the Possession of Mrs Bannatyne of Haldon, Devon* (London: Her Majesty's Stationery Office, 1922).

Marshall, Peter, ed., *The Writings and Speeches of Edmund Burke*, vol. 5: *India: Madras and Bengal, 1774–1785* (New York: Oxford University Press, 1981).

Pickering, Danby, ed., *The Statutes at Large from the Magna Charta to the End of the Eleventh Parliament of Great Britain*, vol. 28 (Cambridge, 1761–1807).

Quincy, Josiah, ed., *The Journals of Major Samuel Shaw, the First American Consul at Canton: with a Life of the Author* (Boston: W. Crosby and H. P. Nichols, 1847).

Raithby, John, ed., *The Statutes Relating to the Admiralty, Navy, Shipping and Navigation of the United Kingdom* (London: George Eyre and Andrew Strahan, 1823).

Ross, Charles, ed., *Correspondence of Charles, First Marquis Cornwallis*, vol. 3 (London: John Murray, 1859).

Spencer, Alfred, *Memoirs of William Hickey* (London: Hurst and Blackett, 19[illegible]9), vols. 1–2.

Van Dyke, Paul, and Cynthia Viallé, trans., *The Canton-Macao Dagregister 1763* (Macao: Cultural Institute, 2008).

Edited Collections of Chinese Sources

Fu, Loshu, ed., *A Documentary Chronicle of Sino-Western Relations* (Tucson: Published for the Association for Asian Studies by the University of Arizona Press, 1966).

Qianlong Chao Shangyu Dang 乾隆朝上諭檔, Zhongguo Di 1 Lishi Dang'an Guanbian, 中國 弟一歷史檔案館編 [Imperial Edicts Archive in the Qianlong Reign], vols. 1–18 (Beijing: Dangan Chuban She, Faxing Xinhua Shudian Beijing Faxingsuo, 1991).

Qinggong Yue Gang Ao Shangmao Dang'an Quanji 清宫粤港澳商貿檔案全集 [A Complete Collection of the Archival Documents on Trade in Canton, Hong Kong, and Macao from the Qing Palace]. Zhongguo Guji Zhengli Yanjiu Huibian, 1652–1911, vol. 5 (Beijing: Zhongguo Shudian, 2002), facsimile.

Xiangshan Ming Qing Dang'an Jilu 香山明清檔案輯錄 [Collection of Xiangshan (County) Ming-Qing Documents, 1624–1911] (Shanghai: Shanghai Guji Chuban She, 2006).

Yang Jibo, Wu Zhiliang, and Deng Kaisong, eds., *Ming Qing Shiqi Aomen Wenti Dang'an Wenxian Huibian* 明清時期澳門問題檔案文獻匯編 [Collection of Ming-Qing Documents Concerning Macao Affairs, 1624–1911], 6 vols. (Beijing: Renmin Chuban She, 1999).

Secondary Literature

Andrade, Tonio, "A Chinese Farmer, Two African Boys, and a Warlord: Toward a Global Microhistory," *Journal of World History,* vol. 21, no. 4 (2011).

——, *The Gunpowder Age: China, Military Innovation, and the Rise of the West in World History* (Princeton, N.J.: Princeton University Press, 2016).

——, *How Taiwan Became Chinese: Dutch, Spanish, and Han Colonization in the Seventeenth Century* (New York: Columbia University Press, 2008).

——, "Koxinga's Conquest of Taiwan in World History: Reflections on the Occasion of the 350th Anniversary," *Late Imperial China,* vol. 33, no. 1 (June 2012): 122–40.

Arasaratnam, Sinnappah, *Maritime Commerce and English Power: Southeast India, 1750–1800* (Brookfield, Vt.: Variorum, 1996).

Ballantyne, Tony, *Orientalism and Race: Aryanism in the British Empire* (New York: Palgrave, 2002).

Bassett, D. K., "British 'Country' Trade and Local Trade Networks in the Thai and Malay States, c. 1680–1770," *Modern Asian Studies* (1989): 625–43.

——, *British in South-East Asia During the Seventeenth and Eighteenth Centuries* (Hull: University of Hull, Centre for South-East Asian Studies, 1990).

——, *British Trade and Policy in Indonesia and Malaysia in the Late Eighteenth Century* (Zug, Switzerland: Inter Documentation Company, 1971).

Batchelor, Robert, "Concealing the Bounds: Imagining the British Nation through China," in Felicity A. Nussbaum, ed., *The Global Eighteenth Century* (Baltimore, Md.: Johns Hopkins University Press, 2000).

Bayly, C. A., *Imperial Meridian: The British Empire and the World, 1780–1830* (London: Longman, 1989).

———, *Indian Society and the Making of the British Empire* (New York: Cambridge University Press, 1990).

Beevers, David, ed., *Chinese Whispers: Chinoiserie in Britain, 1650–1930* (Brighton, UK: Royal Pavilion and Museums, 2009).

Benn, James A., *Tea in China: A Religious and Cultural History* (Honolulu: University of Hawaii Press, 2015).

Berg, Maxine, *Luxury and Pleasure in Eighteenth-Century Britain* (Oxford: Oxford University Press, 2007).

Berg, Maxine, Felicia Gottmann, Hanna Hodacs, and Chris Nierstrasz, eds., *Goods from the East, 1600–1800: Trading Eurasia* (London: Palgrave Macmillan, 2015).

Bickers, Robert, ed., *Ritual and Diplomacy: The Macartney Mission to China, 1792–1794* (London: Wellsweep Press, 1993).

Blake, Robert, *Jardine Matheson: Traders of the Far East* (London: Weidenfeld and Nicholson, 1999).

Blussé, Leornard, *Strange Company: Chinese Settlers, Mestizo Women and the Dutch in VOC Batavia* (Riverton, N.J.: Foris, 1986).

Bowen, Huw, "British Exports of Raw Cotton from India to China during the Late Eighteenth and Early Nineteenth Centuries," in Giorgio Riello and Tirthankar Roy, eds., *How India Clothed the World: The World of South Asian Textiles, 1500–1850* (Leiden: Brill, 2009).

———, *The Business of Empire: The East India Company and Imperial Britain, 1756–1833* (Cambridge: Cambridge University Press, 2006).

———, "Gentlemanly Capitalism and the Making of a Global British Empire: Some Connections and Contexts, 1688–1815," in Shigeru Akita, ed., *Gentlemanly Capitalism, Imperialism and Global History* (New York: Palgrave, 2002).

———, "Investment and Empire in the Later Eighteenth Century: East India Stockholding, 1756–1791," *The Economic History Review,* new series, vol. 42, no. 2 (May 1989): 186–206.

———, "Privilege and Profit: Commanders of East Indiamen as Private Traders, Entrepreneurs and Smugglers, 1760–1813," *International Journal of Maritime History,* vol. 19, no. 2 (2007): 43–88.

Breen, T. H., "An Empire of Goods: The Anglicization of Colonial America, 1690–1776," *Journal of British Studies,* vol. 25, *Re-viewing the Eighteenth Century* (1986): 467–99.

Brewer, John, *The Sinews of Power: War, Money, and the English State, 1688–1783* (New York: Knopf, 1989).

Brockey, Liam, *Journey to the East: The Jesuit Mission to China, 1579–1724* (Cambridge, Mass.: Belknap Press of Harvard University Press, 2007).

Brook, Timothy, *Vermeer's Hat: The Seventeenth Century and the Dawn of the Global World* (New York: Bloomsbury Press: Distributed by Macmillan, 2008).

Bruijn, Iris, *Ship's Surgeons of the Dutch East India Company: Commerce and the Progress of Medicine in the Eighteenth Century* (Leiden: Leiden University Press, 2009).

Bryant, G. J., "Scots in India in the Eighteenth Century," *Scottish Historical Review,* vol. 64, I: no. 177 (April 1985): 22–41.

Bulley, Anne, *The Bombay Country Ships, 1790–1833* (Richmond, UK: Curzon, 2000).

——, *Free Mariner: John Adolphus Pope in the East Indies, 1786–1821* (London: BACSA, 1992).

Burke, Bernard, *General Armory of England, Scotland, Ireland, and Wales; Comprising a Registry of Armorial Bearings from the Earliest to the Present Time* (London: Harrison and Sons, 1884).

Burnett, John, *Liquid Pleasures: A Social History of Drinks in Modern Britain* (New York: Routledge, 1999).

Burton, Antoinette, *Burdens of History: British Feminists, Indian Women, and Imperial Culture, 1865–1915* (Chapel Hill: University of North Carolina Press, 1994).

Cain, Alex M., *The Cornchest for Scotland: Scots in India* (Edinburgh: National Library of Scotland, 1986).

Cain, P. J., and A. G. Hopkins, *British Imperialism: 1688–2000* (New York: Longman, 2002).

——, "Gentlemanly Capitalism and British Expansion Overseas. I. The Old Colonial System, 1688–1850," *The Economic History Review,* new series, vol. 39, no. 4 (November 1986): 501–25.

Carr, Lois Green, and Lorena Walsh, "The Standard of Living in the Colonial Chesapeake," *The William and Mary Quarterly,* 3rd ser., 45 (1988): 135–59.

Carter, Elizabeth, *Letters from Mrs. Elizabeth Carter to Mrs. Montagu between the Years 1755 and 1800 Chiefly upon Literary and Moral Subjects*, 3 vols. (London: F. C. and J. Rivington, 1817).

Catterall, Douglas, "Scots along the Mass, c. 1570–1750," in Steve Murdoch and Alexia Grosjean, eds., *Scottish Communities Abroad in the Early Modern Period* (Boston: Brill, 2005).

Chang, Hsin-pao, *Commissioner Lin and the Opium War* (New York: W. W. Norton, 1970).

Chaudhuri, K. N., *Asia before Europe: Economy and Civilisation of the Indian Ocean from the Rise of Islam to 1750* (New York: Cambridge University Press, 1990).

———, *The Trading World of Asia and the English East India Company, 1660–1760* (Cambridge: Cambridge University Press, 1978).

Chen, Kuo-Tung, *Insolvency of the Chinese Hong Merchants, 1760–1843* (Taipei: Institute of Economics, Academia Sinica, 1990).

Chen, Li, *Chinese Law in Imperial Eyes: Sovereignty, Justice, and Transcultural Politics* (New York: Columbia University Press, 2016).

Cheong, W. E., "Changing the Rules of the Game (The India-Manila Trade, 1785–1809)," *Journal of Southeast Asian Studies,* vol. 1, no. 2 (1970): 1–19.

———, *Hong Merchants of Canton: Chinese Merchants in Sino-Western Trade* (Richmond, UK: Curzon, 1997).

———, *Mandarins and Merchants: Jardine Matheson & Co., a China Agency of the Early Nineteenth Century* (London: Curzon, 1979).

Cipolla, Carlo, *Guns, Sails and Empires: Technological Innovation and the Early Phases of European Expansion, 1400–1700* (New York: Minerva Press, 1965).

Clark, F., *The East India Register and Army List for 1845* (London, 1845).

Clulow, Adam, "The Art of Claiming: Possession and Resistance in Early Modern Asia," *American Historical Review,* vol. 121, no. 1 (February 2016): 17–38.

———, *The Company and the Shogun: The Dutch Encounter with Tokugawa Japan* (New York: Columbia University Press, 2014).

———, "European Maritime Violence and Territorial States in Early Modern Asia, 1600–1650," *Itinerario,* vol. 33, no. 3 (2009).

Cole, W. A. "Trends in Eighteenth-Century Smuggling," *The Economic History Review,* new series, vol. 10, no. 3 (1958): 395–410.

Colley, Linda, *The Ordeal of Elizabeth Marsh: A Woman in World History* (New York: Pantheon, 2007).

Combs, Mary Beth, "'Concealing Him from His Creditors': How Couples Contributed to the Passage of the 1870 Married Women's Property Act," in Tim Stretton and Krista Kesselring, eds., *Married Women and the Law: Coverture in England and the Common Law World* (Montreal: McGill-Queen's University Press, 2013).

Conner, Patrick, *The Hongs of Canton: Western Merchants in South China, 1700–1900* (London: English Art Books, 2009).

Cook, Andrew S., "Alexander Dalrymple (1737–1808), Hydrographer to the East India Company and to the Admiralty as Publisher" (PhD thesis, University of St. Andrews, 1993).

Cormack, A. A., *An Historic Outline of the George Smith Bounty* (Banff, Scotland: Banffshire Journal, February 1952).

——, *More about Founder of Fordyce Academy,* Reprinted from *Banffshire Journal,* January–February 1957 (Petercultern, Scotland: The Author, 1957).

Cunningham, Peter, ed., *The Letters of Horace Walpole, Fourth Earl of Orford,* vol. 1 (Edinburgh: J. Grant, 1906).

Dalrymple, William, *White Mughals: Love and Betrayal in Eighteenth-Century India* (London: Penguin Books, 2004).

Davies, Tim, "British Private Trade Networks in the Arabian Seas, c. 1680–c. 1760" (DPhil thesis, University of Warwick, 2012).

Davis, Natalie Zemon, *Trickster Travels: A Sixteenth-Century Muslim between Worlds* (New York: Hill and Wang, 2006).

Dermigny, Louis, *Cargaisons Indiennes, Solier et Cie, 1781–1793,* 2 vols. (Paris: S.E.V.P.E.N., 1959–60).

——, *La Chine et l'Occident: Le Commerce à Canton au XVIIIe Siècle,* vols. 1–4 (Paris: S.E.V.P.E.N., 1964).

Devine, T. M., *Scotland's Empire, 1600–1815* (London: Penguin Books, 2004).

Devine, T. M., and Angela McCarthy, "Introduction: The Scottish Experience in Asia, c. 1700 to the Present: Settlers and Sojourners," in T. M. Devine and Angela McCarthy, eds., *The Scottish Experience in Asia, c. 1700 to the Present: Settlers and Sojourners* (Cham, Switzerland: Palgrave Macmillan, 2017).

Dickson, P. G. M., *The Financial Revolution in England: A Study in the Development of Public Credit, 1688–1756* (New York: St. Martin's Press, 1967).

Drummond, Mary M., "Monckton, Hon. Edward (1744–1832), of Somerford Hall, Staff," *History of Parliament: The House of Commons 1754–1790*, ed. L. Namier and J. Brook, 1964.

Erickson, Amy Louise, *Women and Property in Early Modern England* (New York: Routledge, 1995).

Erikson, Emily, *Between Monopoly and Free Trade: The English East India Company, 1600–1757* (Princeton, N.J.: Princeton University Press, 2014).

Fairbank, John King, *Trade and Diplomacy on the China Coast: The Opening of Treaty Ports, 1842–1854* (1953; Cambridge, Mass.: Harvard University Press, 1964).

Farrington, Anthony, *Officer Casualties of the Indian Armies 1803-1946 as Reported in the EIC Register, India Office List, Indian Army List* (London: Savannah, 2012).

Fay, Peter Ward, *Opium War, 1840–1842: Barbarians in the Celestial Empire in the Early Part of the Nineteenth Century and the War by Which They Forced Her Gates Ajar* (Chapel Hill: University of North Carolina Press, 1975).

Fichter, James, *So Great a Proffit: How the East Indies Trade Transformed Anglo-American Capitalism* (Cambridge, Mass.: Harvard University Press, 2010).

Finn, Margot, "Anglo-Indian Lives in the Later Eighteenth and Early Nineteenth Centuries, *Journal for Eighteenth-Century Studies,* vol. 33, no. 1 (2010).

Frank, Andre Gunder, *Re-Orient: Global Economy in the Asian Age* (Berkeley: University of California Press, 1998).

Frost, Alan, *The Global Reach of Empire: Britain's Maritime Expansion in the Indian and Pacific Oceans, 1764–1815* (Carlton, Australia: Miegunyah Press, 2003).

Fry, Michael, *The Dundas Despotism* (Edinburgh: Edinburgh University Press, 1992).

Furber, Holden, "Asia and the West as Partners Before 'Empire' and After," *Journal of Asian Studies,* vol. 28, no. 4 (1969): 711–21.

———, *Henry Dundas, First Viscount Melville, 1742–1811* (Oxford: Oxford University Press, 1931).

———, *John Company at Work: A Study of European Expansion in India in the Late Eighteenth Century* (New York: Octagon Books, 1970).

———, "Madras in 1787," in Rosane Rocher, ed., *Private Fortunes and Company Profits in the India Trade in the 18th Century* (Brookfield, Vt.: Variorum, 1997).

———, *Rival Empires of Trade in the Orient, 1600–1800* (Minneapolis: University of Minnesota Press, 1976).

Games, Alison, *Web of Empire: English Cosmopolitans in an Age of Expansion, 1560–60* (New York: Oxford University Press, 2008).

Gardella, Robert, *Harvesting Mountains: Fujian and the China Tea Trade, 1757–1937* (Berkeley: University of California Press, 1994).

Goldstein, Jonathan, *Philadelphia and the China Trade, 1682–1846* (University Park: Pennsylvania State University Press, 1978).

———, *Stephen Girard's Trade with China, 1787–1824: The Norms versus the Profits of Trade* (Portland, Maine: Merwin Asia Publishers, 2011).

Gosh, Amitav, *River of Smoke* (New York: Farrar, Straus and Giroux, 2011).

Grace, Richard, *Opium and Empire: The Lives of and Careers of William Jardine and James Matheson* (Montreal: McGill-Queen's University Press, 2016)

Grant, Frederick Delano, *The Chinese Cornerstone of Modern Banking: The Canton Guaranty System and the Origins of Bank Deposit Insurance, 1780–1933* (Leiden: Brill Nijhoff, 2014).

Greenberg, Michael, *British Trade and the Opening of China, 1800–42* (Westport, Conn., Hyperion Press, 1979).

Guo, Deyan 郭德焱, *Qingdai Guangzhou de Basi Shangren* 清代廣州的巴斯商人 [Parsee Merchants in Guangzhou during the Qing Dynasty] (Beijing: Zhonghua shuju, 2005).

Gurney, J. D., "The Debts of the Nawab of Arcot, 1763–1776" (DPhil thesis, Oxford University, 1968).

Hall, Catherine, and Sonya O. Rose, "Introduction," in Catherine Hall and Sonya O. Rose, eds., *At Home with the Empire: Metropolitan Culture and the Imperial World* (Cambridge: Cambridge University Press, 2006).

Hancock, David, *Citizens of the World: London Merchants and the Integration of the British Atlantic Community, 1735–1785* (Cambridge: Cambridge University Press, 1995).

Hanser, Jessica, "From Cross-Cultural Credit to Colonial Debt: British Expansion in Madras and Canton, 1750–1800," *American Historical Review*, forthcoming.

——, "Teatime in Northumberland: The Consumption of Chinese Exports in North-east England," *Northern History*, vol. 49 (March 2012).

Harlow, Vincent T., *The Founding of the Second British Empire, 1763–1793*, vols. 1, 2 (London: Longmans, Green, 1964).

Harms, Robert, *Diligent: A Voyage through the Worlds of the Slave Trade* (New York: Basic Books, 2002).

Harris, Ron, *Industrializing English Law: Entrepreneurship and Business Organization, 1720–1844* (Cambridge: Cambridge University Press, 2000).

Hellman, Lisa, "Navigating the Foreign Quarters: Everyday Life of the Swedish East India Company Employees in Canton and Macao, 1730–1830" (PhD thesis, Stockholm University, 2015).

Hevia, James, *Cherishing Men from Afar: Qing Guest Ritual and the Macartney Embassy of 1793* (Durham, N.C.: Duke University Press, 1995).

Hodacs, Hanna, and Leos Mueller, "Chests, Tubs and Lots of Tea: The European Market for Chinese Tea and the Swedish East India Company c. 1730–60," in Maxine Berg, Felicia Gottmann, Hanna Hodacs, and Chris Nierstrasz, eds., *Goods from the East, 1600–1800: Trading Eurasia* (London: Palgrave Macmillan, 2015).

Hodson, V. C. P., *List of the Officers of the Bengal Army*, 4 vols. (London, 1927–47).

Hoffman, Philip, *Why Did Europe Conquer the World?* (Princeton, N.J.: Princeton University Press, 2015).

Honour, Hugh, *Chinoiserie: The Vision of Cathay* (1961; New York: Harper and Row, 1973).

Hoppit, Julian, *Risk and Failure in English Business, 1700–1800* (New York: Cambridge University Press, 1987).

Impey, Oliver, *Chinoiserie: The Impact of Oriental Styles on Western Art and Decoration* (New York: Scribner's, 1977).

Jasanoff, Maya, *Edge of Empire: Lives, Culture, and Conquest in the East, 1750–1850* (New York: Vintage Books, 2005).

Jenkins, Eugenia Zuroski, *A Taste for China: English Subjectivity and the Prehistory of Orientalism* (New York: Oxford University Press, 2013).

Jing, Junjian, "Legislation Related to the Civil Economy in the Qing Dynasty," in Kathryn Bernhardt and Philip C. C. Huang, eds., *Civil Law in Qing and Republican China* (Stanford: Stanford University Press, 1994).

Jones, Eric, *The European Miracle: Environments, Economies and Geopolitics in the History of Europe and Asia,* 3rd ed. (Cambridge: Cambridge University Press, 2003).

Kitson, Peter, *Forging Romantic China: Sino-British Cultural Exchange* (Cambridge: Cambridge University Press, 2013).

Kuhn, Philip, *Soulstealers: The Chinese Sorcery Scare of 1768* (Cambridge, Mass.: Harvard University Press, 1995).

Landes, David, *The Wealth and Poverty of Nations: Why Some Are So Rich and Some So Poor* (New York: Norton, 1998).

Latham, Robert, and William Matthews, eds., *The Shorter Pepys* (Berkeley: University of California Press, 1985).

Lawson, Philip, *The East India Company: A History* (London: Longman, 1993).

———, "Women and the Empire of Tea: Image and Counter-Image in Hanoverian England," in David Cannadine, Linda Colley, and Ken Munro, eds., *A Taste for Empire and Glory: Studies in British Overseas Expansion, 1660–1800* (Brookfield, Vt.: Variorum, 1997).

Leonard, Adrian, "Underwriting British Trade to India and China, 1780–1835," *The Historical Journal,* vol. 55, no. 4 (December 2012): 983–1006.

Love, William Davison, *Vestiges of Old Madras, 1640–1800,* vols. 1–4 (London: J. Murray, 1913).

Macfarlane, Alan, and Iris Macfarlane, *Green Gold: The Empire of Tea* (London: Ebury Press, 2003).

Macinnes, Allan I., and Douglas J. Hamilton, *Jacobitism, Enlightenment and Empire: 1680–1820* (London: Pickering and Chatto, 2014).

Mackenzie, John, *Propaganda and Empire: The Manipulation of British Public Opinion, 1880–1960* (Manchester, UK: Manchester University Press, 1984).

Mackillop, Andrew, "Accessing Empire: Scotland, Europe, Britain, and the Asia Trade, 1695–c. 1750." *Itinerario,* vol. 29, no. 3 (November 2005): 7–30.

——, "Europeans, Britons and Scots: Scottish Sojourning Identities and Networks in India, c. 1700–1815," in Angela McCarthy, ed., *A Global Clan: Scottish Migrant Networks and Identities since the Eighteenth Century* (New York: Tauris Academic Studies, 2006).

——, "A North Europe World of Tea: Scotland and the Tea Trade, c. 1690–1790," in Maxine Berg, Felicia Gottmann, Hanna Hodacs, and Chris Nierstrasz, eds., *Goods from the East, 1600–1800: Trading Eurasia* (London: Palgrave Macmillan, 2015).

Mair, Victor, and Erling Hoh, *The True History of Tea* (London: Thames and Hudson, 2009).

Markley, Robert, *The Far East and the English Imagination, 1600–1730* (Cambridge: Cambridge University Press, 2006).

Marshall, P. J., *Bengal: The British Bridgehead, Eastern India, 1740–1828* (Cambridge: Cambridge University Press, 1987).

——, *East Indian Fortunes: The British in Bengal in the Eighteenth Century* (Oxford, UK: Clarendon Press, 1976).

——, *The Making and Unmaking of Empires: Britain, India, and America, c. 1750–1783* (Oxford: Oxford University Press, 2007).

——, "Masters and Banians in Eighteenth-Century Calcutta," in Blair B. Kling and M. N. Pearson, *The Age of Partnership: Europeans in Asia before Dominion* (Honolulu: University of Hawaii Press, 1979), 191–215.

——, "Private British Trade in the Indian Ocean before 1800," in *Trade and Conquest: Studies on the Rise of British Dominance in India* (Brookfield, Vt.: Variorum, 1993).

——, "The White Town of Calcutta under the Rule of the East India Company," *Modern Asian Studies,* vol. 34, no. 2 (May 2000).

——, "William Hickey (1749–1827)," *Oxford Dictionary of National Biography* (Oxford: Oxford University Press, 2004).

Marx, Karl, "Revolution in China and in Europe," *New York Daily Tribune,* June 14, 1853.

McCarthy, Angela, *A Global Clan: Scottish Migrant Networks and Identities since the Eighteenth Century* (New York: Tauris Academic Studies, 2006).

McGilvary, George, *East India Patronage and the British State: The Scottish Elite and Politics in the Eighteenth Century* (London: Tauris Academic Studies, 2008).

Meijers, Esther, *News from the Republick of Letters: Scottish Students, Charles Mackie, and the United Provinces, 1650–1750* (Boston: Brill, 2012).

Mentz, Søren, *The English Gentleman Merchant at Work: Madras and the City of London, 1660–1740* (Copenhagen: Museum Tusculanum Press, University of Copenhagen, 2005).

Mintz, W. Sidney, *Sweetness and Power: The Place of Sugar in Modern History* (New York: Penguin Books, 1986).

Mok, Maria Kar-wing, "Trading with Traders: The Wonder of Cantonese Shopkeepers," in Paul Van Dyke and Susan Schopp, eds., *The Private Side of the Canton Trade, 1700–1840: Beyond the Companies* (Hong Kong: Hong Kong University Press, 2018).

———, "Xieshi Yu Xiangxiang Zhi Jian: Ghangzhou Shangguan Ji Huangbu Bodi Waixiao Hua De Shiliao Yiyi" 寫實與想像之間：廣州商館暨黃埔泊地外銷畫的史料意義 [Between Realism and Imagination: The Historical Meaning of Canton and Whampoa Export Paintings] (PhD dissertation, Department of History, Sun Yat-Sen University, 2017).

Mok, Patrick Kin Wai, "The British Intra-Asian Trade with China, 1800–1842" (PhD dissertation, Department of History, University of Hong Kong, 2004).

Mokyr, Joel, *Lever of Riches: Technical Creativity and Economic Progress* (New York: Oxford University Press, 1999).

Morse, H. B., *Chronicles of the East India Company Trading to China, 1635–1834*, vols. 1, 2, 5 (Oxford, UK: Clarendon Press, 1926–29).

———, 'The Provision of Funds for the East India Company's Trade at Canton during the Eighteenth Century," *The Journal of the Royal Asiatic Society*, April 1922.

Mueller, Leos, "Scottish and Irish Entrepreneurs in Eighteenth-Century Sweden," in David Dickson, Jan Parmentier, and Jane Ohlmeyer, eds., *Irish and Scottish Mercantile Networks in Europe and Overseas in the Seventeenth and Eighteenth Centuries* (Ghent, Belgium: Academia, 2007).

Mui, Lorna, and Mui Hoh-cheung, "Smuggling and the British Tea Trade," *The American Historical Review*, vol. 74, no. 1 (October 1968): 44–73.

———, "Trends in Eighteenth-Century Smuggling Reconsidered," *The Economic History Review*, vol. 28, no. 1 (February 1975): 28–43.

———, "William Pitt and the Enforcement of the Commutation Act, 1784–1788," *The English Historical Review*, vol. 76, no. 300 (July 1961): 447–65.

Muldrew, Craig, *The Economy of Obligation: The Culture of Credit and Social Relations in Early Modern England* (New York: St. Martin's Press, 1998).

Murdoch, Steve, *Network North: Scottish Kin, Commercial and Covert Association in Northern Europe, 1603–1746* (Boston: Brill, 2006).

Murdoch, Steve, and Alexia Grosjean, eds., *Scottish Communities Abroad in the Early Modern Period* (Boston: Brill, 2005).

Namier, Lewis, and John Brooke, eds., *The House of Commons, 1754–1790* (New York: Published for the History of Parliament Trust by Oxford University Press, 1964).

Naquin, Susan, *Shantung Rebellion: The Wang Lun Uprising of 1774* (New Haven, Conn.: Yale University Press, 1981).

Nechtman, Tillman, *Nabobs: Empire and Identity in Eighteenth-Century Britain* (New York: Cambridge University Press, 2010).

Nierstrasz, Chris, "The Popularization of Tea: East India Companies, Private Traders, Smugglers and the Consumption of Tea in Western Europe, 1700–1760," in Maxine Berg, Felicia Gottmann, Hanna Hodacs, and Chris Nierstrasz, eds., *Goods from the East, 1600–1800: Trading Eurasia* (London: Palgrave Macmillan, 2015).

Nightingale, Pamela, *Trade and Empire in Western India, 1784–1806* (Cambridge: Cambridge University Press, 1970).

North, Douglass C., and Barry Weingast, "Constitutions and Commitment: The Evolution of Institutions Governing Public Choice in Seventeenth-Century England," *The Journal of Economic History,* vol. 49, no. 4 (December 1989): 803–32.

O'Brien, Conor Cruise, *The Great Melody: A Thematic Biography and Commented Anthology of Edmund Burke* (Chicago: University of Chicago Press, 1993).

Ogborn, Miles, *Global Lives: Britain and the World, 1550–1800* (Cambridge: Cambridge University Press, 2012).

Parker, Geoffrey, *The Military Revolution: Military Innovation and the Rise of the West, 1500–1800,* 2nd ed. (Cambridge: Cambridge University Press, 1996).

Parker, James G., "Scottish Enterprise in India, 1750–1914," in R. A. Cage, ed., *The Scots Abroad: Labour, Capital, Enterprise, 1750–1914* (London: Croom Helm, 1985).

Parmentier, Jan, *Tea Time in Flanders: The Maritime Trade between the Southern Netherlands and China in the 18th Century* (Ghent, Belgium: Ludion Press, 1996).

Parthasarathi, Prasannan, *Why Europe Grew Rich and Asia Did Not: Global Economic Divergence, 1600–1850* (Cambridge: Cambridge University Press, 2011).

Pearson, M. N., "Merchants and States," in James D. Tracy, ed., *The Political Economy of Merchant Empires: State Power and World Trade, 1350–1750* (Cambridge: Cambridge University Press, 1991).

Peyrefitte, Alain, *Immobile Empire* (New York: Vintage Books, 1992).

Philips, C. H., *The Correspondence of David Scott, Director and Chairman of the East India Company, Relating to Indian Affairs, 1787–1805,* vol. 1 (London: Offices of the Royal Historical Society, 1951).

——, *The East India Company, 1784–1834* (Bombay: Oxford University Press, 1961).

Phillips, Jim, "Parliament and Southern India, 1781–3: The Secret Committee of Inquiry and the Prosecution of Sir Thomas Rumbold," *Parliamentary History,* vol. 7, part 1 (1988).

——, "Private Profit and Imperialism in Eighteenth-Century Southern India: The Tanjore Revenue Dispute, 1775–1777," *Journal of South Asian Studies,* vol. 9, no. 2 (1986).

——, "A Successor to the Moguls: The Nawab of the Carnatic and the East India Company, 1763–1785," *The International History Review,* vol. 7, no. 3 (1985): 364–89.

Plank, Geoffrey, *Rebellion and Savagery: The Jacobite Rising of 1745 and the British Empire* (Philadelphia: University of Pennsylvania Press, 2006).

Platt, Stephen R., *Autumn in the Heavenly Kingdom: China, the West, and the Epic Story of the Taiping Civil War* (New York: Vintage Books, 2012).

Pomeranz, Kenneth, *The Great Divergence: China, Europe, and the Making of the Modern World Economy* (Princeton, N.J.: Princeton University Press, 2000).

Porter, Bernard, *The Absent-Minded Imperialists: Empire, Society, and Culture in Britain* (Oxford: Oxford University Press, 2004).

Porter, David, *The Chinese Taste in Eighteenth-Century England* (Cambridge: Cambridge University Press, 2010).

——, "A Peculiar but Uninteresting Nation: China and the Discourse of Commerce in Eighteenth-Century England," *Eighteenth-Century Studies,* vol. 33, no. 2, "Colonial Encounters" (Winter 2000): 181–99.

Prakash, Om, *European Commercial Enterprise in Pre-Colonial India* (Cambridge: Cambridge University Press, 1998).

Price, Jacob M., *Capital and Credit in British Overseas Trade: The View from the Chesapeake, 1700–1776* (Cambridge, Mass.: Harvard University Press, 1980).

Pritchard, Earl, *Anglo-Chinese Relations during the Seventeenth and Eighteenth Centuries* (New York: Octagon Books, 1970).

——, *The Crucial Years of Early Anglo-Chinese Relations, 1750–1800* (New York: Octagon Books, 1970).

——, "Private Trade between England and China in the Eighteenth Century (1680–1833)," *Journal of the Economic and Social History of the Orient,* vol. 1, no. 1 (August 1957): 108–37.

——, "Private Trade between England and China in the Eighteenth Century (Concluded)," *Journal of the Economic and Social History of the Orient,* vol. 1, no. 2 (April 1958): 221–56.

Puga, Rogerio Miguel, *The British Presence in Macao, 1636–1793* (Hong Kong: Hong Kong University Press, 2013).

Quiason, S. D., *English Country Trade with the Philippines, 1644–1765* (Quezon City: University of the Philippines Press, 1966).

Rappaport, Erika, *A Thirst for Empire: How Tea Shaped the Modern World* (Princeton, N.J.: Princeton University Press, 2017).

Rawsky, Evelyn, *The Last Emperors: A Social History of Qing Imperial Institutions* (Berkeley: University of California Press, 1998).

Richard, Josepha, "Uncovering the Garden of the Richest Man on Earth in Nineteenth-Century Canton: Howqua's Garden in Honam, China," *Garden History,* vol. 43, no. 2 (2015): 168–81.

Rose, Sarah, *For All the Tea in China: How England Stole the World's Favorite Drink and Changed History* (London: Hutchison, 2009).

Rosenthal, Jean-Laurent, and Bin Wong, *Before and Beyond Divergence: The Politics of Economic Change in China and Europe* (Cambridge, Mass.: Harvard University Press, 2011).

Rothschild, Emma, *Inner Life of Empires: An Eighteenth-Century History* (Princeton, N.J.: Princeton University Press, 2011).

Said, Edward, *Orientalism* (New York: Pantheon Books, 1978).

Schopp, Susan E., "The French in the Pearl River Delta: A Topical Case Study of Sino-European Exchanges in the Canton Trade, 1698–1840" (PhD dissertation, Department of History, University of Macau, 2015).

Shammas, Carole, "Changes in English and Anglo-American Consumption from 1550–1800," in John Brewer and Roy Porter, eds., *Consumption and the World of Goods* (New York: Routledge, 1994), 177–205.

Sharma, Jayeeta, *Empire's Garden: Assam and the Making of India* (Durham, N.C.: Duke University Press, 2011).

Singh, S. B., *European Agency Houses, 1783–1833* (Calcutta: Firma K. L. Mukhopadhyay, 1966).

Sinha, H. N., ed., *Fort William–India House Correspondence and Other Contemporary Papers Relating Thereto* (public series), vols. 2–10 (Delhi: Published for the National Archives of India by the Manager of Publications, Government of India, 1957).

Sloboda, Stacy, *Chinoiserie: Commerce and Critical Ornament in Eighteenth-Century Britain* (Manchester, UK: Manchester University Press, 2014).

Smith, Carl T., "An Eighteenth-Century Macao Armenian Merchant Prince." *Review of Culture,* International Edition no. 6 (April 2003): 120–29.

——, "Parsee Merchants in the Pearl River Delta," *Review of Culture,* International Edition no. 10 (April 2004): 36–49.

Smith, Carl T., and Paul A. Van Dyke, "Armenian Footprints in Macau," *Review of Culture,* International Edition no. 8 (October 2003): 20–39.

——, "Four Armenian Families." *Review of Culture,* International Edition no. 8 (October 2003): 40–50.

——, "Muslims in the Pearl River Delta, 1700 to 1930," *Review of Culture,* International Edition no. 10 (April 2004): 6–15.

Smith, John Russell, *The Heraldry of Smith in Scotland with Genealogical Annotations* (London, 1873).

Smith, S. D., "Accounting for Taste: British Coffee Consumption in Historical Perspective," *Journal of Interdisciplinary History,* vol. 27 (1996): 183–214.

Smith, Woodruff D., *Consumption and the Making of Respectability, 1600–1800* (New York: Routledge, 2002).

Smith-Bannister, Scott, *Names and Naming Patterns in England, 1538–1700* (New York: Oxford University Press, 1997).

Souza, George Bryan, *The Survival of Empire: Portuguese Trade and Society in China and the South China Sea, 1630–1754* (Cambridge: Cambridge University Press, 1986).

Spence, Jonathan, *Chan's Great Continent: China in Western Minds* (London: Norton, 1998).

——, *The Memory Palace of Matteo Ricci* (New York: Viking, 1984).

——, *The Search for Modern China,* 2nd ed. (New York: Norton, 1999).

Stern, Philip, *The Company-State: Corporate Sovereignty and the Early Modern Foundations of the British Empire in India* (Oxford: Oxford University Press, 2011).

Subrahmanyam, Sanjay, "Connected Histories: Note towards a Reconfiguration of Early Modern Eurasia," *Modern Asian Studies,* vol. 31, no. 3 (1997).

——, *Political Economy of Commerce: Southern India, 1500–1650* (New York: Cambridge University Press, 1990).

Subramanian, Lakshmi, *Indigenous Capital and Imperial Expansion: Bombay, Surat and the West Coast* (Oxford: Oxford University Press, 1996).

Symonds, P. A., "Petrie, William (1747–1816), of 14 Hanover Street, Hanover Square, Mdx.," Institute of Historical Research, The History of Parliament, http://www.historyofparliamentonline.org/volume/1790–1820/member/petrie-william-1747–1816.

Teltscher, Kate, *High Road to China: George Bogle, the Panchen Lama and the First British Expedition to Tibet* (London: Bloomsbury, 2006).

Thampi, Madhavi, and Shalini Saksena, *China and the Making of Bombay* (Mumbai: K. R. Cama Oriental Institute, 2009).

Thorne, R. G., ed., *The House of Commons, 1790–1820* (London: Published for the History of Parliament Trust by Secker and Warburg, 1986).

——, "Macartney, George, Earl Macartney (1737–1806)," *Oxford Dictionary of National Biography* (Oxford: Oxford University Press, 2004).

Tomlinson, B. R., "The 'Empire of Enterprise': Scottish Business Networks in Asian Trade, 1793–1810," *KIU Journal of Economics and Business Studies,* vol. 8 (2001): 67–83.

——, "From Campsie to Kedgerie: Scottish Enterprise, Asian Trade and the Company Raj," *Journal of Modern Asian Studies,* vol. 36, no. 4 (2002): 769–91.

——, "The Only Merchant in Calcutta: John Fergusson and the Growth of Private Trade in Bengal, 1775–1790," in Toyin Falola and Emily Brownell, eds., *Africa, Empire and Globalization: Essays in Honor of A. G. Hopkins* (Durham, N.C.: Carolina Academic Press, 2011).

Tripathi, Amales, *Trade and Finance in the Bengal Presidency, 1793–1833* (Bombay: Orient Longmans, 1956).

Trivellato, Francesca, "Credit, Honor, and the Early Modern French Legend of the Jewish Invention of Bills of Exchange," *The Journal of Modern History,* vol. 84, no. 2, "The Jew in the Modern European Imaginary" (June 2012): 289–334.

——, *Familiarity of Strangers: The Sephardic Diaspora, Livorno, and Cross-Cultural Trade in the Early Modern Period* (New Haven, Conn.: Yale University Press, 2009).

——, "Is There a Future for Italian Microhistory in the Age of Global History?" *California Italian Studies,* vol. 2 (2011).

Van Dyke, Paul, "The Anglo-Dutch Fleet of Defense (1620–1622): Prelude to the Dutch Occupation of Taiwan," in Leonard Blussé, ed., *Around and About in Formosa: Essays in Honor of Professor Ts'ao Yung-ho* (Taipei: Ts'ao Yung-ho Foundation for Culture and Education; Dist. SMC, 2003), 61–81.

——, *The Canton Trade: Life and Enterprise on the China Coast, 1700–1845* (Hong Kong: Hong Kong University Press, 2007).

——, "Floating Brothels and the Canton Flower Boats, 1750–1930," *Revista de Cultura,* vol. 37 (2011): 112–42.

——, *Merchants of Canton and Macao: Politics and Strategies in Eighteenth-*

Century Chinese Trade, vol. 1 (Hong Kong: Hong Kong University Press, 2011).

———, *Merchants of Canton and Macao: Success and Failure in Eighteenth-Century Chinese Trade,* vol. 2 (Hong Kong: Hong Kong University Press, 2016).

Van Dyke, Paul, and Maria Mok, *Images of the Canton Factories, 1760–1822* (Hong Kong: Hong Kong University Press, 2015).

Van Dyke, Paul, and Susan Schopp, eds., *The Private Side of the Canton Trade, 1700–1840: Beyond the Companies* (Hong Kong: Hong Kong University Press, 2018).

Wakemen, Frederick, *Strangers at the Gate: Social Disorder in South China, 1839–1861* (Berkeley: University of California Press, 1997).

Ward, Kerry, *Networks of Empire: Forced Migration in the Dutch East India Company* (Cambridge: Cambridge University Press, 2009).

Warren, James, *The Sulu Zone, 1768-1898: The Dynamics of External Trade, Slavery, and Ethnicity in the Transformation of a Southeast Asian Maritime State* (Singapore: NUS Press, 2007).

Watson, Ian Bruce, *Foundation for Empire: English Private Trade in India, 1659–1760* (New Delhi: Vikas, 1980).

Watt, Alistair, *Robert Fortune: A Plant Hunter in the Orient* (Kew, UK: Royal Botanic Gardens, Kew, 2017).

Weatherill, Lorna, *Consumer Behaviour and Material Culture in Britain, 1600–1760* (New York: Routledge, 1988).

Webster, Anthony, *Gentlemen Capitalists: British Imperialism in Southeast Asia, 1770–1890* (London: Tauris Academic Studies, 1998).

———, *Richest East India Merchant: The Life and Business of John Palmer of Calcutta, 1767–1836* (Woodbridge, UK: Boydell Press, 2007).

———, *Twilight of the East India Company* (Rochester, N.Y.: Boydell Press, 2009).

Weiller, Kenneth J., and Philip Mirowski, "Rates of Interest in 18th Century England," *Explorations in Economic History,* vol. 27, no. 1 (January 1990): 1–28.

Werner, Michael, and Benedicte Zimmerman, "Beyond Comparison: *Histoire Croisée* and the Challenge of Reflexivity," *History and Theory,* vol. 45 (2006).

Whelan, Frederick, *Edmund Burke and India: Political Morality and Empire* (Pittsburgh, Pa.: University of Pittsburgh Press, 1996).

Wills, John E., *Embassies and Illusions: Dutch and Portuguese Envoys to K'ang-hsi, 1666–1687* (Cambridge, Mass.: Council on East Asian Studies, Harvard University, 1984).

——, *Pepper, Guns and Parleys: The Dutch East India Company and China, 1622–1681* (Cambridge, Mass.: Harvard University Press, 1974).

——, "Review: *Maritime Asia, 1500–1800: The Interactive Emergence of European Domination*," *The American Historical Review*, vol. 98, no. 1 (February 1993): 83–105.

——, "Trade and Diplomacy with Maritime Europe, 1644–1800," in Willard J. Peterson, ed., *The Cambridge History of China*, vol. 9, part 1, *Ch'ing Empire to 1800* (Cambridge: Cambridge University Press, 2008).

Wilson, Kathleen, *Island Race: Englishness, Empire and Gender in the Eighteenth Century* (New York: Routledge, 2006).

Wong, John, "Global Positioning: Houqua and His China Trade Partners in the Nineteenth Century" (PhD thesis, Harvard University, 2012).

——, *Global Trade during the Nineteenth Century: The House of Houqua and the Canton System* (Cambridge: Cambridge University Press, 2016).

Wrightson, Keith, *Ralph Tailor's Summer: A Scrivener, His City, and the Plague* (New Haven, Conn.: Yale University Press, 2011).

Yang, Chih-ming, *Performing China: Virtue, Commerce, and Orientalism in Eighteenth-Century England, 1660–1760* (Baltimore, Md.: Johns Hopkins University Press, 2011).

Zahedieh, Nuala, *The Capital and the Colonies: London and the Atlantic Economy, 1660–1700* (Cambridge: Cambridge University Press, 2010).

Index

Illustrations are indicated by page numbers in *italics*.